THE BOOMER CENTURY 1946-2046

THE BOOMER CENTURY 1946-2046

*How America's
Most Influential Generation
Changed Everything*

Richard Croker
and Alexandria Productions

Foreword by Ken Dychtwald, PhD

SPRINGBOARD PRESS
NEW YORK • BOSTON

Springboard Press
Hachette Book Group USA
237 Park Avenue, New York, NY 10169
Visit our Web site at www.HachetteBookGroupUSA.com

First Edition: April 2007

Springboard Press is an imprint of Warner Books, Inc. The Springboard name and logo are trademarks of Hachette Book Group USA.

Library of Congress Cataloging-in-Publication Data

Croker, Richard.
The boomer century, 1946–2046 : how America's most influential generation changed everything / Richard Croker and Alexandria Productions. — 1st ed.
p. cm.
ISBN 978-0-446-58081-6
1. Baby boom generation — United States. 2. United States. — Social conditions — 1945–
3. Social change — United States. I. Alexandria Productions. II. Title.
HN58.C76 2007
305.240973'09045 — dc22   2006100617

10 9 8 7 6 5 4 3 2 1

Printed in the United States of America

Book design by HRoberts Design

As always,
for Terry and Amanda

Also for former United States Congressman
and Georgia Supreme Court Chief Justice
Charles Longstreet Weltner,
who took a very young "boomer"
under his wing and taught him the meaning of
Moral Courage

Contents

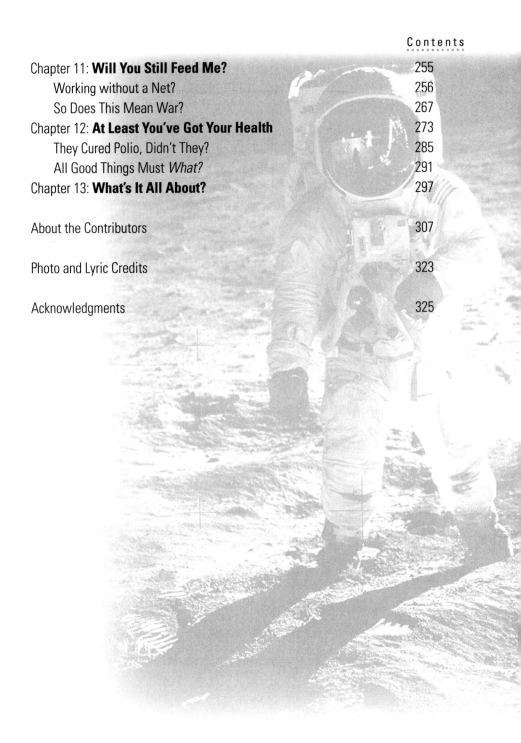

Foreword

or nearly thirty-five years, I have been studying the psychological, social, and marketplace evolution of the baby boom generation. It is my passion, my vocation, and, not coincidentally, my own generation. I have written twelve books about or related to boomers, and I have spoken to audiences totaling two million people. But for a long time, I have dreamed of transforming my theories about this generation into a television documentary. The PBS special *The Boomer Century 1946–2046* is the realization of that dream, and I couldn't be any more proud of the program. Thanks to the generous sponsorship of the Vanguard Group, we were able to produce a thoughtful and comprehensive documentary about the past, present, and future of this incredibly complex generation. However, as we started production, it quickly became apparent that there was far more information and opinion being gathered, and far more that we wanted to say, than the allotted time would permit. So it became obvious that this book was necessary for us to do full justice to the subject.

It has often been said (frequently by myself) that American baby boomers are "the most studied generation in history." You are about to meet the students. Many of the people we have brought together have devoted decades to understanding the impact of this gigantic cohort on the history, social structure, and economy of our nation.

Even with all the study I have done on the subject of this generation, it was fascinating for us to interview such a diverse group. In many cases my research and beliefs were confirmed, but in many others I encountered some challenging and fascinating differing views.

My father never went to college, and he used to say to me, "I want you to get educated so you can see that there are two sides to every story." A few years ago I told my father it didn't quite work out that way. "The more educated I seem to get," I said, "the more I realize there are not two sides to every story—there are a *thousand* sides to every story."

This book contains many sides of the boomer story.

I am often asked by people older and younger than the boomers why we think we are so important. We are often accused of being a self-centered, narcissistic "me" generation. But the truth is, we are important because there are just so many of us. It is the phenomenon often metaphorically referred to as "the pig in the python," as this gigantic "bulge" in the population moves from one stage of life to another. It is because of our numbers that we have overwhelmed every institution along the way. That is one of the key reasons our generation is so important, but what make us particularly interesting are our collective characteristics.

Generalizations are always tricky, and all individuals within a generation are certainly not alike. But it is possible to find characteristics that are shared by enough of a cohort and, to a degree, not found in previous or subsequent generations. Baby boomers are famously antiauthoritarian and idealistic. We also tend to be innovative and self-empowered. Our impact on this nation has been, and will continue to be, measured in terms of both quantity and quality.

But how did we come by those uniquely boomer qualities? That answer will be found in our amazing history and the extraordinary decades of our childhood and adolescence. The peace and prosperity of the fifties gave way to the angst of the sixties and seventies. Television replaced radio; Bob Dylan replaced Perry Como; and civil rights and antiwar demonstrations replaced World War II victory parades. A bomb exploded in Birmingham, and "shots were fired" in Dallas, Memphis, Los Angeles, and at Kent State. Men walked on the moon, and the daughters of Rosie the Riveter demanded to be more than June Cleaver could have ever imagined being. We came to realize that our planet was fragile and should be handled with care.

But my deeper interest has always been in the second half of life. Who will we become next? What will we look and feel like when we're seventy? When we're ninety? How does the world need to be redesigned for our aging bodies? What will we do with the new longevity that science and better living have promised us? Will we simply get entitlements and have a leisurely stroll through the rest of our lives? Or will we use that time to give back, to achieve a state of wisdom, to heal, and, perhaps, to transform the world?

I believe this generation is going to radically redo aging, just as we've changed every other stage of life and institution we've encountered: the way we look, the way we feel, what it means to be sixty, what it means to be ninety, the nature of friendships and relationships in maturity, how long we'll work, who pays, what we might blossom into when we're eighty versus what we thought we were going to be when we were twenty. The whole landscape and mindscape of adulthood are about to be totally and dramatically altered. All this time, we've just been warming up for the big game.

These issues and more will be addressed in this book by some of the sharpest minds and most original thinkers of our time. I know you will be challenged, enthralled, and entertained by *The Boomer Century 1946–2046*. I know I am.

Ken Dychtwald, PhD

Introduction

The *Boomer Century*—both the television documentary and the book—are about the largest and most closely observed generation of Americans in history. Born between 1946 and 1964, boomers have been glamorized and reviled, applauded for their idealism and attacked for their materialism, praised for their innovation and condemned for their rebelliousness.

Whichever of those characterizations may be correct, these seventy-eight million Americans have changed the world—they are changing the world—and they will continue to do so for another twenty, thirty, or forty years to come.

The early chapters of this book are perhaps the most fun, for they are pure nostalgia. From Ricky Nelson to Richard Nixon, we will remember the birth and death of idealism. The middle chapters may be the most challenging, for they are about those days in the middle of our lives when we somehow evolved from "flower children"—emblems of "peace, love, and happiness"—into the "me" generation, set out on a quest for the best and the most. While he wasn't a boomer by definition, Jerry Rubin came to exemplify this bizarre transformation. He went from being one of the infamous "Chicago Seven," parading in front of Judge Julius

Hoffman's bench saluting and shouting "Heil Hitler," to a Wall Street stockbroker. And the final chapters, undoubtedly the most important, perhaps should have been written in Nostradamus-style quatrains, for they predict the future, and it is there, in the next quarter century, that boomers may face their most challenging years and have their greatest impact, for better or for worse, as they begin to experience life after sixty.

The book you hold in your hands is a companion to the PBS documentary *The Boomer Century 1946–2046*. It is a companion, not a clone. The producers of the program interviewed more than thirty of the world's foremost experts in various disciplines and fields of endeavor apropos to the boomer generation, including scholars, authors, entertainers, politicians, and entrepreneurs, as well as experts in the fields of publishing, marketing, economics, technology, gerontology, sociology, religion, and even biochemistry.

The great catch to producing television programming is that such endeavors are by nature enslaved to a relentless and fast-moving clock, and decisions (often heartrending decisions) must be made about what can go in and what must be left out. After sitting down for a series of hour-long conversations with brilliant and fascinating people, producers spent most of their time deciding what not to throw away. So what you have before you is an expanded version of the thirty hours or more of these enticing, edifying conversations. It is here that you will find the nuances, the depth, and the details that fell victim to the producers' merciless stopwatch.

The book is, however, more than a collection of transcripts. We have "virtually" brought these people together, as though simultaneously in a single room, for the most entertaining and informative "roundtable discussion" ever held on the subject. They will agree, and they will disagree. They will vent and rage.

Brief biographies and professional credentials for our experts can be found in the About the Contributors section beginning on page 307. You will find them to be a diverse and most impressive group. Some have PhD's, some have "work/life experience," and some just have very strong opinions.

All are fascinating.

part one

The Times, They Are A-Changin'

The Baby Boom: 1946–1964

Births in Millions

chapter 1

We Are
Born

Beginning in 1946 Americans began growing families at an astounding rate. The Depression was a distant memory, the war was over, times were good, and all was (at last) right with the world. The generation that saw our nation through all those very hard times had jobs and houses and very little fear of anything—and they began making babies, tens of millions of American babies.

The parents of the baby boom have been dubbed "the Greatest Generation" by journalist Tom Brokaw for their sacrifices during all those incredibly trying years. They were Franklin Roosevelt and Audie Murphy. They were the 101st Airborne Division and Rosie the Riveter. And yes, they were also Joe McCarthy, George C. Wallace, and Richard M. Nixon. Nobody's perfect.

David Gergen is a commentator, editor, Harvard professor, and bestselling author who has served as adviser to Presidents Nixon, Ford, Reagan, and Clinton; he has no arguments with Brokaw's assessment. Our fathers' generation gave us victories and values—and a string of seven presidents with different views and from different parties—but with an unquestionable love of country.

3

General Douglas MacArthur was an icon of the Greatest Generation. They believed with him in "those magic words: Duty, Honor, Country." When boomers began shouting "Hell no! We won't go," it was a harsh contrast indeed.

John Kennedy was the first of these Greatest Generation presidents and defined them in his inaugural address as part of "a new generation of Americans: born in this century, tempered by war, disciplined by a hard and bitter peace, proud of our ancient heritage and unwilling to witness or permit the slow undoing of those human rights to which this nation has always been committed."

Gergen sees this sense of duty and patriotism as a common thread connecting all presidents that the postwar Greatest Generation produced: "They gave us a generation of leaders that stretches from Kennedy to George [H. W.] Bush, and for all of them, the forties—especially World War II—was their defining experience. No coincidence that John F. Kennedy had in his inaugural parade a replica of the PT boat sliced out from under him in the South Pacific. . . . Six presidents later, George H. W. Bush has a replica of the Avenger aircraft in his inaugural parade. The Avenger aircraft was shot out from under him when he was in the South Pacific, the youngest pilot to go down. What unites those presidents was that all seven presidents from Kennedy through Bush, all seven wore a military uniform. . . . They came out of that with not only a sense of traditional values, common traditional values, but a sense of common destiny for the country. They had a positive sense of what America could be on the world stage. We just won the war and we just defeated the forces of aggression and fascism. What also united them was not only common values and common destiny, but a sense of common sacrifice. They'd all sacrificed something for the country when they were young, and it gave them a sense that we're all in this together. It made a huge damn difference. Now that's what I think united that World War II generation."

Gergen ends with a reference to Douglas MacArthur's famous farewell address at his beloved U.S. Military Academy:

> The Long Gray Line has never failed us. Were you to do so, a million ghosts in olive drab, in brown khaki, in blue and gray, would rise from their white crosses thundering those magic words: Duty, Honor, Country.
>
> **General Douglas MacArthur**

"Those were real words for that generation," Gergen concludes. "It's not just something you have on a statue at West Point."

It all began with a kiss.

But that generation of Americans gave us more than values, unquestioning patriotism, and leadership. They gave us security and prosperity and, well, they gave us, us. Babies. Before it was over they had produced nearly eighty million of us. This was the "baby boom," and at its height American babies came screaming into this world at a rate of one every eight seconds. That's ten thousand babies a day! Four million a year! From 1946 to 1964, 92 percent of all women who could have children did, and they averaged almost four children each.

It is, after all, a most natural thing. Birth rates trend up after virtually all natural disasters or man-made catastrophes. Millions of lives were lost in the war, and there was in the forties and fifties a biological need to replace them.

Okay. So the boys came home from "over there," and nature just took its course, right? Well, yes and no. Of course nature took its course, but were it that simple the baby boom wouldn't have lasted for eighteen years. Sociologists define the boomer generation as having been born between 1946 and 1964. That's right, *nineteen sixty-four.*

Dr. Joshua Zeitz teaches American history at Cambridge University and has some well-studied theories on why this phenomenon exploded so quickly: "I think you can isolate three principal causes of the baby boom. First is that the generation that came of age in the 1930s would normally have married and had children in their twenties and early thirties but had postponed marriage and childbearing largely because of the economic circumstances of the Great Depression. And so they began to have children in the mid-1940s when America's economy was again on the rise. And they did so at the same time that returning GIs and their wives also began starting families, and that's the second cause of the baby boom. But these two generational cohorts came together, and they were having children at the same time, whereas they would have spaced those children out probably ten to fifteen years had circumstances been more normal. And a third cause of the baby boom is simply America's skyrocketing economy, something that began during the war years and really accelerated in the 1950s."

When the boys came home from "over there," they married, proceeded to get jobs, buy homes, and make babies—one every eight seconds for eighteen years. They produced, in fact, seventy-eight million of us.

"*Accelerated*" may very well be too mild a word. Finance expert Jeremy Siegel takes a closer look at the postwar American economy: "Our parents grew up during the Great Depression and World War II when there was rationing, when there was huge unemployment, when every penny counted and very few people had anything extra. . . . All of a sudden when the boys came home and the rationing was lifted, we had a boom. And when we saw that the financial situation was stable, that we weren't going back into a depression at all . . . I mean, the fifties were very, very good times."

The United States in those days also had a bit of a competitive edge over the rest of the world. The industrialized nations of Europe and Asia had been bombed into rubble over the course of a full decade of war, leaving the United States the world's only economic superpower. If you wanted a car or a toaster, Americans were the only people making them. If you had a nation that needed rebuilding from the rubble up, the tools you needed to do so were all going to be "Made in America."

In addition to all of that, our parents had the GI Bill: thirty-year, government-guaranteed mortgages, and, for the first time ever, consumer loans.

There is one more thing—one more explanation for the boom offered to us by someone who knows a thing or two about how babies happen. Erica Jong, the author of the sexually liberating novel *Fear of Flying,* offers an almost Darwinian insight: "After World War II, as after every war in history that we know about, probably even the Trojan War, people want to make babies. There's a great desire to make babies. People fear the population has been depleted. It's particularly noticeable in Jewish culture, which I belong to. After the Holocaust, where six million Jews were killed, women wanted to make babies and replace the babies who [had] been lost. And it [was] probably true all over Europe. And babies become very valuable after all those deaths; babies become hope, you know. God's way of saying 'human life will continue' is a newborn baby. And everybody feels that. So I think that parents were so dazzled that the war was over and that they were giving new life to the world that they just adored their children.

"Children who are adored grow up with extreme self-confidence. Some of them are a little spoiled; some of them really believe in themselves in a way that's terrific. Lots of confidence, a lot of beans, a lot of 'I can do it—anything.' That's the boomer generation."

Dr. Ken Dychtwald is the moving force behind *The Boomer Century*, both the book and the television documentary. He is a psychologist, a gerontologist, and among the nation's foremost students of the boomer generation. "Every generation has an identity," he tells us, "a personality, a common sensibility. That doesn't mean that everyone holds the exact same values or beliefs, or likes the same food or music. But when a mass of people share similar formative experiences, a generational identity is created."

He compares boomers to Pando—Utah's 107-acre Quaking Aspen grove that is billed as the world's most massive single organism: "If you look at it, it looks like it's tens of thousands of trees, but it's not. It's actually one tree with a common root system."

Of course the "common root system" that boomers all share is the media. Television, radio, newspapers, and classroom experiences could reach every one of us in our formative years, and very quickly. No one was isolated.

Dr. Steven Nock is a professor of psychology and sociology at the University of Virginia: "I think that the historical period, which means *when* we were born, perhaps for one of the first generations, is dramatically more important than *where* we happen to be born.

"The baby boomers certainly learned through open access to communications about everything that was going on in the United States. It happened in my lifetime. I think that the availability of media that is without place is only part of the story. It's true that when you watch the news on TV or you read your favorite Internet blog, it's impossible to know where it's coming from. But the placelessness of my generation is also seen in many other ways. If you walk into a mall—whether it's in Washington, DC, or in Los Angeles—it has the same stores, has the same products at the same prices. If you walk into a fast-food restaurant, is it in Biloxi or is it in Boston? You can't really tell."

This is a point that was brought home strongly for Emmy Award–winning television producer, Joel Westbrook.

When, Not Where

Joel Westbrook
Producer, *The Boomer Century 1946–2046*

When we began the process of developing the television documentary *The Boomer Century 1946–2046,* Ken Dychtwald discussed with us the idea that for baby boomers "when" you were born is more important than "where" you were born. It is a concept that struck me deeply.

I was born on a peanut and cotton farm in south Georgia. The "where" involved dirt roads, outhouses, and rabbit hunting. The "when" was about clear-channel radio stations and eventually television. I first heard the Rolling Stones on WLS from Chicago. We drove into town to watch Elvis on *The Ed Sullivan Show.* There wasn't a major league baseball team in the South, but I watched the Milwaukee Braves on the NBC broadcasts. There wasn't an NBA team in the South, but I was a Bill Russell fan. There wasn't an ocean near us either, but I knew what was down there because I watched Jacques Cousteau. Years later, I would produce television coverage of the Atlanta Braves, I covered the NBA with Bill Russell as one of my announcers, and I worked on documentaries with Jacques Cousteau.

"When" I was born was seven years before a television came to that farmhouse. That timing, even more than the "where" of being rural and southern, would ultimately be the greater influence on my life.

My partner, producer/director Neil Steinberg, was born in Chicago only six years after me. He also heard the Rolling Stones on his "local" radio station,

WLS; he saw Elvis on *Ed Sullivan,* watched baseball on NBC and followed the NBA (he preferred the Cubs and the Bulls' Guy Rodgers), and learned about the oceans from Jacques Cousteau. We first met and worked together in Los Angeles in 1973. Had we been born in those same two places, fifty or a hundred years earlier, we would have had very little in common. But because we were of the boomer generation, by the time we met we had many shared experiences, much common knowledge, and, in spite of my accent, could communicate. Our meeting also happened in Los Angeles—he had lived there for four years and I had just arrived. But absolutely nothing about LA was foreign to me. Riding around LA was pure geographic déjà vu. Remember, I was a child of TV; I'd already spent half my life in LA.

Once, during the time I lived in LA, I returned to visit my hometown, and I drove out to the old farm. As I walked around, I saw our neighbor, Donald Orr, plowing in a nearby field. I went over to say hello. He asked where I lived, and when I told him California, he said, "That's a long way away. I try not to go so far in a day that I can't get home at night." He was born before me. He wasn't a boomer. I am.

So, working on this project, I have come late to identifying myself as a boomer. And in my mind, I know that should be my second grouping after American. The facts are clear—college, drugs, antiwar, VW bus, Volvo station wagon, SUV, a variety of jobs, playing baseball in my fifties, and occasionally drinking bottled water. In my heart, I am still a southerner, but I'm afraid Ken is right: "when" I was born—February 10, 1949—*is* more important than "where"—Randal's Crossing, Georgia.

And yet, like the Aspen trees themselves, our differences are undeniable, "similar formative experiences" aside. In 2006, the oldest of us turned sixty years old while the youngest were in their early forties—that alone makes us a tough group to lump together. And, of course, some of us are black and some of us are white.

Julian Bond was one of the founders of the Student Nonviolent Coordinating Committee in the sixties, is the chairman of the NAACP, and generally concurs with the Aspen grove analogy: "The black/white boomer experience is different in that, while they were younger, the black boomers were likely to be engaged heavily in the movement to eliminate discrimination, the white boomers, less so. The black boomers were finding opportunity bursting around them and coming on them, and so they were adjusting their sights to what was possible for them. I think for the white boomers . . . that opportunity, at least for some, was already there. The black boomers, I think, probably had a more pronounced social conscience about some things than the white boomers did. But I think all of them shared a kind of commonality of 'I'm young. The world is my oyster. I can do things that my mom and dad couldn't think about doing. I am doing some things they don't want me to do.' I think they felt part of a generation, all of them together. There are differences between them, but I think they commonly felt the same things."

Futurist Faith Popcorn, whom the *New York Times* calls "the trend oracle," says that lumping us together, regardless of how broadly, simply cannot be done: "How can there be a group that's forty *and* sixty? How can there be a group that's having babies and getting married, and the other side of it is going through menopause and trying to retire? That's impossible."

Like most of the "leading-edge" boomers, Congressman Tom Price is a bit of a chauvinist when it comes to defining a "genuine boomer." With a smile, he shares his own definition: "If you didn't feel the riots of the sixties, experience the assassinations of the sixties, live the freedom of the sixties, how can you be a boomer? How can you be a boomer if you don't remember the Beatles on *The Ed Sullivan Show?*"

The University of Virginia's Dr. Steven Nock tells us why a generation is so hard to define: "I think most people, when they think of a generation, tend to think of something that defines the members of it in [such] a way that they come to see themselves as alike. Sometimes it's the nature of the economy. Sometimes it's a great experience such as World War II or the Great Depression, facing some common challenge, some common enemy oftentimes. Sometimes it's something like the culture, music, or some other unexpected event. But it's not something that can be defined easily in terms of numbers or in years, although demographers tend to think of a generation as lasting about twenty-five years, about as long as it takes for a child to be born and become of reproductive age."

Of course the boomer generation is too diverse to be categorized or stereotyped, as the scholars readily admit. We don't all agree on anything. Case in point? The bestselling single record of 1966 was "The Ballad of the Green Berets."

Perhaps it need not be pointed out that most of us were *not* at Woodstock, but Dr. Fernando Torres-Gil, the director of the Center for Policy Research on Aging at UCLA, suggests that Woodstock is not the only thing most of us didn't do: "Not all of them were involved in civil rights; not all of them were at Woodstock; not all of them were into drugs, sex, and rock 'n' roll. As a matter of fact, only a relatively small proportion of baby boomers engaged in those activities. The majority of them were just struggling to get through high school, find a job, raise a family. But even that group was ultimately influenced and somehow overshadowed by what that very active segment of baby boomers was doing."

Julian Bond knows how icons get to be icons—and how so many of them are wrong: "I think the snapshot of the boomers as a protest generation, opposing authority, fighting for change . . . was only a single picture . . . and what we've done is squeeze them all together into this single stereotype, and this stereotype wasn't true then, and it's not true now."

Okay. So we're not all one thing and not all the other. But how similar are the similarities, how different are the differences, and how general are the generalities? Just how "hippie" were we?

Dr. Zeitz is specific: "One of the great myths is that everyone was marching and protesting for a cause and that these causes were all on the Left. And in fact, although it's very difficult to come up with precise numbers, at best about 20 percent of college students in the 1960s participated in one or two marches, and only 2 percent or 3 percent identified themselves as 'activists,' which is to say that at least 80 percent of the population was probably apolitical and managed to stay on the sidelines in the 1960s.

"Boomers often like to think that they were responsible for all of the great social and political revolutions of the l960s and the l950s. They like to think, for instance, that they somehow contributed to making America a much more casual and pluralistic society. That's not necessarily the case. There was a great surge in civil liberties activism in the early l940s, around the time of World War II. You also saw, as early as the 1920s, the emergence of a youth culture that was decidedly less formal and more experimental than its parents' generation. This is certainly something that sociologists found in the 1920s, particularly Robert and Helen Lynd when they visited Muncie, Indiana, and undertook their famous study of a typical American town. In that sense, the boomers in the 1950s were really carrying on with trends that their parents and grandparents had initiated.

"Our generations are, in and of themselves, diverse. The boomers are seventy-eight million people from all races, economic backgrounds, ethnicities. They're women; they're men; they're from different sexual identities and backgrounds. They're simply too diverse to reduce to a single entity. They had to share a tremendous amount in common. And they dealt with the changing economy and changing political circumstances to the best of their ability. They probably did it no better and no worse than any other generation because they were so large and they came on the scene in a period when America was achieving a kind of prominence in the world that it had never enjoyed before and may never enjoy again. They just seemed to us to be such powerful agents of change that we can't help but blame them and credit them with things that probably were beyond their control."

Who do you blame when your kid is a brat,
Pampered and spoiled like a Siamese cat?
Blaming the kids is a lie and a shame.
You know exactly who's to blame:
The mother and the father!

From "Oompa Loompa"
(Willy Wonka and the Chocolate Factory)
By Leslie Bricusse and Anthony Newley

Before we were baby boomers, flower children, or the me generation, we were Spock babies. Dr. Benjamin Spock's The Common Sense Book of Baby and Child Care *was more than only an amazing bestseller, it was a cultural revolution.*

But Dr. Dychtwald's definition still stands. Most of us do share "similar formative experiences," making us, in demographic terms, a cohort. "One of the first things to understand about our generation is its size," he says. "There were so many of us that society literally had to reshape itself around us. There weren't enough pediatricians. There weren't enough schools."

There was that. If nothing else, we were huge. And, of course, there was Dr. Benjamin Spock. Dr. Spock wrote *The Common Sense Book of Baby and Child Care,* a book that was a runaway bestseller for the better part of three decades.

Our resident historian, Dr. Zeitz, knows the influence *The Common Sense Book of Baby and Child Care* had on our generation: "It was consulted by over half of all new parents according to some polls. In his book, what Dr. Spock counseled was paying attention to the whole child. It was the so-called progressive ideal of child rearing. It counseled indulgence; it counseled understanding. It placed children and their happiness at the very center of the child-rearing project so they were brought up in nurturing households that placed a lot of emphasis on their education and upbringing. . . . So, it was quite unlike anything that had come before."

Ultimately Dr. Spock's book was translated into thirty-nine languages and sold more than fifty million copies. It was the best-selling nonfiction book after the Bible. It was revolutionary.

In a 1996 interview for PBS's *Nova*, Dr. Spock explained the "before and after": "There have been books, but they were just old, pediatric traditions. They'd say, for instance, thumb sucking is a bad habit. So you paint nasty-tasting stuff on the baby's thumb, or you put aluminum mitts over his hands, or, the cruelest of all, you spread-eagle him in his crib, tie his wrists to the slats of the side of the crib. I knew that this wasn't right. So I tried, first of all, to find out what different people think is the meaning of the thumb sucking, and then I tried to explain to parents what it meant, and then next tried to decide with parents what's the best way of dealing with it."

Dr. Steven Parker is director of Behavioral and Developmental Pediatrics at Boston Medical Center and an associate professor of pediatrics at the Boston University School of Medicine. He is the author of *Behavioral and Developmental Pediatrics: A Handbook for Primary Care* and is coauthor of the 1998 edition of *Dr. Spock's Baby and Child Care*. On that same PBS program, Dr. Parker reflected on the impact of Dr. Spock's work: "To really understand the success and impact of Dr. Spock, you have to remember the context in which he burst upon the scene. Child-rearing advice at the time was an incredibly dismal affair. Parents were told don't touch your child; don't kiss them; don't hug them; feed them on a schedule; let them cry; prepare them for a tough world by not being emotionally involved. And he came to it saying, 'Well, wait a second. Trust yourself. No parent inherently feels that way. Do what feels right for you, and you probably won't go wrong.' And he based it too on his . . . understanding of child development, which included the importance of attachment and the emotional relationship between parent and child, and most of all, that children needed to feel loved. And if they felt loved, almost everything else would follow from there. That was revolutionary in 1946, believe it or not."

Ultimately the "rebellious" nature of the "Spock generation" would be blamed by some on this man they called "the father of permissiveness."

In the early years we generally had in common nurturing mothers, an economically secure environment, the power of numbers, and one more thing—television.

Television: What America Wasn't

WALLY: Boy, Beaver, wait'll the guys find out you were hanging around with a girl. They'll really give you the business.

BEAVER: But gee, Wally, you hang around with girls, and the guys don't give you the business.

WALLY: Well, that's because I'm in high school. You can do a lot of stuff in high school without getting the business.

From **Leave It to Beaver**

Dr. Zeitz reminds us that the emergence of television as a national medium came about very swiftly: "In 1948, there were something like 172,000 televisions throughout America, and four years later, by 1952, there were over fifteen million TVs in American living rooms."

Any real boomer can easily flash back in time and find himself sitting on the living room floor absolutely mesmerized by those beloved Saturday morning cartoons. For many of us, those cozy Saturday mornings led us directly to careers in that magical, whirling, swirling world of television production.

Richard Chapman has had a long career writing and producing television programs in both the entertainment and documentary segments of the industry, and he, like most of us, remembers Buffalo Bob as an old and beloved childhood friend: "Watching television, drinking delicious hot cocoa, and getting a decoder badge to boot? What boomer doesn't have fond memories of Captain Midnight and his goofy sidekick Icky? Or Buffalo Bob and his honking compadre Clarabelle? Pat Brady and Nellie-Belle? Joey, Pete, and Fury? It was a glorious era of courageous masked men, straight shootin' singing cowboys, a stone-faced Indian named Tonto, and an entire menagerie of animated mischief makers like Hekyll and Jekyll and Woody Woodpecker. Boomers

From Beverly Sills to Elvis Presley and the Beatles, Ed Sullivan provided us all with some unique "shared formative experiences." Here, he conducts a live, in-depth interview with the ever-popular Topo Gigio.

sat in pajamas, mesmerized by a parade of guys in space suits and white hats, spouting truth, justice, and the American way, while in the 'real world' Joe McCarthy was busy blacklisting many of the actors who played them.

"Boomer television was actually Sunday School a day early. It promoted honesty, cleanliness, and made it okay to have freckles. Dick Clark got you through puberty. Ed Sullivan brought the family together at least one night a week . . . and Roy and Dale gave you a happy trail of memories to last a lifetime."

Rob Reiner is another boomer who found a career in TV, and who better to talk about the impact of early television than *All in the Family*'s "meathead" himself? "There was no television when I was born. I was born in 1947. I mean, there was a little, but nobody had a television, really, not until the fifties. As a matter of fact, my father [Carl Reiner] was on television before we had a television. So, when I remember that as a four-year-old in 1951, . . . I could watch my father on television, that was also a very strange thing to be doing. But we grew up on television. So that has always been part of our lives. . . . I tell my kids now, I was born at a time when there was no television—they can't even imagine that. So we have an affinity for television, we're connected to television, and we're hooked on it."

Many historians and sociologists believe that more than security, more than numbers, more than nurturing and loving mothers, it was television that provided the shared similar formative experiences that make baby boomers a cohort.

Emmy Award–winning television documentarian Joel Westbrook refers to the early days of television as "the communal gathering place—history's largest tribal campfire."

Because of the limited number of stations and programs, the impact of television was perhaps greater in the fifties than at any time since. By the millions we gathered round a glowing box to share in *The Adventures of Ozzie and Harriet*, each and every week.

Regardless of the fact that his father was a regular on *Your Show of Shows*, along with Sid Caesar and Imogene Coca, the very young Rob Reiner sat and stared at the box with the rest of us: "Like everybody else, I watched all the sitcoms. I watched *Leave It to Beaver,* and *Ozzie and Harriet,* and *Father Knows Best,* and *The Donna Reed Show.* I loved all the sitcoms, but I also loved the Westerns, the *Mickey Mouse Club,* and *Spin and Marty,* and all that stuff. There was an idealized version of suburban life in the fifties that was portrayed on television. It didn't really exist, but we all wanted it to exist. We all aspired to having a father like James Anderson, who always did the right thing, and Ozzie who never had a job. But it was interesting; he just was always at home and didn't have a job. But we always wanted that kind of nice suburban lifestyle; we aspired to that."

Miss Kitty: Mat, you can't account for everything that happens to people who touch you. You know, I learned a long time ago, there are some things in this life that you just accept the way they are.
Mat Dillon: That's pretty deep for a redhead.
Miss Kitty: I'm a pretty deep redhead.

From Gunsmoke

If you are a professor of American history with an interest in the late twentieth century, the cable network Nickelodeon may well be a valuable (and tax-deductible) research tool. Such a person can watch Nick@Nite and see hours of fifties and sixties dramas, sitcoms, and Westerns, and apparently Dr. Zeitz does just that. He tells us that early television did more than entertain us, it molded us: "If you look at the kinds of television shows that were popular in the 1950s and early sixties, they definitely tell us a great deal about that generation. For instance, seven out of the eleven most popular television shows in the late fifties were Westerns, and these Westerns, shows like *Gunsmoke,* really talked about a mythic period in American history, when you had rugged individuals who went out and tamed the frontier, and that said a lot about the generation that was growing up amid tremendous economic prosperity and confidence. This was a generation raised to believe that it could simply

21

June Cleaver was always dressed for dinner, always deferential to Ward, and rarely seen outside the home. In the fifties, the June Cleaver model of the "modern" American woman was the stereotypical vision of the perfect mother and wife.

tame and conquer and defeat any possible enemy and really meet any possible challenge."

But it was the sitcoms, the situation comedies, that may have most impacted the psychology of our generation, one way or another. A half century later, some view them as harmless, idealized stereotypes, while others look back on them as deceitful propaganda.

Let the debate begin.

In addition to being a professor of sociology at the University of Virginia, Dr. Steven Nock is also director of the Marriage Matters project and the author of *Marriage in Men's Lives:* "I like to tell my students that every stereotype has an element of truth behind it. When we think of the family of the fifties, we think of *Ozzie and Harriet* and *Leave It to Beaver* and *Father Knows Best*. And if we strip those down to their core, what we see is families that are based upon marriage; families that are organized so that the primary honor is to the husband; and families with relatively large numbers of children—two, three, four children. That's probably more true than false; that is, the fifties are remembered as a period of high—*very* high—marriage rates, low divorce rates, and very high fertility that is the nature of the baby boom itself. On the other hand, the portrait of the fifties as monolithic, and 'everyone living this way,' is a true exaggeration.

"Television shows in the fifties, and even into the sixties, were all about the way things *should* be. Family problems should be able to be resolved; couples should be able to stay married; life should be happy as long as people abide by the basic rules."

Even motion picture director Oliver Stone, who would become renowned for his rebellious nature, grew up a victim of "the myth," casting his own father as Robert Young's character in *Father Knows Best:* "I loved, I respected and admired my father, and I loved Robert Young at the same time. I saw my father very much in that role, sure; I went to him for wisdom."

While it may be difficult for us to believe today, even Stone was subject to the mandated conformity of the age: "I ended up going along for the ride and being in the system, and I was very, very conformist. I wanted Goldwater to win in 1964. I was raised Republican. I didn't know much. I grew up a conformist. I went to a school where you wore a jacket and tie, you did the same thing, and you did it like everybody else, and you tried to stay out of trouble."

Tony Snow is a journalist and the press secretary for President George W. Bush, and he remembers that while television in the fifties was generally "sanitized," the Cleaver household wasn't too different from the norm: "It was a different country then. In the early sixties, my first memories are life in a neighborhood where people would always come next door to borrow a cup of sugar. Your doors were always open. People would walk in. It was a much smaller nation."

But the woman who wrote and performs *The Vagina Monologues* (as might be expected) begs to differ. Eve Ensler has different memories than Tony Snow—and a drastically different perspective: "I was highly suspicious always of *Father Knows Best* and *Leave It to Beaver,* because I lived in a family that *looked* like that. You know, I actually had a white picket fence in front of my house, and yet it was the complete opposite. It was full of enormous violence; it was full of rage, it was full of alcoholism. It was a nightmare, it was a nightmare; and everybody was telling me how grateful I should be for living this upper middle-class life in this white community when, in fact, it devastated my soul. To be perfectly honest, it took fifty years to recover from it."

It was possible, and probably even common, for an American town of the fifties to be both idyllic and disgraceful at the very same time. While John Chane is an Episcopal bishop today, back in the fifties, he was a typical child in a typical family living in a small and fairly typical Massachusetts community: "We lived in a great neighborhood, but we didn't have a lot of things. We had great neighborhood friends, and so in the summers we were out on the streets playing stickball every evening. So growing up in that neighborhood in a Massachusetts small town of twelve thousand was really neat because it seemed as if everybody cared for everybody else. I look at that time now, and I look at the way in which my own children have grown up, and I think they've really missed a lot. What we didn't have in terms of things, we made up for in terms of our care for one another.

"My mom was a real estate broker, and I remember when she sold a home to the first African American to buy a home on the west side of this town. And about five days after the home was sold, someone threw a Molotov cocktail on the front porch of our house and threw a rock through our window with a note on it that said, 'Nigger lovers aren't welcome in this town.'

"And it was really painful to begin to realize that the town that I grew up in was pretty intolerant. But it really reflected, I think, many of the towns in that part of the country."

So we are not all of a single tribe. Some of us are black, and even middle-class African Americans in the fifties had a different perspective.

Julian Bond is too old to be an "official" boomer, but he has his own memories of the days of *Leave It to Beaver* and *Ozzie and Harriet:* "When you looked at TV then, you saw families, because it was all about families. All these shows were about families that could have been yours, except you weren't them, and they weren't you. . . . You wanted to enjoy it for what it was, but you knew it was off-putting in the sense that you never saw yourself there, except as a maid or a janitor or some person doing menial work. So you liked it, and it repulsed you at the same time.

"Television not only created a kind of disconnect, but it also created a kind of aspiration of what could be. It gave you pictures of a world that you could live in, so the possibility was there. You weren't there, but you *could* be there, and in many ways it taught you how that world behaved. I can remember watching *American Bandstand,* and they usually had one black couple there, a boy and girl who could dance with each other, and I lived in the country then, and a chance of seeing these people was like seeing an eclipse of the moon. But I think seeing them, not just for me, but for the white kids who were watching TV, this show particularly, but all these shows, gave them a look at a world that they weren't in, but could be in, and for them it was an exciting world. It was an appealing world. So this medium did an enormous job in both creating aspiration and demonstrating how far you were from that aspiration."

Shirley Franklin, now mayor of Atlanta, grew up in a middle-class black family in Philadelphia, and in her youth she was relatively isolated from bigotry if not from segregation: "I remember the first time I saw a young black woman on television. It was Cab Callaway's daughter and she was dancing. She was in a dance program on *Ed Sullivan,* I think, and everyone in the neighborhood went home to watch that show because it was such an unusual occurrence. Of course, it was very similar to when Jackie Robinson played baseball. There was no one outside playing. Everyone was around the radio, listening to the game."

And Franklin offers another recollection from the perspective of a young, black boomer watching white people on TV: "I tended to like the women on television who had a swarthy complexion, because they looked more like me than the others, like Annette Funicello."

So black or white, male or female, we all knew that the Andersons, the Cleavers, the Nelsons, and the Ricardos were works of fiction and were different from "real" American families. The extent of that fiction was left for each of us alone to determine.

Television wasn't the only mass media that impacted boomers in the late fifties and early sixties. With our pockets full of quarters, the boomer generation headed out to the movies.

Movies: The First Rebels

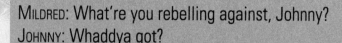

MILDRED: What're you rebelling against, Johnny?
JOHNNY: Whaddya got?

From **The Wild One**
Screenplay by Ben Maddow,
based on a short story by Frank Rooney

When the boomers came of age, apparently the Beaver and company had somehow failed to fill a need, so we went shopping for something a little more "real," and Ron Reiner remembers that what we found had an edge to it—a darker side: "We latched on to James Dean and Marlon Brando because they were irreverent, they were renegades, and even though they were in the early fifties, we still latched on to them as our icons."

In listing his favorite movies by decade, Oliver Stone starts with Brando's masterpiece, *On the Waterfront.* It wasn't about a white middle-class suburban family. It was about the fight game, dock workers, corrupt union bosses, murder, love, and lost dreams. "I could have been a contender" may be the classic line of fifties films.

Every director in Hollywood went off in search of "the next Brando" until Elia Kazan found James Dean and cast him in the 1955 film *East of Eden.* As the first boomers approached their teen years, Dean gave us a role model unlike anything we had ever seen on television, and *East of Eden* showed us a father-son relationship that was, to say the least, diametrically opposed to Ward and the Beaver. The Moviefone biography of Dean tells why: "Playing a hell-raising teenager who yearned openly and unashamedly to be loved and accepted by his rigid and taciturn father [Raymond Massey], Dean 'spoke' to the disenfranchised youth of the Eisenhower era far more eloquently than any previous actor."

And the age of the brooding and rebellious teenager was born. As Oliver Stone puts it, "The kids on *Father Knows Best* were revolting against the father."

Blue jeans, T-shirts, and leather jackets became the uniform of our generation, and our parents became concerned. A new phrase came into vogue in the late fifties: suddenly we were a bunch of "juvenile delinquents."

Dr. Zeitz seems to picture these early films glorifying rebellion as more of a reflection than a cause: "There was a tremendous amount of concern in the 1950s about the youth problem, the adolescent problem, and delinquencies, certainly. If you look at movies, particularly the James Dean movies, even early Marlon Brando movies, they reflect those anxieties."

We began to look at what American television was showing us and to wonder whether it was harmless fiction or not. Was television showing us the way we were or telling us how we were expected to behave? Dr. Dychtwald lists the core influences on the early boomers as "the nuclear family unit. A dad who works. A mom who stays home and devotes herself to her 3.8 kids per household."

Dr. Steven Nock agrees: "I do believe that the fifties and sixties were dominated by a particular view of what was right and proper. It was cohesive . . . for better and for worse. There was a more or less shared moral sense of what things should be. And I believe the media in those days focused more upon the ideal. They were all about the way things should be, not necessarily the way things were."

And it was this vision of how America should be that we saw on TV. But, as we were beginning to discover, it was far distant from the real America of the fifties.

The America That Television Didn't Show

Leonard Steinhorn is associate professor of communications at American University and author of *The Greater Generation: In Defense of the Baby Boom Legacy,* and he reveals the harsh realities of America in the fifties: "So, what was really going on in the 1950s for a lot of Americans? Well, black people were kept separate. Women were told to stay in the home. Gays were told to stay in the closet. People who prayed to a different God or wanted to do their own thing or express their own personal freedom or who even wanted to protect the environment were told to stay silent. And so, we had a society, which on its surface, seemed like a nice placid peaceful place. But for a lot of minorities, for women, for people who were anything outside the mainstream, it was an uncomfortable terrain.

"Eighty percent of Americans said if a woman was unmarried, she was sick, neurotic, or immoral. Women couldn't gain credit. They couldn't get home mortgages. There were limited jobs available to women.

"If you were gay, you could be imprisoned. If your parents suspected you were gay, they might put you up for electroshock therapy or induced vomiting, certainly psychotherapy.

"In the 1950s, if you were a man with a beard walking in a community, the police might stop you and ask what you [were] doing. In fact, it wasn't unusual if you grew a beard to be told you might be a Communist."

Racism was institutionalized in America, and while most may today believe that those restrictions existed only in the South, where Jim Crow laws were prominent and enforced, there were bigots everywhere. Racism was everywhere.

Dr. Zeitz teaches that on a national level there was a quiet and perhaps more sinister institutionalized racism: "The [Federal Housing Administration] redlined all of its mortgages, which is to say it didn't consider areas that were racially integrated or economically integrated as safe for investment. If you were a white baby boomer, you probably grew up in a suburb; if you were an African American or Asian or Latino baby boomer, you probably didn't, and that was in large part because of the way the federal subsidies worked."

From an age when Ozzie and Harriet slept in separate beds, and "bad girls" simply vanished, Erica Jong recalls another fear of the fifties: "I remember the fear of pregnancy when I was in high school. I remember the terror. The girls who vanished, who went to the wilds of New Jersey and then were admitted to a New York hospital hemorrhaging. And some of them never returned. And some of them were sterilized for life. And some of them wanted to have babies later on and couldn't. So it was really scary."

It was here, Dr. Dychtwald says, that the divide began to form between us and our parents: "For many of us there was a disconnect between what we saw on the screen and what we saw in our communities. Raised by our parents to think for ourselves, we suddenly looked around and saw hypocrisy everywhere."

The "generation gap" was beginning to spread. That is not to say that the fifties were an entirely happy and complacent time and that with the turn of the decade we all suddenly became screaming revolutionaries. No. The sixties actually began with a new breath of idealism when, on January 20, 1961, a young, auburn-haired war hero placed his hand on a Bible and said, "I, John Fitzgerald Kennedy, do solemnly swear . . ."

chapter 2

....

Camelot

> We shall pay any price, bear any burden, meet any hardship, support any friend, oppose any foe, in order to assure the survival and success of liberty.
> **President John F. Kennedy**
> **January 20, 1961**

The most beautiful days God gives us, it seems, are those that follow the storm, and so it was on the first of the "Thousand Days" of the Kennedy administration. A blizzard struck Washington over the two days and nights before Inauguration Day and buried the nation's capital under a layer of snow that was measured in feet. But January 20 dawned cold and clear, America's soldiers were mobilized to clear the streets, and the great event, which had been in danger of cancellation, went on as scheduled.

It was a spectacularly bright and beautiful day. It was a grand inaugural address.

Best remembered for urging Americans to "ask what you can do for your country," it was almost exclusively a foreign policy speech in which the new president pledged to the world that "we shall pay any price, bear any burden, meet any hardship, support any friend, oppose any foe, in order to assure the survival and the success of liberty."

The Cold War was raging all around the globe after all. The war in Korea festered in a permanent cease-fire (as it continues to do today). The communists in the Soviet Union had influence or

On January 20, 1961, a youthful president challenged a young generation "to bear the burden of a long twilight struggle, year in and year out, 'rejoicing in hope, patient in tribulation'—a struggle against the common enemies of man: tyranny, poverty, disease, and war itself."

total control over governments in Europe, Asia, Southeast Asia, the Middle East, South America, and, worst of all, Cuba. The closing years of the Eisenhower administration had seen the shooting down of Francis Gary Powers and his U-2 spy plane over the Soviet Union, followed by a deceitful denial. In 1957 the Soviet satellite Sputnik orbited the earth, and suddenly and unexpectedly the godless communists had a basketball-sized "thing" way up in *space,* orbiting the earth and beeping! *We* didn't have a beeping basketball in space, but the Russians did!

The launching of Sputnik by the Soviet Union may have been our generation's first shared "Oh, my God" moment, but even the oldest of us were very young at the time. There would be more such moments.

And, of course, on Kennedy's spectacularly bright and beautiful Inauguration Day, boomer boys and girls were well practiced at "duck and cover" air-raid drills because both sides had "The Bomb."

The phrases space race,
missile gap, and mutual
assured destruction were
all part of our childhood
vernacular. Duck and cover,
boys and girls!

MAJOR T. J. "KING" KONG: Well, boys, I reckon this is it—nuclear combat toe to toe with the Rooskies. Now look, boys, I ain't much of a hand at makin' speeches, but I got a pretty fair idea that something doggone important is goin' on back there. And I got a fair idea the kinda personal emotions that some of you fellas may be thinkin'. Heck, I reckon you wouldn't even be human bein's if you didn't have some pretty strong personal feelin's about nuclear combat.

From **Dr. Strangelove, or: How I Learned to Stop Worrying and Love the Bomb** *Screenplay by Stanley Kubrick*

Regardless of all that, on his first day in office, John Fitzgerald Kennedy both challenged us and gave us hope. He called that beautiful Inauguration Day "an end as well as a beginning." Dr. Dychtwald agrees: "For many boomers, Kennedy represented a hope for a new and more hopeful era in America. Raised to believe that we could pursue our own dreams, we saw the youthful Kennedy as an emblem of our own idealism and our belief in a better future for all."

In those days Shirley Franklin was a very young, African-American female boomer growing up in a middle-class Philadelphia family where she was among those who got caught up in the young president's promise: "Well, President Kennedy was the first politician [whose campaign] I got actively engaged in. . . . I was a high school student, . . . and I wouldn't let anyone come in the house who would not commit to me to vote for President Kennedy. It was my way of spreading the word about this amazing young man with this big vision. What I was attracted to was how young and vibrant he was. Not to take anything away from the other presidents before him, but he had a vibrancy about him and an inclusiveness."

David Gergen, on the other hand, was a young, white southerner, and he, coming from such a drastically different background than Franklin, was caught up in the Kennedy idealism as well: "I think that John Kennedy's call to action, his challenge, his inspiration was enormously influential in kicking off the sixties, in sort of opening the door to what followed. I had the opportunity to go hear him speak. . . . He was one of these figures who just had this heroic quality but also spoke with this idealism that cut right through all the crap, and it really moved you.

"You're throwing a Frisbee, you're studying somewhere—you go find a television set to watch John Kennedy on television."

But beneath the hope for the world lay a festering feeling of hopelessness for America.

While the civil rights movement was well begun, it had made dramatic but only brief appearances on the front pages of our papers, only to recede until the next violent drama demanded our attention. The earth-shattering Supreme Court decision called *Brown v. Board of Education of Topeka* was six years old and had since been watered down by "Brown II," which allowed for progress toward desegregation of our schools at "all deliberate speed." There were no more troops in Little Rock, the Montgomery Bus Boycott was resolved, and Rosa Parks was fading from memory. The new administration in Washington had global wars to fight, "cold" and otherwise.

The space race continued at full tilt. Four months into Kennedy's administration, the Soviet Union again made international headlines, but this time it wasn't a beeping basketball, and it wasn't a dog or a monkey like the previous "Russians" that had traveled in space. This time it was a living, breathing, communist human being named Yuri Gagarin who was orbiting the earth. But less than a month later, Alan Shepard became the first American in space, and we all felt better.

President Kennedy felt *a lot* better. As he stood in the well of the House for his first State of the Union speech, he shocked the nation by raising the bar:

I believe that this nation should commit itself to achieving the goal, before this decade is out, of landing a man on the moon and returning him safely to the Earth. No single space project in this period will be more impressive to mankind or more important for the long-range exploration of space; and none will be so difficult or expensive to accomplish. . . . In a very real sense, it will not be one man going to the moon—it will be an entire nation.

President John F. Kennedy
May 25, 1961

Dr. Martin Luther King Jr. and the peaceful protesters in the South were, at best, a distraction. The Cold War, the space race, and the missile gap were far more important to the administration and the media than were a bunch of black kids sitting at a lunch counter in Nashville, Tennessee. After all, segregation may not have been fair, but it was "just the way things are."

David Gergen remembers growing up white in North Carolina: "I lived in an all-white community, and we were told that people across town whom we never saw, unless they came to cut your lawn, that they were happy and that this was the way people liked it to be. And Negroes went to one place, and you went to another place. You had one water fountain. They had another water fountain. You could go to one restaurant, but they couldn't. Everybody said that's the way they'd like it to be. And you thought that was paradise. And then you grew up a little later in the sixties, and you realized that's *not* the way they wanted it to be. I'm always grateful for growing up in the South. I'm also equally grateful to those young African-American kids who rode in buses and sat down in lunch counters in Greensboro and got their heads beaten in, because they changed the South. They opened our eyes to what was going on."

While all of this was happening, the earliest boomers were still too young to participate, but we were not too young to watch. We had spent our childhood watching Lucy and Beaver, and now, in that same glowing box, we began to see something different, something real—something ugly—and we began to figure out that the America we'd been watching on TV all our lives was a lie.

Leonard Steinhorn calls it a "disconnect": "America had gone through some rough times, the Depression, World War II. I think people wanted to feel better about themselves, and television reflected that. But, television also did some other things, because this was the birth of television news. And all of the 'Beaver Cleavers' and 'Father Knows Bests' couldn't smother the images of black people being hosed down when they were trying to eat at a lunch counter, or German shepherds attacking them when they were trying to vote, or angry police chiefs trying to beat them up when they tried to ride in an interstate bus. Television couldn't hide that.

"Boomers grew up believing in 'truth, justice, and the American way'; grew up believing that America was a good country; that America had fought the bad people overseas and had triumphed on behalf of democracy and freedom.

"The bottom line for boomers, though, is that they saw a society which extolled freedom, extolled justice, extolled equality, yet wasn't fully living up to it. So young people growing up at that time saw these things in front of them and said, 'There's a disconnect here. We're taught all these good values—thank you, Mom and Dad. Thank you for teaching us these good values. But why aren't people living up to them?'"

African Americans saw something more than only the injustice. For the first time on TV, Shirley Franklin and others like her began to see heroes of their own, and she remembers to this day the thrills and the fear she felt for the young activists who risked their lives for her: "I believe when I heard about the Freedom Riders I thought they were the craziest people I'd ever heard of. Getting on a bus, knowing that you're going to be beaten, possibly killed. It seemed to be that they were crazy but terribly coura-geous."

Julian Bond says that virtually all African Americans in those days had a similar experience—and it was an experience that unified and galvanized a race: "They had seen black people. Even if they didn't know them, they'd seen them on TV. They had been exposed by the media to Dr. King and the onrush of this move-ment. They saw young people like themselves, black young people, sitting at lunch counters, and they said, 'These kids are no differ-ent than I am.' So the whole society sort of tilted in a way to say to them, 'Come on. Join this. This is something great you can do for your country, something great you can do for yourself.' I think they just felt compelled to go into it. . . . You saw how you could join this fight. You didn't have to be a lawyer like Thurgood Marshall. You didn't have to be a magical speaker like Dr. King. If you could do what I'm doing, if you could sit down, you could join this movement. All of us can sit down. And so all of a sudden, the movement became accessible to us, and we had the feeling from these earlier victories that victory could be won, and the lunch counter sit-ins were victorious relatively quickly. In Greensboro, a matter of months after the sit-ins began, the lunch counters inte-grated. And in the upper South, these victories just came like that, and I'm living in the lower South, in Georgia, but I didn't make distinctions between Georgia and North Carolina. If they could do it in North Carolina, we could do it in Georgia too."

And so the preboomer protesters in the civil rights movement began to bleed their way into the newspapers and onto the evening news, and the Kennedy administration was dragged, kicking and screaming, into the fray.

In May 1961, two busloads of Freedom Riders were beaten badly in Anniston, Alabama. A photograph of a bombed and burn-ing Greyhound bus appeared above the fold on front pages across America. It looked like something that might happen in Eastern Europe, but it wasn't. It wasn't in Southeast Asia. It wasn't even in some Third World, poverty-stricken, junta-run, despotic South American dictatorship.

It was in Anniston, Alabama.

Attorney General and presidential brother Robert Kennedy sent his friend and associate, John Seigenthaler, south to try to calm things down. He explains: "We were trying to get the movement *in* the courts and *off* the streets."* And, one would assume, off the television screens. Seigenthaler's efforts failed to the point that he himself was beaten unconscious in Montgomery, and Robert Kennedy was furious. He sent in federal marshals.

In October of that year, James Meredith attempted to become the first black student to enroll at the University of Mississippi. The Kennedys sent in five thousand marshals, and in the rioting that ensued 160 marshals were wounded (twenty-eight by gunfire) as were two bystanders.

But naturally the media continued its habit of covering the civil rights movement only when it bled. Like the Kennedy administration, the media remained focused primarily on things like the rise of communism and the space race.

Tony Snow went on to a career in journalism and ultimately became President George W. Bush's press secretary—a life journey that began sitting at home watching the news: "The interesting thing about the sixties is it was the first time the dramatic moments were played out on TV. In our case, wheeling the television into the gymnasium at the elementary school so you could see Alan Shepard taking off and Gus Grissom taking off and John Glenn taking off—John Kennedy addressing the nation on the Cuban missile crisis."

Oh yeah. That.

The Cuban Missile Crisis

The Russians were building missile launch sites for nuclear weapons on the island nation of Cuba, just ninety miles off our shores. The armed forces were placed on full alert and mobilized. The

---

John Seigenthaler, personal interview with the author, 2005.

nation was mesmerized when U.N. Ambassador Adlai Stevenson—live on television—confronted the Russians with U-2 photographs of the launch sites and demanded answers, answers we were prepared to wait for "until hell freezes over."

And then, President Kennedy went on television as well.

It shall be the policy of this nation to regard any nuclear missile launched from Cuba against any nation in the Western Hemisphere as an attack by the Soviet Union on the United States, requiring a full retaliatory response upon the Soviet Union.

President John F. Kennedy
October 22, 1962

Oh, my dear God.

Coming fresh on the heels of the construction of the already infamous Berlin Wall, the "Kennedy Doctrine" had us practicing the old drills with a new urgency: Duck and cover, boys and girls. We are poised on the brink of thermonuclear war. It could really happen this time. But Kennedy and Khrushchev worked a deal, and the day of reckoning was postponed.

In a speech before the United Nations, President Kennedy once said, "Every man, woman, and child lives under a nuclear sword of Damocles, hanging by the slenderest of threads, capable of being cut at any moment by accident, or miscalculation, or by madness."

We spent our youth living under this terrible sword, practicing "duck and cover," and stocking up on canned goods enough to survive the "nuclear winter" that would follow whatever accident, miscalculation, or madness that might come.

Dr. Daniel Goleman is a cutting-edge psychologist whose best-selling book, *Emotional Intelligence,* opened up an entirely new field of study. It is his contention that there is a great deal more to "smart" than IQ and that life lessons that teach us self-awareness, self-discipline, and empathy (emotional intelligence) often counterbalance intelligence quotient. He also contends that growing up under the constant threat of the end of the world had an undeniable impact on our collective emotional intelligence: "The boomer generation grew up having routine A-bomb drills. You may remember if you're of [a] certain age, that every few weeks, we would stop what we were doing and get under our desk and put one arm over our eyes and the other behind our neck, to protect ourselves from nuclear annihilation. If you grow up with that as a routine part of your reality, I think it forces you to consider deeply where we're going in this world.

"The formative movement in the collective character of the boomer generation was the world in which we were created. It was a world that had just seen catastrophe and come back from the brink, and [that] continued through the Cold War. We grew up with the doctrine of mutually assured annihilation. We were raised facing the grimmest prospects. Even though we were born in a time of great prosperity, it was this odd combination of having more materially than any other generation of Americans, and at the same time having to face the existential dilemma that it all could end."

While the Cuban Missile Crisis was undoubtedly a terrifying time, our ultimate "Oh, my God" moment—the generationally defining "Oh, my God" moment—was still more than a year away.

In the meantime America was under invasion, but not by the Soviets. Once again, the British were coming.

The Rock 'n' Roll Revolution

The oldest boomers had been listening to Elvis, Buddy Holly, and the Big Bopper for some time now, and while young Mr. Presley's pelvic gyrations sent many of our parents into fits of near apoplexy, he had finally been endorsed by none other than Ed Sullivan himself as "a fine young man." But Elvis was only the beginning.

41

Boomers thought Elvis Presley's hip-swiveling gyrations were cool, while many of our Glenn Miller–loving parents thought they were vulgar.

Enter: The Beatles.

The first single by "the Fab Four" to be released in America sold six million copies in less than three weeks. While the lyrics to "I Want to Hold Your Hand" may have been less than revolutionary, the music was.

"Turn that racket down!"

But it wasn't a racket to us. Dr. Nock knows that it was a great deal more than dance music: "Part of what happened with the baby boom coming of age in the early and midsixties is the British invasion of music, which was heralded as rebellious. . . . It involved drugs, it involved clothing, it involved appearance, and it involved lyrics that were quite strange and unusual. . . . It was also in that period when African-American music filtered into mainstream music for the first time."

And so a line was drawn between Benny Goodman and the Beatles, and it was a hard line. It was more than a matter of taste. Leonard Steinhorn says it was a huge and sometimes angry cultural divide: "You had authorities in town shutting down concerts for kids; you had authorities burning Beatles' records and saying that they were anti-Christian. You had people saying that our soul music was jungle music and was encouraging the intermingling of the races. And young people looked up and said, 'You know, why is this reaction going on to our music?' And I think music had a powerful force of fueling generation identity, by making boomers wonder why people were so angry at this fun music that everyone wanted to dance to and sing aloud and that everybody knew . . . and listened to together. Why were people angry with it?

From "I Want to Hold Your Hand" to "I Am the Walrus," most boomers knew the words of all of their songs. As the Beatles evolved, we learned that change is good.

"'Hmm, why are these authorities, why are our parents, why is that generation saying all these bad things about things that are really fun? Really good?'"

If it separated us from our parents, Julian Bond knows well how that "new" music began to unite black Americans and white Americans: "The advent of rock 'n' roll music, the popularity of the music that your parents hated, that you loved therefore all the more—all of these things created a kind of a mix of excitement in the air, and I think young people of this period felt free from the restraints that their older brothers and sisters, and certainly that their parents had felt, and therefore felt free to participate in the civil rights movement, a movement that not only wasn't there in the same way when their parents were their age, but was more appealing to them now because of the experiences they've had.

"You know radios in the boomer age had dials, so if you wanted some music that you knew you wanted to listen to, you had to turn that dial and find it, and those dials were not segregated, and the music

43

that came through the box wasn't segregated the way the music makers were and music listeners were before the boomer age. But what that did, as white kids are attracted to this music, it exposes them to a world—and in their view, it's a stereotype world, it's not the true world—but exposes them to a world of excitement, of some sexual excitement, of some romantic excitement. It exposes them to a world that is greatly attractive to them, and I think it opened the doorway for their later participation in the movement for civil rights. Not all of them, but some of them. You know, I've talked to many white people roughly in this group who tell me stories of sneaking away to go sit upstairs in the Atlanta City Auditorium, where whites had to sit for black shows, and coming downstairs to the ground floor, where the black kids were and dancing with them. And this was the first interracial experience these people had, and it's okay, it's all right. So what Mom and Dad had told them about these things, they are not true. And so [they understand they] can do it again in some other context."

And of course there was all that hair! As laughable as it may seem today, many of our spit and polish, crew-cut fathers decided that the Beatles' hair length was proof positive that they were communists—or "girls." They probably meant something different by calling them "girls," but the oldest of us were still only sixteen and may have missed altogether whatever other implications there may have been. Regardless, hair became an issue, and, on this issue at least, Dr. Nock thinks our parents may well have been right: "When I look back at the shows and the pictures and the recordings of Woodstock, I realize how grungy everyone looked. And maybe that was part of it, maybe the long, greasy, unkempt look with the beard and everything was the most obvious departure from the clean-cut GI look of our parents. And after all, they were GIs."

And we weren't. Erica Jong cuts to the heart of the whole hair thing: "It was about differentiating yourself from your parents, I think. I mean look at the kids now. They shave their heads. Why do they shave their heads? They shave their heads because they don't want to look like their parents—and that's the long and the short of it."

In addition to the British invasion, 1963 would see the release of Betty Friedan's *The Feminine Mystique* and the dismissal of Dr. Timothy Leary from his professorship at Harvard for experimenting with psychedelic drugs. We had rock 'n' roll, and sex and drugs were right around the corner. But first, we all had to survive 1963.

Only the Good Die Young

In his inaugural address on January 14, 1963, Alabama Governor George C. Wallace vowed, "Segregation today, segregation tomorrow, and segregation forever!" May of that year brought bombings and riots to Birmingham, and, since people were bleeding, television news brought the pictures into our living rooms as that city's commissioner of public safety, Eugene "Bull" Connor, attacked peaceful demonstrators with fire hoses and attack dogs. On June 11, Wallace symbolically stood "in the schoolhouse door" in defiance of a court order that the University of Alabama should admit black students Vivian Malone Jones and James Hood.

Kennedy had had enough. On that same day, he submitted to Congress a piece of civil rights legislation that he promised would provide "the kind of equality of treatment which we would want for ourselves." On the following day, in Mississippi, NAACP field director Medgar Evars was assassinated by members of the Mississippi Ku Klux Klan.

It was with all of this fresh on his mind—with all of this fresh on the mind of the nation—that Dr. Martin Luther King Jr. stood in the shadow of Abraham Lincoln on a bright August day and told us all of his dream "that one day this nation will rise up and live out the true meaning of its creed: 'We hold these truths to be self-evident: that all men are created equal.'"

To many Americans it must have seemed an impossible dream, and to many others his dream of "race mixing" was not a dream at all. It was their most feared and looming nightmare.

Denise McNair, Carole Robertson, Addie Mae Collins, and Cynthia Wesley were boomers who still had some time to wait before reaching the legal driving age. Denise was eleven, and the others were fourteen. On September 15, 1963, less than three weeks after King's speech, these four little girls had just gotten out of their Sunday school class at Birmingham's 16th Street Baptist Church when a Klan-planted bomb exploded and ended whatever dreams they may have had—and shocked a nation.

Oh, my God.

Until now, all the pictures, all the events, all the national traumas had featured our fathers. Denise, Carole, Addie Mae, and Cynthia were us, the very first boomers to make national headlines.

It was this moment, many believe, that "segregated" the civil rights struggle into two camps in the minds of young boomers— one that was right, and one, quite simply, that was wrong. The contrast between real and ideal was being brought home to us most harshly in 1963. These weren't vague differences to be found in television's shades of gray. They were stark. Television had shown us Beaver Cleaver and Bull Connor, and it wasn't difficult for us to figure out that the Beaver was fiction and the bombings were real.

The civil rights movement had now finally bled enough to push the Cold War below the fold in the newspapers and make civil rights the lead story on the CBS Evening News until . . .

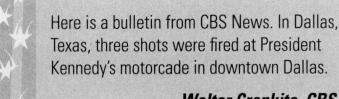

Here is a bulletin from CBS News. In Dallas, Texas, three shots were fired at President Kennedy's motorcade in downtown Dallas.

Walter Cronkite, CBS News
November 22, 1963

Oh, my dear God!

The oldest of the boomers were in our adolescence, at our most impressionable age, and the impact on us of that day and of the mournful days that followed cannot possibly be overstated. We gathered around our television sets—our new communal gathering place—and we wept. Other generations had experienced assassinations and the funerals that followed, but only from afar, reading the cold words and glancing at the bad, day-old photographs on the front pages of their daily papers. But we, the boomers—thanks to television—*attended* the Kennedy funeral. We saw the flag-draped casket and heard the muffled drums and felt agonizing grief, many of us for the very first time, when we witnessed, as it happened, that heartrending moment when John-John saluted his father good-bye.

John-John was a boomer too.

UCLA sociologist Fernando Torres-Gil believes that we took away from those days more than only the grief and the anger: "Each generation in this country appears to have a defining moment, which helps us to understand how they are as a group and how they're different from the other generations. The defining moment for baby boomers, in my opinion, was the assassination of President Kennedy. Every one of us [old enough to remember] knows exactly where we were, how we felt the moment we heard that President Kennedy had been assassinated. That began our continual journey into skepticism, into frustration, into a lack of belief that government and society can do good and can be trusted. We're still living with that legacy."

Dr. Daniel Goleman may be the world's foremost expert on how these types of traumatic moments can impact the psyche, and hence the future actions, of a generation: "Kennedy was the guy who saw us through the Cuban Missile Crisis, where there was almost a nuclear war, and he found his way through. He was the leader that we were hoping would lead us to all the right answers and—all of a sudden—he was gone. I think that that death, in a certain psychological way, emotionally compelled the boomers to become activists themselves."

The assassination of President Kennedy was perhaps our most traumatic "Oh, my God" moment. While many of us can still hear the muffled drums and the emotional missed note of taps being played at Arlington National Cemetery, the John-John salute is our most persistent memory of those heartrending days. John-John was a boomer too.

The youthful idealism of the Kennedy administration has come to be remembered as "Camelot." It survived for just over one thousand days. For many boomers it remains "one brief, shining moment."

Perhaps it did that, but it also may have set us on another path as well. In light of the subsequent murder of accused assassin Lee Harvey Oswald and the doubts arising from the Warren Commission's report on the assassination, some of us have taken that feeling well beyond skepticism and into the realm of "conspiracy theory." To Oscar-winning director Oliver Stone, it's not a theory at all: "If you're a baby boomer, you could go back and say that was the beginning of the great deception that went on and on. But of course it is a big event, and I do believe that [Kennedy] was 'gotten rid of' because I think he was a very dangerous man for change. And all the things that he said and did in '63 indicate a sea change in the man. So there was more change coming because he was definitely going to win in '64, and that's what they were scared of—whoever 'they' were—and I think it doesn't have to be a huge group of people, by the way. It is a small group that is very concentrated, and very military like, and they got rid of him."

Civil rights activist Julian Bond has a retrospective view, not so much about the Kennedy assassination as about the Kennedy "myth." While those "Thousand Days" of the Kennedy administration are remembered by many boomers as "Camelot," Bond, somewhat reluctantly, points out that even King Arthur had his flaws: "I think John F. Kennedy—and it's hard to say—benefited from dying young, and because he died young without having completed his first term, you're able to impose upon him what you thought he *would have* done. You thought he would have withdrawn from Vietnam. You thought he would have been more vigorous in pursuit of civil rights than he actually was. You thought he would have acted in a very different way than we know he was acting then, and he was also lucky enough to have a circle of supporters and admirers who very quickly created an image of him that was different from the truth.

"When my students hear about his vacillation toward civil rights, they are astounded, because they see him as part of a group of great figures leading us toward a better world. I don't want to denigrate him, he did some good things, but he didn't do what popular memory says he did. The popular memory is wrong."

The memory was still fresh of that sunny noon a thousand days ago when the young and vibrant Kennedy had taken the oath and challenged us to "explore the stars, conquer the deserts, eradicate disease, tap the ocean depths, and encourage the arts and commerce." That magical memory stood in dreadfully stark contrast to the image of a man, who seemed incredibly old to the boomers of the day, standing next to the grieving and blood-soaked former first lady in a dark and cramped *Air Force One,* as he placed his hand on a Bible and said, "I, Lyndon Baines Johnson, do solemnly swear . . ."

Only two months later the man who would come to be known as "the voice of a generation" released a new and surprisingly prophetic album. "The times," Bob Dylan said, "are a-changin'."

Etched into our collective memories is this vivid image of the day youthful idealism died.

chapter 3

"Your Sons and Your Daughters Are Beyond Your Command"

During the first six months of the Johnson administration, it seems that Americans were anxious to get past mourning for our slain president—especially young Americans.

The Beatles were greeted by twenty-five thousand screaming boomers as they touched down in America for the first time. Two days later they made their "historic" appearance on *The Ed Sullivan Show,* and, thanks to millions of teenaged boomers, destroyed all rating records. In March, the first Ford Mustang rolled off the assembly line. *Gilligan's Island* premiered in 1964, and Emmys went to Dick Van Dyke and Mary Tyler Moore. We were, we found out, still able to laugh. While the civil rights movement was in a kind of winter hibernation, Sidney Poitier became the first black actor to win a leading role Oscar for his performance in *Lilies of the Field.*

Come mothers and fathers all over this land
And don't criticize what you can't understand.
Your sons and your daughters are beyond your command.
Your old role is rapidly agin'.
Please get out of the new one if you can't lend a hand
For the times they are a-changin'.

From "The Times
They Are A-Changin'"
By Bob Dylan

But in Washington, the business of governing continued. On May 27, President Johnson met with National Security Adviser McGeorge Bundy about the "situation" in Vietnam. Bundy tape-recorded President Johnson's words:

> I'll tell you, the more that I stayed awake last night thinking of this thing, the more I think of it, I don't know what in the hell—it looks like to me we're getting into another Korea. It just worries the hell out of me. I don't see what we can ever hope to get out of there with, once we're committed. I believe that the Chinese Communists are coming into it. I don't think we can fight them ten thousand miles from home. . . . I don't think it's worth fighting for, and I don't think we can get out. It's just the biggest damned mess that I ever saw.

With the summer heat, racial rioting broke out, and not only in the South. Blacks and whites clashed in New York, New Jersey, Illinois, and Pennsylvania as well. What captured the largest headlines, however, *was* in the South. On June 21, three young civil rights workers—Andrew Goodman, twenty, Michael Schwerner, twenty-four, and James Chaney, twenty-one—disappeared near

It was an uneasy partnership between an African-American preacher and a Texas-born politician that brought about the Civil Rights Act of 1964 and the Voting Rights Act of 1965.

Meridian, Mississippi. Their car was found burning late in the day. President Johnson took personal command of the search for the three young men—it was a search that would last for forty days.

On June 19, while the search for the three civil rights workers continued, President Johnson signed into law the Civil Rights Act of 1964. The bill had survived an eighty-three-day filibuster in the U.S. Senate and was approved by a vote of 73–27. Segregation in public places was now against the law in the United States of America.

David Gergen believes that this was a masterful political victory that changed America for the better, and forever, and that there were few other people in the world who could have pulled it off: "I don't think there's any doubt that Lyndon Johnson was one of the few Americans who could deliver on civil rights and that John Kennedy could not have, as much as John Kennedy came to believe in it over time. Johnson delivering on civil rights was like Nixon going to China.

"Even though he was not as eloquent, by any means, as Kennedy, he was not as inspirational as Kennedy, Lyndon Johnson still spoke from the heart, and when he got up there in that speech and he said, 'We shall overcome' to Congress—that refrain from the song that had joined together the civil rights movement—that was one of those memories that just sticks with you."

Gergen also understands, as did Johnson, what that victory would cost both the president and his party: "He understood that the South would break with the Democratic Party, and especially it broke with Bobby Kennedy when he was over at the justice department. And so you saw the riots of the George Wallace movement, and then after Wallace was shot, then you saw that vote start to go to Richard Nixon in '68, and Nixon started to bring it into the Republican tent. And of course by 1980, when Ronald Reagan ran, it was almost a 'solid South' again. It has become much more solid since then. It's the reddest of the red states, with a few exceptions."

Finally, on June 21, the bodies of Goodman, Schwerner, and Chaney were found buried in an earthen dam near Philadelphia, Mississippi. Federal prosecutors brought conspiracy charges against eighteen Ku Klux Klansmen, eight of whom were found guilty. None served more than ten years on those convictions. No murder charges were filed at the time. (Klansman Edgar Ray Killen was finally charged with and convicted of murder—but not until 2005.)

In issuing the light sentences to the Klansmen, Judge William Cox said, "They killed one nigger, one Jew, and a white man—I gave them all what I thought they deserved." It was yet another example of injustice within "the system" that boomers could add to their ever-growing list of lies. It also served to prove that while the Civil Rights Act was a victory for the movement—a major battle won—the war was far from over.

As the civil rights war was at its height, another war, halfway around the world, was just getting started. One way or another, boomers would get caught up in both.

On July 27, the president sent five thousand new troops to Vietnam. Then came the bombing of the North, and then came the Gulf of Tonkin Resolution that was little less than a declaration of war. "Mission creep" had begun.

While these were the things on Mr. Johnson's desk, an item or two coming out of the University of California at Berkeley might have escaped his attention. College students, it seems, were taking a page out of the Mahatma Gandhi/Martin Luther King Jr. book of nonviolent civil disobedience. The university prohibited the passing out of civil rights and other political pamphlets on the campus, and when the police arrived to arrest Jack Weinberg for doing so, students surrounded the squad car in a protest that resulted in a thirty-two-hour standoff. The campus activist movement had begun.

Spock Babies Go to College

This was in the fall of 1964, and the first of the boomers—the 1946 babies—were college freshmen. It is an appropriate time to note that while the first of the boomers were starting college in 1964, the last of the boomers were just being born. But, once again, simply by our sheer numbers, another great American institution was overwhelmed. The number of college students tripled between 1965 and 1975.

Historian Joshua Zeitz thinks the boomers came into an archaic environment of traditional rules and regulations that must have seemed like boot camp to "Spock babies": "Colleges and universities were still governed by *en loco parentis* rules which regulated *what* someone could do, *where* he or she could do it, and *when* he or she could do it. These college campuses kept close guard on their behavior and conduct, and it was almost bound to create friction. And it did.

"And increasingly college campus activists came to equate these *en loco parentis* [rules] with Jim Crow laws governing African Americans in the South, and so they became more conscious of the incursions against their own liberties on college campuses, and it only turned up the heat. 57

> BOBBY: I'd like an omelet, plain, and a chicken-salad sandwich on wheat toast, no mayonnaise, no butter, no lettuce. And a cup of coffee.
> WAITRESS: A Number 2, chicken salad sand. Hold the butter, the lettuce, the mayonnaise, and a cup of coffee. Anything else?
> BOBBY: Yeah, now all you have to do is hold the chicken, bring me the toast, give me a check for the chicken-salad sandwich, and you haven't broken any rules.
> WAITRESS: You want me to hold the chicken, huh?
> BOBBY: I want you to hold it between your knees.
>
> **From Five Easy Pieces**
> **Screenplay by Adrien Joyce**

"[They] also rubbed up against the injustices they saw on television coming from the South, from Vietnam, and they took a sense of entitlement and a sense of purpose and mission and injustice, and they spiraled it out of control. And that narrative works to a certain extent. I don't think you can blame Dr. Spock or indulgent suburban parents for the behavior of their kids.

"In many ways, the things that happened in the 1960s were probably a demographic inevitability. You couldn't have so large a cohort filing into institutions which were . . . by their nature not very malleable, and you couldn't help but have a tremendous amount of conflict. And that conflict could be very creative."

As young as we were, we had already decided that we didn't like the rules.

Dr. Dychtwald recognizes that the newfound freedom of college had effects on us, both good and bad: "There wasn't anybody looking over your shoulder. You could be all kinds of things: illegal, legal; common, uncommon; weird, straight. It was this fertile ground for personal discovery or for personal indulgence. And you got exposed to a new 'authority class' who were professors, who, by and large, were better educated, more intellectually sophisticated than the adults you had been hanging out with."

Boomer defender Leonard Steinhorn adds another intriguing observation. There were huge numbers of students from every conceivable background demanding to go to college. Higher education was no longer the sole prerogative of the progeny of the rich and famous, and some well-ensconced ivory towers were about to come crashing down: "Instead of universities and colleges being schools for the elite, as many of them had been in years past, you had a wider and more diversified student body on these campuses. And what they were finding was that they had common perspectives; they had a common sense of the music they listened to; they had common experiences by even watching television; they were reading *MAD Magazine* together; they were looking at the hypocrisy of America through the same prism.

"So, what was forged on the college campuses of those days was increasingly not a class identity as it was in years past at Harvard or Yale or the other elite institutions that the William Buckleys would go to and pine away for. But it was a generational identity. And that generational identity began to spread from the campuses to the rest of the generation, through alternative papers, music, and other types of medium. So, in effect, even though you could talk about previous generations back then, this, I think, was the first time on a widespread scale that people were thinking about generational identity and how that shaped their personalities and character."

And the early boomers were about to have their personalities and characters shaped in some odd and mysterious ways. They hit the campuses like a tidal wave in the sixties, and what many found there was a growing atmosphere of dissent. The free speech movement at Berkeley had won its first victory, as, very early in 1965, University of California at Berkeley officials relented to the demonstrators and announced a new policy that permitted political expression on campus. This on the heels of the Civil Rights Act combined to convince boomers that "Hey, this stuff works." With our "defining moment" behind us, the boomer generation was about to embark on our "defining decade."

> It was the best of times, it was the worst of times; it was the age of wisdom, it was the age of foolishness; it was the epoch of belief, it was the epoch of incredulity; it was the season of Light, it was the season of Darkness; it was the spring of hope, it was the winter of despair; we had everything before us, we had nothing before us; we were all going directly to Heaven, we were all going the other way.
>
> *From* **A Tale of Two Cities**
> **By Charles Dickens**

We will be defined as pot-smoking, bra-burning, draft-dodging hippies, and some of us were. But most of us weren't. The images of the relatively few protesters on campus obscured the fact that most students were attending to their studies. Much as with Kennedy's Camelot, myth not only overwhelmed reality, it also became our perception of our own history.

David Gergen reminds us that the protesters "did not represent the majority of the people in their generation. So if you actually look at the polls on Vietnam, you'll find that the people who hung in the longest in support of the war, who stayed there the longest with approval ratings, were actually people between eighteen and twenty-four. And the crevices we saw opening up in the sixties and seventies have become canyons today. People are at war with each other for cultural values. And very importantly, the sixties and seventies brought us the Vietnam War, and the Vietnam War put an ax right down the middle of this generation, . . . because some people went and some people didn't. And the people who went always resent those who didn't.

"A lot of what you believed often depended on where you grew up and where you went to school. So if you went to the University of Oklahoma, you typically came out with a very different perspective on Vietnam than if you went to the University of Wisconsin.

You know, if you've been in Oklahoma, you tended to be prowar, believed that these are persons who are out there trying to stop this thing and we ought to stand up for the country "'cause we're fighting the commies.' But if you were out of Madison, Wisconsin, you came out of there thinking, 'Oh, my God. We're the imperialists, and we're savaging these poor people!'"

Dr. Zeitz agrees that it's dangerous to label a generation as having one single persona:

"We should remember that not all activists in the sixties were necessarily activists on the Left, and, in fact, although there's a great kind of historical cult that's emerged around [Left-wing groups like] the Weathermen and around their kind of more respectable predecessors—the Students for a Democratic Society, SDS—it's really important to remember that the Young Americans for Freedom, the YAF, which was the conservative counterpart to the SDS, actually had a substantially larger membership in the 1960s."

"Damned right we'll go!" Not every boomer burned his draft card. A great many boomers went to Vietnam—many even volunteered— and far too many never came home.

So the stereotypes of us as youthful boomers, like most stereotypes, are exaggerated if not downright wrong. Civil rights activist Julian Bond has spent a lifetime disproving stereotypes, and the popular view of the boomer generation is no exception: "If you look at all the people who marched, who protested, who did this and the other, this is a small part of this large, large group of people. But now we have taken the large group of people and said, 'You are all alike,' and you weren't. You were different then, and you are

61

different now. You had different values then among you; you *have* different values now among you; and so it's no surprise that now that you're in control you behave differently than we thought you would, because you never were what we thought you were. You were always a mix. The ones of you who fit that single snapshot made the most noise, wore the strangest clothes, smoked the most dope, danced in the streets, while your compatriots, your colleagues, were doing regular ordinary things."

That having been said, what historians do is backtrack footprints, and people who stand quietly in the middle of the herd, never moving left or right, leave none. The ground in the middle is so churned up that no individual footprints can be discerned. Those in the middle can be studied only by economists and sociologists using trends and statistics and actuarial tables, which may be far more accurate but are anything but iconoclastic. There are no images seared into America's collective memory of the "good" boys and girls sitting behind their desks, studying for tomorrow's biology exam. So all that is left for historians to backtrack are the footprints and photographs of the bold ones who dared to step out into the fringes, and what may differentiate the boomers from previous generations is the fact that there were so many who did. But it must be remembered that for every iconic image of an antiwar demonstrator, there is another of a Vietnam soldier. Look closely at every photograph of a baby boomer civil rights activist being beaten, and you may find that it's another boomer doing the beating. At least some of the National Guardsmen sent in to quell the demonstrations at Kent State were probably boomers too, and this diversity within our sociological cohort continues to divide us and impact our nation even to this day. As Gergen concludes, "A lot of the value splits that we see in the country today started back in Vietnam and in the civil rights movement."

Nonetheless, in 1965, it was the activists on the Right who wanted America to stay the same, and those on the Left who wanted it to change. And the times, indeed, were "a-changin'."

Look closely. The soldier is a boomer too.

"We Shall Overcome"

In 1965, the Beatles were in full swing. "Yesterday" hit number 1 on the charts, and on August 15, they performed at Shea Stadium before fifty-five thousand fans who screamed so loud throughout the entire concert that the music couldn't be heard—even by "the Fab Four" themselves.

The Sound of Music smashed box office records, and the small screen premiered *I Dream of Jeannie, Get Smart,* and *The Smothers Brothers Comedy Hour,* which ended up being about more than only comedy.

Also in 1965, the civil rights movement refocused its efforts on voting rights, and to this day March 7 of that year is remembered as "Bloody Sunday." On that day, a group of six hundred protesters, led by a young man named John Lewis, attempted to march from Selma to Montgomery, Alabama, to put an end to the racial discrimination that existed at the voting booths.

What happened in Selma is part of a far larger movement which reaches into every section and state of America. It is the effort of American Negroes to secure for themselves the full blessings of American life. Their cause must be our cause too, because it's not just Negroes, but really it's all of us who must overcome the crippling legacy of bigotry and injustice. And we shall overcome.

President Lyndon Johnson
March 21, 1965

David Gergen interviewed Lewis a third of a century later for PBS's *The NewsHour with Jim Lehrer,* and Lewis recalled just how blatant the restrictions against black voting were: "In Selma only 2.1 percent of blacks of voting age were registered to vote."

And so they started to march from Selma, Alabama, heading for the state capitol in Montgomery: "We all started walking in twos. On the other side, at the foot of the [Edmund Pettus] bridge, we saw Sheriff Clark, the sheriff of Dallas County in Selma, with his posse. We saw men on horseback, and we heard a man, Major John Clough of the Alabama State Troopers, say it is an unlawful march, and 'I give you three minutes to disperse and return to your church.' In less than a minute and a half, he said, 'Troopers advance.' And these men came toward us, beating us with nightsticks, bullwhips, trampling us with horses. They were on horses, and they trampled us. They used tear gas. I was beaten. I had a concussion. But to this day, I don't know how I made it back across that bridge, crossing the Alabama River, back through the streets of Selma, back to the church. I don't recall, but I was knocked unconscious. I had a concussion, but somebody apparently gave me a lift or carried me somehow in some way. I wish thirty-three years later that I knew the person or persons just to say thank you. But I thought that day I was going to die. I think I saw death."

Lewis saw death, and America saw Bloody Sunday. There were probably few if any boomers at the Edmund Pettus Bridge that Sunday, but thanks to the media, many of us witnessed the beatings of these American citizens who were only attempting to exercise their First Amendment right "peaceably to assemble," and most of us (one would hope) were appalled, particularly in light of the fact that the entire reason they were marching was to gain for themselves the most basic of all democratic privileges—the right to vote.

While Bloody Sunday may or may not have reached the level of an "Oh, my God" moment for boomers, it was unarguably another dagger to the heart of trust in the laws and traditions of our fathers. Bloody Sunday demonstrated, at least to the Left-leaning boomers, that both the First and Fifteenth Amendments to the U.S. Constitution were simply lies. It also showed, once again, that nonviolent civil disobedience could work. Eight days later, President Johnson called a joint session of Congress and demanded that it pass an act that would guarantee *and enforce* the rights of all Americans to vote.

It is a wonderful proof positive of the success of Bloody Sunday to note that Lewis, who "saw death" on that day, not only won the right to vote, but the right to run for office—and to win. He was first elected to Congress in 1989 and will continue to serve as Atlanta's Congressman for as long as he chooses.

Only three weeks after Bloody Sunday, demonstrations against the war in Vietnam began to make some below-the-fold headlines, as on April 17, Students for a Democratic Society held its first anti–Vietnam War protest rally in Washington, DC. Seeming not to notice, on July 28, President Johnson announced he was increasing the number of American troops in South Vietnam from 75,000 to 125,000.

Two days later he signed into law another piece of landmark legislation that may end up being the most important of all for the entire baby boom generation, though it may not have seemed so at the time. In fact, in gigantic, adolescent, "never trust anyone over thirty" numbers, we may not have even noticed the passage of a law designed to help old people. On July 30, 1965, Lyndon Johnson signed into law the Medicare Bill.

Then, on August 2, something extraordinary happened. Sent to Vietnam by CBS, correspondent Morley Safer filmed a U.S. soldier setting fire to a Vietnamese hut with a Zippo lighter. It was extraordinary because the U.S. military was unaccustomed to having reporters show Americans anything other than, well, propaganda. Throughout World War II, "the Greatest Generation" of reporters were little more than a public relations arm of the Pentagon, with their filmed moving images highly censored and shown only in movie theaters. The Safer piece was harshly critical, highly disturbing, and it appeared in millions of our living rooms—and dorm rooms—just like all the other "Oh, my God" moments.

Leonard Steinhorn believes that these incredibly disturbing pictures profoundly impacted the boomers: "When people watch television, they remember images, not words. So when you saw the assassination of John Kennedy, that was a powerfully emotional experience about what was happening to our society. When you saw the Edmund Pettus Bridge or what was going on in Birmingham and when you saw the police attacking people, just for being citizens of the United States and wanting to exercise their rights and freedoms as citizens, that had a powerful emotional impact. . . . When you saw the Vietnam War and the children running naked from the napalm attacks, with their skin being stripped off their bodies, that had a powerful impact."

Richard Chapman is a veteran screenwriter and producer in film and television with particular interest in the ways journalists report on war. He is currently producing *Shooting the Messengers,* a feature-length documentary about how war correspondents in Vietnam covered that conflict.

The Television War

Richard Chapman

Many network television news reporters covering the Vietnam War in 1965 were closer in age to the boomer generation than to their older viewers. Morley Safer identified more strongly with the post–World War II boomers than with their parents, who had followed previous wars from Ernie Pyle's newspaper accounts or were in the trenches themselves. On the other side of the TV looking glass, boomers relied on these fearless young journalists out risking their lives in an uncensored war to tell them the truth. From the outset, a strong bond of trust developed between the correspondents and their younger audience.

Initially, boomers found themselves supporting the war, as television brought heroic imagery of GIs fighting to defend democracy in the rice paddies of Vietnam. Recruitment levels were healthy and reflected a generally optimistic view of the future. The picture changed dramatically with Morley Safer's footage of Marines torching the thatched roofs of Cam Ne with their Zippo lighters. As reports became more critical of the troops' treatment of villagers and more iconic images of brutality lit up the boomers' living rooms, attitudes began shifting.

The Tet offensive of 1968 outraged boomers, with NBC's shocking footage of a South Vietnamese officer literally blowing out the brains of a Vietcong captive in downtown Saigon. Boomers learned from TV news reporters that their own government was bending the truth. A credibility gap developed as doubt and confusion flooded young viewers' minds. Was their own government lying to them about the progress of the war?

Further cynicism was fueled by reports coming straight off the battlefield, as TV news crews were given free rein from the military to pursue any story and interview young soldiers under fire. CBS News's Ed Rabel gave many a boomer some grim food for thought on Thanksgiving Day 1970, with a gut-wrenching interview of the buddies of a soldier freshly killed by a mine. These GIs, boomers themselves, expressed their true feelings, declaring this war senseless. This loss of innocence was felt throughout the boomer community and marked a new wave of strong antiwar activity. The boomers took to the streets, and the antiwar movement was born.

The most memorable moment for many younger news viewers during the Vietnam War came with "Uncle Walter" Cronkite's pronouncement that the conflict was unwinnable and that it was time to find our way out and home. The boomers' yearning to find a way out and home didn't end there. For many, it continues to this day.

"Television couldn't hide the terrible things that were going on in Vietnam," Steinhorn remembers. "How we were hurting people and stripping the skin off of their bodies because of the napalm. So television accomplished a number of things. It showed an idealized image of America, but it also showed the realities. As the first mass media generation, baby boomers saw both of those things, and said, 'We want to have the good things, but why are these bad things happening? We've got to fix America and make it better.'"

But in summer 1965, Cronkite's report still lay in the distant future. The civil rights movement was gaining success, the antiwar movement was gaining momentum, and yet we were still able to find a new and perhaps even more exciting revolution to add to the list—and this one was sexual.

chapter 4

Sex, Drugs, and Rock 'n' Roll

The sixties was a period of enormous change in America, one of the most profound being in sexual relationships. Erica Jong was a student and a "literary junkie" in those days, and saw a new freedom to write about formerly taboo subjects, such as S-E-X. "We couldn't read Henry Miller's *Tropic of Cancer* in this country until 1962. You had to smuggle it from Paris. All of a sudden, because of Barney Rosset and Grove Press you could buy *Tropic of Cancer* in the United States. All of a sudden you could read *Lady Chatterley's Lover*, which was published in 1928, in a private printing in Florence, Italy, and now it could be published in paperback in the U.S. So suddenly there was this wave of freedom, and as a writer you had to be aware of it.

MRS. ROBINSON: Benjamin, I want you to know that I'm available to you, and if you won't sleep with me this time . . .
BENJAMIN: Oh, my Christ.
MRS. ROBINSON: If you won't sleep with me this time, I want you to know that you can call me up anytime you want, and we'll make some kind of arrangement.

From **The Graduate**
*Screenplay by Buck Henry**

"I mean, Philip Roth published *Portnoy's Complaint*. John Updike published *Couples*. He was on the cover of *Time* magazine for *Couples*. Suddenly you could write about sex without using asterisks. And I thought, 'Yeah, this is open now, but women aren't doing it.' And I remember thinking when I read *Portnoy*, 'This is fabulous. This is terrific. This is funny. This is brilliant. But where's the woman's story?' And I was inspired to write the book that didn't yet exist."

And so she did. It was about a modern woman who not only actually enjoyed sex but was exuberant about it! She called her book *Fear of Flying*, and people read it. *Lots* of people read it.

In 1960 the U.S. Food and Drug Administration licensed the birth control pill (hereafter referred to as "the Pill") that gave women a greater sense of sexual freedom than any other contraceptive device that had come before. It was an almost instant success. The baby boom births ended in 1964.

Coincidence?

I don't think so.

By the time the seventies rolled around, more than ten million women were taking the Pill.

MIKE STIVIC: You've got a hang-up about sex.
ARCHIE: I ain't got a hang-up about . . . that.
MIKE STIVIC: See, you can't even say it.
ARCHIE: I don't use four-letter words in front of women, ya dope.
GLORIA: Daddy, you shouldn't be afraid of sex.
ARCHIE: Listen, little girl, if I was afraid of it, you wouldn't be here. Right, Edith?

From **All in the Family**

The Power of "the Pill"

Eve Ensler of *Vagina Monologues* fame, as one might suspect, has an opinion about the power of the Pill and "free love." Dr. Steven Nock is the director of the Marriage Matters project at the University of Virginia, and he, too, has a perspective on the long-term social consequences of the "uncoupling of sex and marriage" that resulted from the availability of the Pill.

So let's have a little debate, shall we?

Ms. Ensler—you go first.

"I think the fact that women finally had reproductive rights, that we could protect ourselves, that we weren't going to get pregnant when we had sex, absolutely freed women to begin to experiment with sex and to know sex.

"If you control a woman's body in terms of determining that she has to have children every time she has sex, aren't you really controlling her sexuality as well? Aren't you telling her that you can only have sex to procreate? And I'm a great believer in sex. I think that sex is the great healer. I think that when we have great intimacy and delicious contact with other human beings, we heal parts of ourselves that cannot be healed through any other way.

"When I was growing up, everybody just had sex all the time with everybody. And we were very happy about it, and it was very relaxed and very natural and very wonderful and very crazy, and it was fabulous. I was so in the moment, to be perfectly honest with you, I didn't think past my twenties. To be honest with you, I didn't think I was going to *live* past thirty. I really didn't. I was living a very fast, hard, and incredibly self-destructive life, which had a lot of great, crazy, wonderful moments. But for the most part, it was pretty self-destructive. I never even thought of a career. I didn't think of growing up. I didn't think of being part of the mainstream. I didn't think of having an apartment. I didn't think of having a boyfriend or a husband or a girlfriend. I just was here and now with whomever I was with and that was my life.

"Would I go back and erase those years? Not for a second. You know, I'm so happy not only that I lived through it but that I *survived,* because there was a period right after where people didn't survive that kind of lifestyle. So for me, I grew up at that point where everybody just took off their clothes and took off masks and took off taboos and experimented and discovered, and that absolutely shaped who I am.

"Sex was the thing that taught me about being undone, that taught me about surrender, that taught me about the dissolution of the ego, that taught me about living outside of duality, that taught me about ambiguity and mystery. . . . I really feel for people who came after, the post-AIDS generation, because they've never had that freedom, and it's certainly being manipulated and used now by the Right to get people back into that family structure and to that, you know, no sex until you are married . . .

"All the people who were opposed to *The Vagina Monologues,* and there aren't many, I want to say, but there is a Right-wing fringe of the Catholic Church, and they say things to me like, 'Are you saying you believe in masturbation?' And I'm like, 'Uh-huh, I believe in masturbation, that's correct.' They say it to me as if it's some horrible thing to know your body, to give your body pleasure, to know what gives you pleasure. And I will fight with my life for the right of women to have sex when they want it—with whomever they want it. I trust women to be responsible. I trust women to know what's right for them. I don't think women are insensitive and careless and frivolous with their love. And I think all women have the right to experiment sexually and to know what feels good and to discover how their bodies can have pleasure. And I'd be horrified if we were to go backwards."

There are those who might contend that going "backwards" might not be such a bad thing. The uncoupling of sex and marriage, sex and fertility, sex and any number of other possible repercussions, had a downside that continues to cost us in more ways than one even to this day.

Dr. Steven Nock, director of the Marriage Matters project at the University of Virginia, will continue our debate.

"Prior to birth control, there were few options for having sex except in marriage. The law criminalized sex outside of marriage as adultery or fornication; children born to unmarried women were labeled as bastards and illegitimate children; communities stigmatized illegitimacy. Sex in all forms except marital sex was actually prohibited by law. And that made a great deal of sense in a time, in a historical period, when communities were responsible for offspring that were born to people who were not able to care for them themselves, and when there was no way of preventing births to people who were sexually active. The introduction of birth control had prodigious consequences that I think we're just beginning to recognize, because what it allowed for the first time was for people to engage in sex without it meaning that they were going to have children.

"Once childbearing becomes voluntary, then all of the social arrangements that were predicated on the idea that it isn't voluntary—and if you have sex, you're going to have babies—begin to change. So marriage was mandatory if you're going to have sex, because having sex almost inevitably meant that you were going to have babies. Once we uncoupled that, then everything that was based upon it began to uncouple as well. I personally think that we are midway through a redefinition of marriage and childbearing that was produced by the introduction of birth control. Sex became more or less optional. People could or could not engage in sex, but fertility became *completely* optional. And once that was true, then marriage and sex became uncoupled. And once marriage and sex became uncoupled, then sex and childbearing, of course, became uncoupled. And before long, everything related to sex and marriage was uncoupled.

"We're just beginning to understand the wide range of consequences of unmarried births. You can look at this from two perspectives. You can ask, 'What is the consequence to society of having high numbers of births to unmarried women?' And you can also look at it from the perspective of the offspring. 'What is the consequence to a child, of being born to an unmarried person?' Both of those are topics of great research. From the societal perspective, the primary consequence that attracts attention, other than the issue of morality, is [the] economic consequence of high rates of unmarried births. Increasingly, poverty in the United States is concentrated among single mothers and their children. This has been labeled the 'feminization of poverty' by some, and, despite some debates about it, it is true that single moms and their kids have the highest rates of poverty in the United States. So from a public-policy perspective, high rates in unmarried births produce high rates of poverty and high claims upon tax resources. From the individual perspective, we're beginning to understand that children born to single moms, especially never-married moms, struggle in terms of their childhoods and their early adult years. They typically finish fewer years of education; they typically have higher rates of poverty and higher rates of delinquency. There's a great debate, though, as to whether these things would have happened to those children anyway, and we're still resolving that. But I think from the social side of things, the collective side, there's little question that high rates of unmarried births put a huge claim on welfare and other social services."

So, once again, boomers have agreed to disagree. Either the Pill gave us a greater appreciation of our bodies, ourselves, and each other, *or* it is at least indirectly responsible for the moral and fiscal breakdown of the social structure that once held this nation together.

But, as Dr. Ken Dychtwald points out, the sexual revolution was actually only a momentary blip: "The sexual exuberance and indulgence of the sixties actually didn't last very long. Within a decade, AIDS and other sexually transmitted diseases radically curtailed much of the boomers' experimentation and excesses." He agrees with Dr. Nock, however, that it had a profound impact on our society.

In the early seventies, Erica Jong bridged the gap between the sexual revolution and the feminist movement with *Fear of Flying*. She says "if you give kids in their late teens and early twenties a kind of protection against accidental pregnancy, the hormones are going to go wild. That's a big thing. But also I think, it was a 'fuck you' to our parents." She also believes that, to a large extent, this particular revolution was a "media myth."

Historian Joshua Zeitz contends that the sexual revolution actually predated the Pill—and the boomers. It began (God forbid) with our *grand*parents! He explains: "The work of Alfred Kinsey, who is the famous sexologist studying the question of American sexual behavior in the 1940s, was polling people who came of age in the 1910s and 1920s. But Kinsey found that there was a quiet sexual revolution on the build for decades and decades preceding the 1960s."

Be that as it may, in order to be a "common defining experience" for a modern generation, "media myths" have very nearly the same impact as "media facts," and, as a media fact, the perception of moral decay among the boomers served to drive another wedge not only between the boomer generation and the Greatest Generation, but also between the boomers on the Left and the boomers on the Right. It was one of those things that further widened the ever-growing generation gap.

Another of those things was drugs.

Killer Weed

It probably surprises no one that Eve Ensler imbibed in drugs back in those crazy, psychedelic, mind-altering, "if it feels good, do it" days. What may surprise is that she remembers. "There was something about the liberation of drugs. . . . There was something about going to the Fillmore East and watching Grace Slick and being stoned, and just being high and exploring those boundaries that was amazing. Was it dangerous? Would I recommend it to children? No, I wouldn't. But do I regret it? No. Not at all. I was wild; I was wild; and that wildness allowed me later on to be wild intellectually, to be wild politically, to create a life of my own, to invent my life."

As with the sexual revolution, boomers didn't invent the drug culture either. Leonard Steinhorn points out that "drugs have

BUREAU OFFICIAL: Here is an example: A fifteen-year-old lad apprehended in the act of staging a holdup— fifteen years old and a marijuana addict.
DR. CARROLL: Yes. I remember. Just a young boy . . . under the influence of drugs . . . who killed his entire family with an ax.

From **Reefer Madness**
Screenplay by Arthur Hoerl,
based on a story by Lawrence Meade

never been missing from the American scene. You look at the 1890s, and it was not uncommon for a lot of the people to be taking cocaine. There was a reason why marijuana was made illegal in the 1930s; it was because a lot of people were smoking it."

While Dr. Andrew Weil is best known for his work with healthy habits, he knows a bit about the unhealthy ones as well: "Until the time that the boomers came of age, [marijuana] was really being used in subpopulations. For instance, jazz musicians, African Americans in the South, Mexican Americans along the border. But it really hadn't made the jump into middle-class America. And when the boomers started smoking pot, that was really the first time that drug jumped into middle-class white America. And I think that's what caused a great deal of the rumpus, that it was a newer drug that had been associated with deviant subpopulations and excluded minorities that had very different values associated with them."

In *The Psychedelic Experience* (1964), Dr. Timothy Leary et al. told us to "turn off your mind, relax, float downstream," and a great many of us did. And we did it because it felt good. But Leary suggested in that same book that LSD could stand for "Let the State Disintegrate."

Dr. Weil suggests that there was something more at play here than only "getting a buzz on": "I think it was a multitude of factors that drew that generation toward experimentation with drugs. Some of it was the spirit of the times, because it's something we saw, really, all over the world. I think some of it was the particular time and place. Some of it was the availability of substances that up to then had been either not available or only in certain small subpopulations.

"There's no question that as boomers came to experiment with drugs like marijuana, that this was a chief reason they began to question authority. Because the authorities were telling them that marijuana would kill you and lead to insanity and cause brain damage. And they very quickly found out that that was not so. And I think that fabrication extended into the drugs like LSD, being told that it broke your chromosomes or that if you took it you'd think you could fly and jump out of a window. These were all fabricated stories or based on really shoddy research. And it wasn't very hard to see through them. So, I think, once you begin to see that the authorities are giving you that kind of laughable misinformation, it's not very hard to look at the other areas where they seem to be doing that, such as about the war in Vietnam.

"And it involved them in a stance toward society that I think has carried through to the present. And I think the actual psychological effects of that experimentation also were enormous. That is, really giving people a sense that there are other ways of seeing reality; that your experience of external reality is influenced by what goes on inside your head. I think those are very profound changes from the way that the previous generation looked at things."

They told us that marijuana would make us want to rape and kill; that marijuana led to hashish, and hashish led to LSD, and LSD led to heroin, and heroin was suicide. Therefore, marijuana leads to suicide. For some people that was true. But for a vast majority of marijuana users, we found that marijuana led only to a gigantic plate of brownies and a huge glass of milk. The only thing that it killed was ambition. So, once again, "they" were lying.

It is Leonard Steinhorn's theory that "the relationship between boomers and drugs was less the appeal of drugs, and it goes partly

The ultimate photo op. This image of Richard Nixon, of all people, trying to appear "hip" alongside Elvis Presley, gave boomers the impression that our leaders would lie to us about anything.

to the issue of 'Am I getting the truth from the people who are telling me that these things are bad?'

"So, what happened is that when boomers first tried marijuana, as other generations did, they did it on college campuses. And again, college campuses became this sort of a formative place for generational identity, and they said, 'Hah! This stuff doesn't seem that bad. It doesn't seem like it's as bad as what the authorities are telling me.' So, the drug issue actually got caught up into the relationship with authority at the time. Are the authorities telling me the truth? And it's very interesting. If you go back to a 1972 document that was commissioned by the Nixon administration, called the Shafer Commission, . . . they concluded that young people were doing drugs because they really couldn't trust the facts that were being given to them by the authorities about the drugs. And that commission actually recommended the legalization or decriminalization of marijuana.

"The commission report was squashed and never endorsed. But drugs go beyond just people partaking of the individual drug. It was part of our culture and the relationship with what people were being told and seeing that some of these things didn't seem as harmful as everyone was saying they were."

He concludes that the tendency to associate boomers with drugs is "a bad rap": "Had they been told the truth about some of these things—what really are the harmful ones, what are some of the drugs that are less harmful, how do they distinguish those drugs from alcohol—I think people might have rebelled less on the drug issue than they did at the time."

It's an interesting observation that marijuana actually bridged the peace-war gap that existed between boomers of the sixties (and continues to do so even to this day). Peaceniks and Marines were twistin' 'em up in those days. It may have been one of the few things we had in common.

So for some, the drug culture opened up a "new reality," but for others, like Jimi Hendrix and Janis Joplin, it put an early end to their turbocharged lives.

John Chane was a rock 'n' roller in those days—"The Chane Gang" was his band—and they had some success. And like most successful or nearly successful groups, John and the rest of the boys in the Chane Gang had to deal with the sex, drugs, and rock 'n' roll culture every night: "We got way out with drugs first of all. I was one of those guys who was pretty clean, but drugs were available.

"I had an agent who at the end of a show, when we would go back to the hotel, to keep us out of trouble and to keep the groupies and the hangers-on away, he would put a guard outside the door and he would throw in a bag of marijuana and say to the guys in the band, 'Have a great time folks; watch the test patterns.' I mean, it was insane; everything was insane.

"In terms of sex, you would travel around the country, and you would in many cases be followed. It was like an armada of people who would follow you. And you had choices to make. I mean everybody had choices to make. And I'm fortunate enough to have made, I think, the right choices based on the way I was raised. But it didn't keep me away from seeing the ravages of it. People who think the 'generation of love' was a great generation need to really reflect on it.

"Later on, you look at what happened to Jimi Hendrix, Janis Joplin. I mean, you can run the table with great, great talent that just literally threw itself away on a lifestyle that was absolutely crazy and self-destructive.

"Two of the guys that I toured with died of overdoses."

John apparently did make the "right choices." He got out of rock 'n' roll and is now a bishop in the Episcopal Church.

For people like Tony Snow, the out-of-control drug-crazed sixties at least taught us an important lesson: "Drugs certainly messed a lot of people up. I was doing the 'drug talk' with my kids the other day, and I started going back and recollecting friends who've died from overdoses or totally messed up their lives—who've gone away and never come back. And on the sex part, you know, what seemed fun—people forget about commitments. And you also had people whose lives got all chopped up by that as well.

"The one thing that we learned in the sixties is that there was a reason why certain values and institutions have persisted for thousands of years. The other thing we learned is we couldn't remake the world as much as everybody wanted to remake a brand-new world. 'We're going to remake values; we're going to start from the beginning.' It doesn't work that way, and I think a lot of people learned that the hard way."

But for the Left-leaning boomers of the sixties, the sexual revolution and the drug culture were battles fought as a part of a much larger rebellion, a rebellion against, well, virtually everything.

The generation gap grew wider, it seemed, with each passing day—wider and angrier.

Make Love, Not War

There was no greater wedge driven between us and our fathers than the Vietnam War. The Greatest Generation fought the fascists in Europe and in the Pacific, and everybody joined in the fight one way or another. Virtually everybody adored Franklin Roosevelt, and "doing without" was patriotic. We were the good guys, and they were the bad guys, and we kicked their butts. John Wayne was the archetypal American hero, and, by God, don't you dare, young man, utter a word against the good ol' Red, White, and Blue.

But wait a minute! Why does the Bill of Rights protect freedom of speech if we can't speak out against our government? What's the point of freedom if it only protects those who cheer? They have freedom to cheer in the Soviet Union, for crying out loud! But that was something the Greatest Generation, many of whom subscribed to the "my country, right or wrong" theory of patriotism, was not ready to hear.

Dr. Dychtwald reminds us that by 1965, 41 percent of all Americans were under the age of twenty. Add in the "war babies," the preboomers born just before and during World War II, and that means that by 1965 almost half of all Americans had no personal memory of D-Day, Iwo Jima, and V-J Day, or the monumental effort that went into winning that war. During those war years, the people and the government were one. When Uncle Sam called, Americans answered without pause. And now, only twenty years later, to the boomers, our parents' revered Uncle Sam was a liar.

Therefore, Dychtwald tells us, "The war in Vietnam and the sixties created a definite generation gap between the boomers and our parents. Rebellion had become popularized, even glamorized by the media. It was cool to defy authority and to break the rules. The sheer number of us and our refusal to accept the status quo produced the most prolonged domestic turmoil of the century in the years between 1964 and 1970.

"It sounds silly when we talk about it now, but I do believe that we thought that we had feelings of bravery to fulfill the American destiny and the American dream—that, not only was it *not* anti-American, as many accused us of, but many of us felt it was deeply American. It was an expression of freedom and thoughtfulness and the desire to create a great new future."

Dr. Nock not only studies the generation-gap phenomenon, he lived it: "My parents and I got into arguments about whether or not the United States should be in Vietnam. We fought about it because as a war protester I was seen as unpatriotic. My father, as a veteran, felt that he held the value of service to his country, and if you are called, you go."

David Gergen has served as an adviser to four presidents and has experienced firsthand the residue of this gap that continues to divide us, even today: "[Vietnam] opened up these great gaps between what people believed, so that you had these new values that were being embraced largely on the coasts and largely in some of the Big Ten schools versus the old traditional values. And we've seen this in our boomer presidents. We have Bill Clinton, who represents the new values, and George W. Bush, who represents the old values. The old values tended to be more traditional; they tended to be more about the spirit, more religious. They tended to be a lot more about thrift, working hard, making your way, individualism. And the new values tended to be more about equality.

"The sixties and seventies were a time that began to pull the country apart in terms of values."

Oliver Stone was one of those who went and was awarded the Bronze Star. He wrote and directed both *Born on the Fourth of July* and *Platoon*. Like many boomers, when he returned from Vietnam, his parents didn't recognize him—or accept him: "It opened my eyes. To go to the bottom of the bag and see what is going on. I became another person over those fifteen months. The country became so divided in Vietnam. It was like the American Civil War,

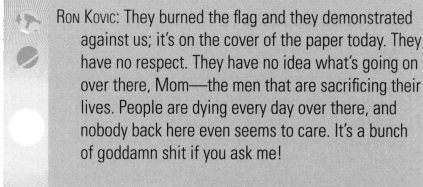

RON KOVIC: They burned the flag and they demonstrated against us; it's on the cover of the paper today. They have no respect. They have no idea what's going on over there, Mom—the men that are sacrificing their lives. People are dying every day over there, and nobody back here even seems to care. It's a bunch of goddamn shit if you ask me!

From **Born on the Fourth of July**
Screenplay by Oliver Stone,
based on the book by Ron Kovic

and *Platoon* was based on that feeling of division in every unit I was ever in.

"When I got back to the States, I talked, my father said, like a black man. You know, 'cause I was like, 'Hey, man,' everything was 'Like, man.' I was probably a pain in the ass, a dope smoker, all of that, and dangerous. It was not easy for my father to accept me. I was no longer little Oliver. And my mother was shocked at how my clothes had degenerated and all of that. So it was a personal thing."

It was a scene repeated a million times over in the seventies, and the arguments had only just begun. The gap continued to widen. Or should we say, the gaps? There were gaps between fathers and sons, gaps between brothers and sisters, gaps between blacks and whites, and gaps between men and women.

Male Chauvinist Pigs!

It is clear that boomers weren't the first antiwar activists or the first civil rights activists, and it is perhaps even more clear that the women's movement in America did not begin in the 1960s. It may have begun on March 31, 1776, when Abigail Adams wrote a letter to her rebellious husband John, then involved in the work of independence.

> I long to hear that you have declared independency. And, by the way, in the new code of laws which I suppose it will be necessary for you to make, I desire you would remember the ladies and be more generous and favorable to them than your ancestors. Do not put such unlimited power into the hands of the husbands. Remember, all men would be tyrants if they could. If particular care and attention is not paid to the ladies, we are determined to foment a rebellion and will not hold ourselves bound by any laws in which we have no voice or representation.

His response? "As to your extraordinary code of laws, I cannot but laugh."

A line of American feminists that begins with Mrs. Adams must include Sacagawea, who not only displayed the same "undaunted courage" as the men on the Lewis and Clark journey of discovery, but gave birth en route as well. There were Clara Barton, Susan B. Anthony, and Eleanor Roosevelt, just to name the most famous.

The feminist movement had won major victories prior to the sixties (the 1960s) including having given women the right to vote in 1920. It may surprise some people to know that (at least constitutionally) black men could vote in this country more than a half century before women could. But Abigail Adams's dream of having a "voice and representation" had at long last been won by the time the boomers came along. "Unlimited power," however, still remained in "the hands of the husbands," not only by social custom, but by law.

Betty Friedan's *The Feminine Mystique* became a gigantic best-seller in the middle of the decade, and the feminist movement was reborn in an effort to make come true the rest of Mrs. Adams's dream. Friedan held that "modern" views of the role of women in society were based in large part on the archaic and sexist perceptions of one Dr. Sigmund Freud—who was so very, very wrong.

The fact is that to Freud, even more than to the magazine editor on Madison Avenue today, women were a strange, inferior, less-than-human species. He saw them as childlike dolls, who existed in terms only of man's love, to love man and serve his needs. Freud grew up with this attitude built in by his culture—not only the culture of Victorian Europe, but that Jewish culture in which men said the daily prayer: "I thank Thee, Lord, that Thou hast not created me a woman," and women prayed in submission: "I thank Thee, Lord, that Thou has created me according to Thy will." *

In 1963, Betty Friedan debunked "the feminine mystique" and all of the Freudian attitudes that went along with it. Her book was read by millions, and an entire generation of boomer women began demanding more.

---

*Betty Friedan, The Feminine Mystique (New York: W. W. Norton, 1963), 108.

The boomer women read this and looked at their mothers and at June Cleaver and at the television commercials of the sixties, and they took offense, and they began to demand that they be treated with dignity and respect and that they be given equal opportunities—*and* equal pay—in the workplace.

Ultimately the women's movement would have every bit as much impact on the America of the future as did the civil rights movement.

Dr. Nock, who is an expert on the institution of marriage, contends that the women's movement changed more than only the workplace of the future; it changed the very foundation of the American family. It changed motherhood: "People who studied the fifties believed that parents doted upon their children more than prior generations had. It's known as a period of intensive mothering, when children were regarded as fragile and needing lots and lots of supervision and parental input. One of the justifications for the single-wage-earner family, in fact, among middle-class Americans, was the idea that children needed moms to raise them properly.

"Baby boom women had their lives redefined in profound ways. They gained control over their childbearing; they got access to higher education; they got access to credit; they got access to housing. The nature of what it means to be a woman, what it means to be a mother, was redefined in the course of a single generation."

Like tens of thousands of other women, for Eve Ensler the women's movement was much more than a concept. It changed her life forever: "Women were still marginalized in all the major movements. In the antiwar movement, in the civil rights movement, women were still pretty marginalized. I think the good news about the sixties was that women started coming into their power.

"Look, I would never have written *The Vagina Monologues* had I not grown up in the women's movement. I never would have felt that I could trust my own self enough, or my own ideas enough, or my own ways enough, or my own self in the world enough, had I not had that backing and not had that kind of support or influence early on. So I think it was fantastic for women in a lot of ways.

"I am really fortunate in that I grew up at the height of the women's movement, at the height of the antiwar movement. And those movements absolutely created who I am. You know, they are mainlined into my consciousness. So I grew up believing that I had not only a right but also an obligation to devote my life to making the world better."

Shelly Lazarus is certainly one who has benefited greatly. She is a boomer who graduated from Smith in 1968 and from Columbia in 1970. She has risen through the ranks to become CEO of Ogilvy and Mather Worldwide—one of the world's most respected advertising and marketing firms—and she looks back on the very significant changes the women's movement has made in her life:

As a Friedan disciple, Shelly Lazarus was among the first to break through a "glass ceiling" and become CEO of Ogilvy and Mather Worldwide.

As a youngster, Dr. Sally Ride wanted to be a tennis player. Instead, she became a physicist, and on June 18, 1983, she became the first American woman to orbit the earth. It was no longer only little boys who wanted to grow up to become astronauts.

"I think the change in the role of women has been extremely dramatic. To me, it's one of the most significant things that's happened in our generation. I graduated from college in 1968, and I went to Smith, an all-women school. It was a school that had very high academic standards and attracted women who were achievement oriented, certainly in academic pursuits. And yet the whole time we were there, the goal was to get married and have kids. So up until 1968, there was a whole set of expectations we had of ourselves, that as smart as these other women were and as capable as they were, what they really aspired to was to get married and to have children who would then go to Smith and Yale, you know, and the pattern just repeats itself.

When Nancy Pelosi became the first female Speaker of the House of Representatives, she said that she had broken through "the marble ceiling," and this mother of five children thanked her family for giving her the confidence to "get out of the kitchen and into the Congress."

"I actually go around and I show advertising from the 1960s to young women, because I want them to remember where we were—where women were promised romance, love, satisfaction, and all that from using skin cream or making the perfect cup of coffee. Or all of a woman's value was derived from her husband's shirts being really white to the point that people noticed. And I do think that a lot of what happened to women was a reaction to all that. I actually think advertising helped trigger women to say, 'But wait a second, that's not enough. I mean, I'm not going to derive my value from how white my husband's shirts are. There is more to life than this.'

"In my class there were a few women who wanted to be lawyers, and a few who were going to medical school, and a few who were doing some other sort of acceptable things for women. But you certainly had no one who aspired to be successful in business or thought that they would go into the corporate world except to work for a little while to find the man who they would marry and then move off to a dreary end. But something happened, because I graduated with women who had those expectations, and yet I, and many women of my age, wound up entering the business world and staying. I think we all entered. Entering was not the surprising thing. The staying part was the change."

Some of our shared, formative experiences are tragic, and some are inspiring. Some are uniting and some are divisive. Some are hugely important and others are downright silly. But can a shared, formative experience be both silly and important at the same time?

At least one can.

The Battle of the Sexes

A tennis player and 1939 Wimbledon champion by the name of Bobby Riggs called himself a "self-proclaimed male chauvinist pig," and in 1973 he challenged Billie Jean King to a match that would prove once and for all time that only males could be athletes. "Girls" who played sports were "tomboys" and nothing more.

On September 20 that year, before a packed Astrodome and a television audience estimated at fifty million, Riggs was escorted onto the court by scantily clad models he called "Bobby's Bosom Buddies," and, not to be outdone, King appeared in a Cleopatra-esque sedan chair held aloft by four strapping, young male "slaves."

King skewered the pig in straight sets, 6–4, 6–3, 6–3.

Game. Set. Match.

Okay, that's the silly part. But how is it "important"?

The match, which had inexplicably captured the imagination of the nation, was played when the ink was still wet on Title IX of the Education Amendments of 1972. Title IX prohibits discrimination on the basis of gender in programs and activities at educational institutions that receive federal funds. It is an omnibus education law affecting all curricular and *extracurricular* programs.

(That means sports, folks.) Its goal was to level the playing field for our daughters, and, while that remains more a goal than a reality, thirty years later it meant that 45 percent of athletic scholarship dollars went to women. At the high school level, Title IX has provided millions of girls the chance to play varsity sports. One of every 2.5 high school girls now participates in varsity sports compared to 1 in 27 in 1972.*

"The Battle of the Sexes" gave Title IX (and "tomboys" everywhere) an image, a proof, and a hero.

In 2006, after signing a $20 million endorsement contract and winning over $1 million as the Women's U.S. Open Champion, Maria Sharapova thanked Billie Jean King. And well she should.

So add "women's lib" to the list of boomer movements of the sixties and seventies.

As girl boomers burned bras, boy boomers burned draft cards.

Rules are for sissies.

---

*Women's Sports Foundation, http://www.womenssportsfoundation.org/cgi-bin/iowa/issues/ article.html?record=1017.

chapter 5

Hell No!
We Won't Go!

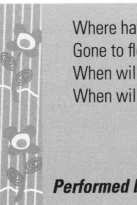

Where have all the soldiers gone?
Gone to flowers every one.
When will we ever learn?
When will we ever learn?

*From "Where Have All
the Flowers Gone?"
Performed by Peter, Paul, and Mary
Lyrics by Vera Lynn*

s the body count continued to grow and the gap over Vietnam continued to widen, the antiwar protests became a magnet for Left-leaning boomers. There were rallies and protests and "teach-ins," and, maybe most important, there was the draft.

All to Whom the Presence May Come, Greetings

In 1966 Muhammad Ali applied to the Selective Service for conscientious objector status based on his position as minister in the Nation of Islam. His application was rejected, and he still refused to serve. "No Vietcong ever called me nigger," he said. He was found guilty of draft evasion and stripped of his world heavyweight boxing title. It would be five years before the U.S. Supreme Court would reverse Ali's conviction, but in the meantime, the cry of "rich man's war, poor man's fight" began to permeate the civil rights community, and the lines between it and the antiwar movement became blurred.

Many civil rights activists, like Julian Bond, were active in both movements: "I think Vietnam became divisive because, first, we knew a great deal about it—there were these teach-ins around the country. People learned the history, the struggle of the Vietnamese people themselves to be free from colonialism; the victory they had won over the French, and then our replacing the French as oppressors and colonizers. So the facts were relatively well known among the generation that was being called upon to go fight this war.

"The draft was an awful spur to antiwar sentiment, as you can imagine. You're eighteen, nineteen years old, and the possibility of your being sent thousands of miles away to fight against an enemy who had never lifted a hand to you, that helped people propel themselves into the antiwar movement. The general feeling of rebellion that was in the air—if the government says do something, there must be something wrong with it.

"All of these things didn't affect everybody, but the combination of them together just made this something we did not want to do. We thought it was wrong in every possible way. We didn't believe what the government was telling us about it and found out that we were right; they were wrong. So this mix just created this enormous antiwar sentiment."

Was that "enormous antiwar sentiment" inspired by injustice or by something more personal? Were we really against America fighting in Vietnam, or were we only against being forced to go over there and fight it ourselves? To pose the question bluntly, were we crusaders for peace, or were we cowards? It's a question that many of us cannot answer honestly even to this day.

Of course, it's not that simple. It was neither and it was both. According to Rob Reiner, it was a combination of issues that all converged at a single pivotal moment in history: "Our generation was the first generation in a long time to really be lied to by authority. And we learned that lesson: to 'listen, trust, but verify,' as they say. And we were asked to fight and die, and we were being drafted and we didn't like that.

"Now, you have a lot of similar kinds of things, where the authority is lying in certain ways or at least deceiving us about why we're going to war, but you don't have a draft. So, you don't have

> I went over to the sergeant, said, "Sergeant, you got a lot a damn gall to ask me if I've rehabilitated myself. I mean, I mean, I mean that just, I'm sittin' here on the bench, I mean I'm sittin' here on the Group W bench, 'cause you want to know if I'm moral enough to join the army, burn women, kids, houses, and villages after bein' a *litterbug.*
>
> *From "Alice's Restaurant"*
> *By Arlo Guthrie*

an impetus to galvanize young people to the kind of loudness, the screams, that we all felt during that period. And so I think if you had a draft now, you'd see a lot of antiauthority sentiment today."

Leonard Steinhorn puts the draft cynicism aside and gives us credit for doing right simply because it was the right thing to do: "Vietnam was a different war. It was never fully justified. It was never clear what our goals were. It was never clear if we had a strategy. It was never clear that the people over there really wanted us over there.

"What we were supporting in South Vietnam was a military dictator. It wasn't really a democracy we were supporting; these were corrupt governments that were going on. And we were sending baby boomer after baby boomer after baby boomer to fight and possibly die for a war that ultimately turned out to be pointless and, from a political sense, duplicitous. And so, boomers also fought against the pointlessness and duplicity of that war and protested it, because there wasn't a good rationale for it. So, yes, **97** we have those bookend wars: one is a war that boomers always said they would have fought in. . . . Even protestors during the Vietnam War said, 'If this were World War II, I would have fought against Hitler, no question, but this is not World War II.'"

By this time many of us were almost addicted to rebellion, seemingly for rebellion's sake. There was a rush, a buzz, an emotional adrenaline that pushed us forward. There was very little we were *not* rebelling against.

From *Leave It to Beaver* to the Bill of Rights to drugs to the war in Vietnam to white supremacy to male supremacy, many boomers thought we were being lied to and had been since birth, and with every passing news event, that belief seemed to be more justified. It seemed that everyone in authority was lying to us about virtually anything that mattered, and nobody trusted anybody. At least nobody over thirty!

Never Trust Anyone over Thirty!

Like self-reliance and idealism, antiauthoritarianism, Dr. Dychtwald reminds us, is another of the major traits of this generation: "Raised to think for ourselves, to question everything, we began to challenge all rules and conventions. 'Don't trust anyone over thirty' became our mantra. That meant parents, teachers, politicians, and particularly those who led us into Vietnam."

By spring 1966, there were some 215,000 U.S. soldiers in Vietnam, and very nearly that many Americans met in New York for the largest antiwar demonstration to date. Julian Bond had been denied a seat in the Georgia legislature simply for opposing the war in Vietnam.

"There was a reason why there was an antiauthoritarian bent to our generation," Reiner remembers. "We always heard that expression, 'Never trust anybody over thirty.' The reason for that is the people over thirty were running the show, and they were lying to us. They were lying to us about the Vietnam War, and we were asked to go fight and die. So it polarized the country, and it galvanized us to speak out against what we thought was an illegal and immoral war."

Oliver Stone's perspective makes "the establishment" more sinister yet: "We inherited this tremendous Promethean power, from World War II, that was like thunder. It was like lightning. And this generation, as perhaps our generation would have been, or any other generation possibly, is corrupted by power, or it becomes arrogant with power.

"That bloated generation became the commanders in Vietnam. They were all World War II veterans. They knew what they were doing, supposedly. And they were completely full of shit, excuse me. They were full of shit. From Westmoreland down, they were lying through their teeth, from day one."

Then everything is a lie? *Absolutely* everything?

Is God Dead?

On March 4, 1966, John Lennon told a magazine reporter in England that the Beatles were "more popular than Jesus now."

All hell broke loose.

A priest in Cleveland threatened to excommunicate any parishioner who listened to Beatles music. The KKK burned the Fab Four in effigy and nailed their albums to fiery crosses. Across America, bonfires melted the vinyl disks from hell into hard, black gobs.

Lennon tried to set the record straight (so to speak): "I believe Jesus was right, Buddha was right, and all of those people like that are right. They're all saying the same thing—and I believe it. I believe what Jesus actually said—the basic things he laid down about love and goodness—and not what people say he said. . . . If Jesus being more popular means more control, I don't want that. I'd sooner they'd all follow us even if it's just to dance and sing for the rest of their lives. If they took more interest in what Jesus—or any of them—said, if they did that, we'd all be there with them."

Less than a month later, the cover of *Time* magazine blasphemed, in giant red type over a stark black background:

99

Is God Dead?

From the oddest possible source the story came. From Emory University, a highly respected Methodist college in, of all places, Atlanta, Georgia, and a group of professors who called themselves "Christian atheists." The article belabors the debate over twelve pages, but offers this as a softening tone: "Less radical Christian thinkers hold that, at the very least, God in the image of man, God sitting in heaven, is dead, and—in the central task of religion today—they seek to imagine and define a God who can touch men's emotions and engage men's minds."*

An interesting additional note in the article addresses itself directly to the young boomers of the day: "Particularly among the young, there is an acute feeling that the churches on Sunday are preaching the existence of a God who is nowhere visible in their daily lives. 'I love God,' cries one anguished teenager, 'but I hate the church.'"

By now the Beatles were blatant drug users, which only proved what our fathers had known all along about these long-haired hippies, and the "Jesus thing" served to widen the gap between the boomers and our parents even more. The Lennon controversy continued for *nine months*—an aeon in media time—until in December of that year he held a press conference in Chicago and issued perhaps the most disingenuous and halfhearted apology ever uttered in the history of the world: "I'm not saying that we're better or greater," he said, "or comparing us with Jesus Christ as a person or God—as a thing or whatever it is. . . . I wasn't saying whatever they're saying I was saying. I'm sorry I said it. Really. I never meant it to be a lousy antireligious thing. I apologize if that will make you happy. I still don't know quite what I've done. I've tried to tell you what I did do, but if you want me to apologize, if that will make you happy, then okay, I'm sorry."

It was also in 1966 that George Harrison led the Fab Four to India, where he wanted to buy a really nice sitar. But there they came under the influence of Maharishi Mahesh Yogi and had

---

"Toward a Hidden God," Time, April 8, 1966.

This is my simple religion:
There is no need for temples;
No need for complicated philosophies.
My brain and my heart are my temples;
My philosophy is kindness.

Dalai Lama

their picture taken with this odd-looking man (to Western eyes) with a long beard and elegant robes. For most Westerners, it was their first introduction to Eastern music, meditation, and mysticism. Not to mention Hare Krishna.

While we were engrossed in a theological debate that actually had begun with Nietzsche and apparently concluded with Lennon, America's predominantly white churches were, in the retrospective view of many, completely ignoring their ethical responsibilities, burying their collective heads in the sand, and wishing that all of the moral dilemmas of the day would just go away.

Bishop John Chane is one who remains embarrassed by the memory: "I always felt that the only reason why the civil rights movement gained the energy and steam that it did was because of the black church in America. It certainly wasn't because of the energy of the white church or what I would call the standard white denominations in this country. And that was very painful."

Leonard Steinhorn agrees and further suggests that not working hard, or not taking a stand, is just another form of deceit, aka lying: "In his book *Why We Can't Wait,* Martin Luther King said, 'The tragedy of Birmingham in 1963 was not the anger and the hatred of all the nasty bad people, it was the silence of the good people.' And I think baby boomers heard that silence. They went to church, and they didn't hear their ministers preaching against racial segregation or the Vietnam War. So they wondered who were their elders, and what were they saying. They tried to speak up at schools, and they were told to stay silent, that young people

101

should be seen and not heard. And they wondered how a society that could respect all of those wonderful values could not be fulfilling them.

"So I think the formative experience for boomers was a sense that America wasn't living up to its ideals, that there was something awry, that the people in power, the authorities, the leaders, they weren't telling us the entire truth, and something had to be done about it."

On the civil rights front, there came a rebellion *within* the rebellion as Stokely Carmichael was elected chairman of the SNCC, and "black power" was on the rise. They didn't trust white people.

Julian Bond remembers: "My organization, the Student Nonviolent Coordinating Committee, expelled our white members pathetically and sadly, so it's almost as though the world as you knew it was coming apart. You'd won some things—they were great things—but there was more, and you didn't know how to go at the 'more,' and being unable to go at the 'more,' things just fell apart." And they were about to get worse.

Oh, My God! Not Again!

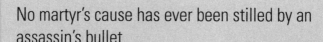

No martyr's cause has ever been stilled by an assassin's bullet.

Robert Kennedy
April 5, 1968

On January 5, 1968, Dr. Benjamin Spock, pediatrician to a generation and the man many people blamed for the rebelliousness of the boomers, was indicted for his antiwar activities. In the final week of that month, the North Vietnamese began the Tet offensive. Early in February, Saigon's police chief executed a Vietcong officer with a pistol shot to the head in a gruesome scene captured by photographer Eddie Adams. It became the shot *seen* round the world. On February 8, former Alabama governor and staunch segregationist George C. Wallace announced his candidacy for president of the United States. And then, on February 27, came the famous commentary by CBS newsman Walter Cronkite that the war in Vietnam was unwinnable. In addition to being "the most trusted man in America," Cronkite was an icon not of the boomer generation but of the "Greatest." Less than three weeks after Cronkite's report, Robert Kennedy decided to run against Lyndon Johnson for the democratic nomination for president, and then—a bombshell:

> I shall not seek and I will not accept the nomination of my party as your president.
>
> ### President Lyndon B. Johnson
> ### March 31, 1968

America would have a new president.

Boomers on the Left rejoiced and looked to the younger brother of their slain president to end the madness in Vietnam. Long forgotten were Johnson's contributions to the cause of the elderly and to equal rights for all, even by many of those who had gained the most.

Julian Bond remembers standing outside the White House chanting, "Hey, Hey, LBJ. How many kids did you kill today?": "When I did that, I wasn't thinking of the Lyndon Johnson who had taken Kennedy's Civil Rights Bill and made it his and passed it through the Congress. I wasn't thinking about the LBJ who passed the Voting Rights Bill. I wasn't thinking of the LBJ who began the war on poverty. I wasn't thinking about that LBJ. It is the war that just overwhelmed him. I think more and more historians are saying you have to look at a large mixed performance, some of it great, some of it not so great. But, yes, the war just erased in the popular memory everything good that he did." 103

The man who led us into Vietnam, the most powerful man in the world, had been forced from office. "The boomers who had opposed the war saw that their protests had not been in vain," Dr. Dychtwald says. "They witnessed for the first time the enormous political power they possessed when they acted together."

Then, a rifle shot in Memphis, and a pistol fired in L.A.

Oh, my God! Not again!

First Dr. King fell to an assassin's bullet, and two months later senator and presidential candidate Bobby Kennedy fell as well. For the boomers, the oldest of whom were only twenty-two at the time, it was a childhood nightmare revisited. Dallas all over again, times two. To many—hopefully to most—it was devastating.

The impact of these assassinations on the older boomers cannot be overstated. Dr. Steven Nock is one of us, and all of us: "The assassinations of great leaders shaped me. They shaped me in ways I think I'm just beginning to understand. They made me appreciate the risk that some people are willing to take—knowingly. I think the great leaders recognize that they may die in the name of their cause.

"They saw a grand vision of the way the world might be."

Now the trumpet summons us again—not as a call to bear arms, though arms we need; not as a call to battle, though embattled we are—but a call to bear the burden of a long twilight struggle, year in and year out, "rejoicing in hope, patient in tribulation"—a struggle against the common enemies of man: tyranny, poverty, disease, and war itself.

President John F. Kennedy
January 20, 1961

Robert Kennedy took up the mantle of his slain brother and suffered the same fate. It was another in a series of tragic "Oh, my God" moments for leading-edge boomers.

With those words, on that cold and beautiful January morning, a young president had challenged us. Then a young preacher, and then a young senator, and they all spoke to an incredibly young generation and inspired us to step out and make the world a better place. And then—they were gone.

David Gergen thinks it was more than only the loss of the men, it was the death of optimism and idealism that wounded us most. These leaders had taught us that "you can go out and actually change the world," he says. "And then we had a series of assassinations that I think just left people feeling empty. And then you realized, to a significant degree, you couldn't depend upon the leaders who were out there to change the world. You had to rely upon yourself because they might disappear. You couldn't count on them being there."

Dr. Dychtwald thinks that the loss of these leaders also left us even more cynical and suspicious: "The combination of these three powerful, charismatic men, cut down in their prime, under circumstances that raised deep suspicions among the public, had a profound impact on the country. The official investigations that followed the assassinations were met with skepticism and distrust. It was a time of great anguish and upheaval in America, especially for the young."

Following the death of Senator Kennedy, Vice President Hubert Humphrey arrived at the Democratic National Convention in Chicago to claim his now virtually unopposed nomination, only to be greeted by some of the most violent antiwar demonstrations to date. The protesters were met there by Chicago's finest, with tear gas and billy clubs and paddy wagons, and it looked like Bloody Sunday all over again. When CBS correspondent Dan Rather was manhandled on the convention floor, Walter Cronkite called Chicago "a police state."

In the wake of the assassinations, both the peace movement and the civil rights movement found themselves suddenly leaderless. It was perhaps a more difficult challenge for the civil rights movement, because it had been so successful. Julian Bond remembers that they had not only lost their leader, but they had also lost their way: "It was harder to rally people to more abstract things like poverty, like poor housing, and hard to figure out, how do you fight that? Do you picket a bank because people are poor? No, that's not the way. What do you do? King himself struggled with how to make poverty an issue in America and did settle on this Poor People's March before he died. For many people, he was the maximum leader, and without the leader you felt directionless. Then the black-white tensions within the movement itself began to be exacerbated."

On hearing of the death of Dr. King, Mayor Shirley Franklin feared that the dream had died with him and that "the civil rights movement would just come to a standstill": "In part that is out of my own ignorance, because Dr. King had many followers, and there were many leaders of the movement who really picked up the baton and continued. The continuation of the movement, both by his wife and many, many other people, like John Lewis and Vernon Jordan and Andy Young and just tons of other people, really kept the movement alive, and it has continued to be an inspiration to me. To both know people who were so courageous in the civil rights movement but who continued the struggle, even after Dr. King's death, and now to be mayor of Atlanta, which is his birth home, is just beyond words."

In 1968, while America mourned two young fallen leaders, individual parents, wives, and children wept over the flag-draped coffins of the 16,589 young Americans who died in Southeast Asia that year, most of them boomers—16,589.*

In 1969 Richard Milhous Nixon became president of the United States. He, like Lyndon Johnson before him, had run as a peace candidate. Maybe the war would soon be over. Maybe the lying would stop.

Maybe.

Maybe not.

One way or the other, the sixties—the boomer decade—was coming to a close.

The Nixon Years

The Nixon presidency began well enough. In his inaugural address, he told us that "we cannot learn from one another until we stop shouting at one another." He also gave both antiwar demonstrators and the soldiers in Vietnam a glimmer of hope when he said, "The greatest honor history can bestow is the title of peacemaker. This honor now beckons America," and in July troop levels began to be reduced from the peak levels of more than a half million. Then the bombing of Cambodia began, secretly.

---

*U.S. Military Casualties in Southeast Asia, http://thewall-usa.com/summary.asp.

So much for good beginnings.

The final stanza of the sixties featured the release of the last album recorded by the Beatles, *Abbey Road*, and a very public denial by Paul McCartney that he was dead. Also in 1969 police found the title of their song "Helter Skelter" scrawled in blood on the walls of the home of brutally murdered actress Sharon Tate.

> People have got to know whether or not their president is a crook. Well, I'm not a crook.
>
> **President Richard Nixon**
> **November 18, 1973**

They had come on the American scene in 1963 with "I Want to Hold Your Hand," charted fifteen number 1 singles, and were so amazingly popular they were able to top the album charts with a double LP that had no cover art. To this day it is known worldwide simply as "the white album." There is not a genuine boomer around today who cannot sing, word-for-word and note-for-note, about two dozen Beatles songs, now more than thirty years after they broke up. The Beatles were perhaps the most enduring of what Dr. Dychtwald calls our "common formative experiences": "The Beatles arrived in America when many of us were teenagers and looking for something new. And here they came in their suits and their strange, mop-top hairdos. . . . Everybody was listening to the Beatles, and everybody was talking about them. . . . But what we really loved about the Beatles was their fantastic capacity to change, to take risks and transform themselves again and again.

"Just as John Kennedy is an icon of boomer idealism, the Beatles are a personification of the boomers' enthusiasm for change."

That eagerness to embrace change is a character trait common to most boomers that has remained with us, and will continue to do so, Dychtwald says, throughout our retirement years and right up to our final moments.

It was also in that final year of the sixties that many of us were reminded how they began, with President Kennedy, our icon of

There were many things that divided us, but the magic moment of "one giant leap for mankind" united us in awe.

In what may have been some sort of cosmic convergence, this vision appeared to us fresh on the heels of Cleveland's Cuyahoga River fire. Less than a year later, twenty million people participated in the first Earth Day and the environmental movement was born.

idealism, standing in the well of the House of Representatives, giving words to his dream "of landing a man on the moon and returning him safely to the earth." In July 1969, right on schedule, we gathered around our tribal campfire and heard Buzz Aldrin report, "Houston, Tranquility Base here. The Eagle has landed."

The first man on the moon was not only a common formative experience for American boomers, it was also a common formative experience for everyone in the world old enough to remember. As on that dreadful day in Dallas, we all remember where we were and who we were with when man first walked on the moon. For most Americans, it involved a television set. What may make the first man on the moon unique for boomers is that it is the first common formative experience that we *all* can remember. The oldest boomers were twenty-three years old, and the youngest—the 1964 boomers—were six, and perhaps just old enough to recall hearing, "That's one small step for a man, one giant leap for mankind." It was an event that signaled mankind's giant leap into that final frontier as well as the beginning of a technological revolution that would change, and continues to change, the world.

Apollo 11 was not an event that stood alone in those final months of 1969. In retrospect, it might appear that it was a part of some kind of cosmic convergence. The month before, the Cuyahoga River in Cleveland, Ohio, caught fire. The industries along the banks of that once beautiful river had no problem with the cheap and easy dumping of toxic and flammable waste products directly into the river, and a spark (it is believed) from an overhead train trestle ignited the resulting oil slick. In fact, it was not a particularly alarming story in Cleveland on that day and didn't even get front-page coverage in the newspapers. But the story slowly oozed out, and America was disgusted.

Then the men of *Apollo 11* gave us a spectacular view of the blue earth as seen from the heavens, unquestionably a classic icon of the sixties: a beautiful, fragile, and borderless globe floating alone in space.

In September 1969, inspired by the antiwar protests, Senator Gaylord Nelson of Wisconsin announced the first Earth Day. Initially it was planned and run by two members of his senatorial staff, but, on the heels of the Cuyahoga River fire and the new perspective of our vulnerable planet, the response was so great and it became such a "happening" that soon a headquarters had to be opened and a staff of volunteers took over.

By the time April 22, 1970, rolled around, organizers estimated twenty million people participated in the first Earth Day, most on college campuses. Even in the age of "What's good for General Motors is good for the U.S.A.," Americans, it seemed, were at last ready to agree on something. The defiling of mother earth must stop.

But of course a man on the moon wasn't the ultimate event of the sixties for the boomer generation.

That would be . . .

Woodstock

Jimi Hendrix played "The Star Spangled Banner" on electric guitar, and hundreds of thousands of hippie boys and girls did drugs and frolicked (some of them naked) in the mud and listened to Richie Havens; Joan Baez; Blood, Sweat, and Tears; Creedence Clearwater Revival; Crosby, Stills, Nash, and Young; Joe Cocker; Arlo Guthrie; the Grateful Dead; Janis Joplin; Jefferson Airplane; Ravi Shankar; Sly and the Family Stone; Santana; Johnny Winter; and the Who, among others. It has gone down in history as a gigantic orgy of "sex, drugs, and rock 'n' roll." Estimates say that as many as 400,000 of us attended, which means, of course, that 77,600,000 of us did not.

Woodstock was further proof that music, above all else, fanned the flames of rebellion. Perhaps more than in any other way, boomers expressed their rebellion in their choice of music. Rather than being something to dance to, or romance to, like the tunes so dearly loved by the Greatest Generation, the new music, our music, was about rebellion, defiance, and protest.

"The celebrity voice of that time was the protest voice," Dr. Dychtwald says. "It wasn't a Pat Boone thing—it was Bob Dylan, it was Arlo Guthrie, it was Joni Mitchell—commanding voices of protest that were basically stoking the fires of a generation. It was a generation that was being trained to look under the surface, and what they saw were lies in their parents, their community, and their church."

That colossal party at Yasgur's farm put a gigantic exclamation point at the end of the decade of "sex, drugs, and rock 'n' roll." A brand-new decade beckoned us. The first of our adolescence. The oldest of us were fourteen the last time the cosmic calendar ticked over a new decade. In the seventies, we would reach adulthood. In the seventies, we hoped all that we had begun would be finished, and maybe, just maybe, it would be the dawning of a new age.

It was, at least, a new age in television, as our communal campfire had finally decided to make their sitcoms look more like the "real" America and launched a program that was *about* the gap. It made fun of the gap. And it was a huge success. It was . . .

Dr. Ken Dychtwald is not only one of the world's foremost experts on boomers, he very obviously is one.

All in the Family

In this show, Carroll O'Connor would portray "them," and Rob Reiner would play "us." Of course, these are stereotypes, and Reiner warns us against stereotyping even Archie and the "Meathead": "It's two generations, but it's also two characters who are politically diametrically opposed. I mean, there were certainly people in Archie's generation who were more liberal, more Left leaning, who were against the war, who didn't like Richard Nixon, and so on. So, it was generational, but it was also a character separation as well."

Still, without the stereotypes, there would have been no *All in the Family*. Reiner recalls a classic moment when the show flashed back to the first meeting of Michael Stivic and Archie Bunker: "We had such a great built-in conflict between those two characters, we just wanted to explore the genesis of that conflict. That's all. Just that moment when these two characters first laid eyes on each

113

Archie and the Meathead: The groundbreaking sitcom All in the Family *featured Rob Reiner as the liberal "us" and Carroll O'Connor as the reactionary "them." Of course it was never that simple. Even today, boomers are not all one thing or all the other.*

other, and the explosion that would happen, that instantaneous explosion, and everything spoked out from there. I remember screaming, 'You're prejudiced,' and he was singing 'God Bless America.' And that just was like the total epitome of the dichotomy between those two characters.

"I just was playing a character that was fairly close to myself and was expressing the social and political ideas that I felt during the time of that generation. So it was a perfect opportunity for me to get certain ideas, feelings, thoughts, across in a debate . . . in a debate format with Archie."

The seventies would begin with what might have been another "Oh, my God" moment but wasn't. It certainly had that potential

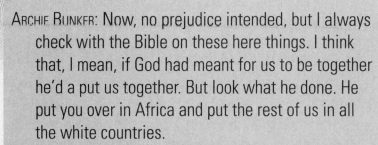

ARCHIE BUNKER: Now, no prejudice intended, but I always check with the Bible on these here things. I think that, I mean, if God had meant for us to be together he'd a put us together. But look what he done. He put you over in Africa and put the rest of us in all the white countries.

SAMMY DAVIS JR.: Well, He must've told 'em where we were because somebody came and got us.

From All in the Family

when we first heard the words, "Houston, we've had a problem here." After days of fervent prayers by millions of the earth's inhabitants, the men of *Apollo 13* were returned "safely to earth," and billions of people heaved a worldwide sigh of relief.

But the safe return of *Apollo 13* was only a brief respite. Less than three weeks later, the headlines would come not from outer space, but from a campus in the heartland of America.

Kent State.

"The Age of Aquarius" would have to wait just a little bit longer.

There's a Man with a Gun over There!

By May 1970 the American public was aware that the rationale for the Gulf of Tonkin Resolution that had authorized President Johnson to commit our troops in Vietnam had been a sham, perhaps the biggest lie of them all. Also the government had discontinued the 2-S student draft deferment, throwing college students into the pool with everybody else. And finally Nixon's "secret" invasion of Cambodia was a secret no longer. Apparently President Nixon, in the eyes of the antiwar movement, intended to bomb his way into his role as "peacemaker."

The students of Kent State began their protest on May 1, and it spilled over into the next day, and the next day, and the next. Rocks were thrown at policemen, windows were broken out, and the already abandoned ROTC building was set on fire. Firefighters had rocks thrown at them, and demonstrators cut their hoses.

Governor James Rhodes called the protesters "the worst type of people that we harbor in America. I think that we're up against the strongest, well-trained, militant, revolutionary group that has ever assembled in America." Apparently Governor Rhodes considered the minutemen and General Washington's Continental Army to be some kind of exception. Be that as it may, he called out the National Guard to put down the current revolution. They were badly trained, badly prepared, badly led, and young. They were, however, well armed.

There is little doubt that many if not most of them were boomers themselves.

They fixed their bayonets.

They loaded their rifles.

They panicked.

And they fired.

A Kent State student took a photograph of a young lady, screaming in shock and terror, while kneeling next to the lifeless body of Jeffrey Miller, which lay facedown on a sidewalk. By the following morning, it would have been difficult to find a solitary American who had not seen it, boomer or otherwise.

Oh, my God!

John Filo's Pulitzer Prize–winning photograph did more than inspire the antiwar movement to greater efforts. It reinforced the already pervasive view of the government as the enemy—and now they're shooting at us; they're killing our children. Our mothers and fathers, the Greatest Generation, were moved by the tragic image as well, and support for the war in Vietnam was, by now, negligible at best. The tide against the war had fully turned. Or at least so we thought.

In 1972, the Democrats nominated an adamant "dove," who advocated immediate withdrawal from Vietnam. But the campaign of George McGovern was amateurish at best and incompetent at worst, and Richard Nixon defeated him in one of the most lopsided elections in American history.

Our resident historian, Dr. Joshua Zeitz, notes that that particular election established a trend that continues to this day: "In 1972, the first year that eighteen- and nineteen- and twenty-year-olds had the right to vote, barely half of those who bothered to show up to vote voted for George McGovern the Democrat, [and] about half voted for Richard Nixon. During the Vietnam War, the opinion on the war shifted within the boomer generation cohort with the same kind of predictability it shifted among older Americans, which is to say when the war seemed to be going well, most boomers supported it, and when it was going poorly, most boomers opposed it."

We still had years to wait before the fall of Saigon, and President Richard Nixon would not be in the White House to see it. He would resign the presidency in disgrace following the disclosures of the cover-up of the infamous Watergate break-in. Congress held dramatic investigations, open and televised for all to see, demanding to know, "What did the president know, and when did he know it?" The White House refused to hand over documents "on grounds of national security" that obviously had nothing to do with national security. They erased a critical eighteen and a half minutes of a tape that might have incriminated Nixon, and after the House Judiciary Committee voted a bill of impeachment to the full House, the president resigned.

"Our long national nightmare" was over, but, according to David Gergen, not before it had driven the last nail into the coffin of trust in the government: "You can look at the polls, and you'll see that from the early days of polling, which go back to the 1940s, even back to the 1930s, there is a very, very high degree of trust in government to do the right thing—for people who are leaders in government to do the right thing. And that breaks around 1967. What you find is there's a sharp drop around 1967, and then it just 117

Most boomers felt that they had been deceived by the government for decades. The deceptions of the Watergate scandal were the last nail in the coffin of trust in leadership, and many boomers remain cynical to this day.

keeps going down, sliding, sliding, sliding, right through Watergate. And since that time, we've never really rebuilt, restored faith in people in government or people in politics. So we paid a heavy price for Vietnam and Watergate."

But was it really a price we paid, or was it a lesson well learned? Leonard Steinhorn points out, "America has a long tradition of being distrustful of authority. You go back to the founding documents of our culture: the Declaration of Independence is a declaration basically against the misplaced and misguided authority of the British government; the Constitution itself is a document that has distrust of authority built into it—there's separation of powers, balance of powers, and that no one should get too much power. We as a country get nervous when people get too much power, particularly when they do things that they're not held accountable for. So I think what was happening in the 1950s and sixties is boomers were saying, 'people in politics doing and saying things, not facing consequences, sending people to war without even a vote to go to war, based on false information.' So how could you not distrust authority at that time?"

A man who may rank as the nation's leading "conservative" agrees. When Newt Gingrich was Speaker of the House, a young lady stood up at a town hall meeting and asked him, "Mr. Speaker, can we trust you?" Gingrich answered, without pause, "No. Never trust anybody with power."

Had we trusted what our government was telling us in the fifties, sixties, and seventies, things might never have changed. So distrust, for lack of a better word, is good. It was because so many of us rebelled against those things that were wrong with America that America changed and, most would agree, changed for the better.

Julian Bond was there, and active, and can evaluate the impact of the boomers' activism from an almost unique perspective: "Because I am older than the baby boomers, when I'm asked to measure progress, I measure it over a longer time, and I look back to my college days in the late fifties, and I can see we have come an enormous way since then. When I was in college I couldn't go to restaurants in downtown Atlanta; I couldn't work at most white-collar jobs in Atlanta no matter how well I did in school. That didn't mean much in the white world I lived in, and it does mean something now.

"[The boomers] are the people who helped eliminate racial segregation by law in this country. These are the people who gave life to an environmental movement that is still with us. These are the people who took an older women's movement and gave it new life. These are the people who took an older Hispanic movement that was long lasting, long existing in the United States, and gave it new impetus. These are the people who set the model for all these other groups, for how they should behave and how they should fight for their freedoms. The great demonstrations we are seeing now of Hispanics are a legacy of the civil rights movement

119

of the 1960s and really a legacy of the baby boomer generation. So it's not that the baby boomers invented these things, far from it, but they gave life to them. And because their numbers are so great, they've made them a permanent part of American life and culture."

It is amazing to look back now at all the movements we gave life to. The environmental movement that began with Earth Day in 1970 started us down a road that has led to the establishment of the U.S. Environmental Protection Agency and the Clean Water Act, the Clear Air Act, and the Endangered Species Act, and has kept us focused on earth issues. Our planet may still be in trouble, but these issues remain front and center thanks to the twenty million who came together on that day, and to the two hundred million who came together "earthwide" in 1990. Since then, they've simply stopped counting.

Far out.

We had ended a war.

Cool.

We made the world a better place for women and minorities.

Groovy.

But now comes the midseventies, and it is time—God forbid— to get a job.

Bummer.

part two

Get a Job!

chapter 6

Jack and Jill

The sixties are over. The war in Vietnam is lost. The Civil Rights Act and the Voting Rights Act are law. Lyndon Johnson has been exiled to his ranch near Austin, Texas; Richard Nixon, pardoned for his crimes, lives in posh disgrace in Yorba Linda, California; and it's time for the oldest boomers to leave school or get out of the army or give up on their dreams of being the next Jerry Garcia or Janis Joplin and move out into the "real" world.

When we were six years old, we magically appeared on the doorsteps of America's elementary schools, and they weren't quite ready for us. When we were eighteen years old, we tsunamied our way onto the nation's college campuses, and they weren't quite ready for us. And when we were in our early twenties and enlisted in the largest army of job seekers ever in the history of the world, well, American businesses weren't quite ready for us then either.

Dr. Dychtwald gives us a brief history of American economics: "America began as an agricultural society where grandfather, father, and son often plowed the same fields together. Women also helped in the fields, raised the kids, and, of course, managed the household.

"The industrial revolution created new kinds of work—hard, dirty, physical labor best suited for the young and able bodied.

The farm-based family split up. Men went to work in the mills and the factories, and the women remained at home to look after the kids.

"But then the manufacturing society gave way to a white-collar world. Corporations replaced factories as the center of business in America. Employees spent their entire career working for the same company. A job was almost like a marriage—'till death do us part.' After twenty-five or thirty years of work, a man could expect to retire with a comfortable pension and a gold watch."

Between 1969 and 1976, some eight million baby boomers entered the labor force—twice the number that began working in the seven previous years. We were self-empowered, idealistic, anti-authoritarian, and eager, not only to embrace change, but also to cause it. Our women were "liberated" and our men were confident. And one more thing—in greater numbers than ever before, we were single and living alone.

The director of the Marriage Matters project at the University of Virginia, Dr. Steven Nock, thinks that this is another "first" in American history, and another reason boomers are unique: "The baby boomers left home at higher rates than their parents had or their grandparents had—there's no question about it. We are a mobile society and always have been, but the baby boomers moved as individuals as opposed to as families. They left home, they moved away, and they lived on their own. They created a new stage of life.

"In the colonial era, people were not permitted to live alone. Single men in particular were viewed as a threat to social order and they could be prohibited from living alone in the North or taxed heavily for living alone in the South.

"Now the census of 1900 shows a very high percentage of American households having boarders and lodgers, and these were people who were simply living with another family because they were either apprenticed or they were going to school, but they were not yet married and on their own.

"The baby boomers almost take it for granted that when you leave home, you can live on your own. There's this wonderful period of life that's been created in the last forty or fifty years, between when an individual leaves home and when they form their own family, and it can last ten or fifteen years. And it's historically unprecedented."

It had been America's industrial might that had carried us through the Victorian era and won World War II. The "smoke-stack industries" were the economic engine of the day and the employers of our fathers who by now had put in twenty years or more and had their pensions and gold watches in sight. "But boomers were not brought up to be the same 'company men' that their fathers had been," Dr. Dychtwald tells us. "They wanted more from their work than a nice salary and lifelong security. They wanted their jobs to be more flexible, more fulfilling, and even fun!"

Harvard economist Dr. D. Quinn Mills agrees: "The idea that work was supposed to be fun is an idea that came with the baby boomers. They brought it to us, and I think they thought life was supposed to be fun, which was very different than their parents and preceding generations, who saw life as duty and obligation."

Of course there was a culture shock waiting to happen. In addition to being single, independent minded, and antiauthoritarian, for the first time a large percentage of this gigantic army of job seekers were women.

I Am Woman—Hear Me Roar!

It is difficult to conceive, looking back from the twenty-first century, that in 1946, the year the first boomers were born, American women had had the right to vote for only twenty-six years.

"You've come a long way, baby!" Boomer women had burned their bras and finished their educations. They had read *The Feminine Mystique* and *Fear of Flying*. They were single and smart and, along with their brothers, they had just changed the world. They had earned a place in the workforce and expected to be hired, respected, and given equal pay for equal work.

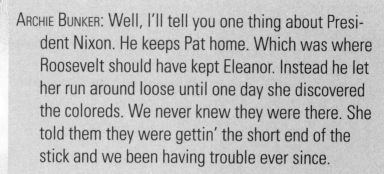

ARCHIE BUNKER: Well, I'll tell you one thing about President Nixon. He keeps Pat home. Which was where Roosevelt should have kept Eleanor. Instead he let her run around loose until one day she discovered the coloreds. We never knew they were there. She told them they were gettin' the short end of the stick and we been having trouble ever since.

From **All in the Family**

In June 1978, for the first time in U.S. history, the proportion of women aged sixteen and older in the labor force surpassed 50 percent. No longer limited to nurse, teacher, or secretary as an occupation, women entered the workforce en masse, drastically changing the office dynamic. The American workplace would never be the same.

Historian Dr. Joshua Zeitz says that by the seventies and eighties, 70 percent of all boomer women were employed, and the Ward and June Cleaver model was a thing of the past for two reasons: "Part of the reason why many middle-class and upper-middle-class women had not been in the workforce prior to the 1970s is simply that these opportunities didn't exist, and so part of the mass entry of boomer women into the workforce can be explained by economic calculation, and part of it can be explained by the simple opening up of opportunity. The second thing, however, which characterized boomers, is that they married later than their parents and they had children later than their parents, and, in part, this is because they were growing up in an era of grand expectations economically, but they came of age in an era of diminished economic opportunities and limited resources."

Having worked her way up to the presidency of Ogilvy and Mather Worldwide, Shelly Lazarus is one of the great success stories of the early boomer women in the workplace. She recalls her personal journey: "I was very open to admitting at the time

While our dads were off at war, our moms went to work in the war effort, and many found out that they liked having a job and earning a salary. Suddenly the June Cleaver model of the stay-at-home mom was doomed.

that I went to get an MBA because I didn't want to type. And in 1968 when you graduated from college and you wanted to enter the business world, the commercial world, you almost certainly had to type. I actually was so discouraged by this fact that some woman who was in some corporate HR department tried to make me feel better and said, 'You know, I bet if you got an MBA, they couldn't make you type.' And I thought, 'Well, I'll look into this MBA thing.'

"I came to an organization that was a true meritocracy. I didn't know it at the time—it took me a while to figure out what had actually happened—but I came to work for Ogilvy, which was a company that was founded by a very unusual and fabulous Englishman who believed a lot of things. This was in the seventies now. One of the things he believed was that in any organization, people should only be judged by their actual contribution, that issues of where you went to school, your social background, your gender, your religion, how you dress, what you believe, were absolutely irrelevant, and that there was only one thing that counted, and that was how good you were at what you were asked to do . . . how big a contribution you could make. And what I learned is, when you have a true meritocracy, women succeed. I mean they succeed as often as men do. And so I always speak out and say, 'You know, women don't need remedial help. We don't need programs and mentors and all of that stuff that people throw at us. What we really need is a truly even playing field,' and then my belief, my observation, is that women will succeed in equal numbers as men will."

Cathleen Black was also among the first of the boomer women to break through the so-called glass ceiling. She began her career selling advertising and is currently the president of Hearst Magazines, which publishes 115 editions that range in appeal from *Cosmopolitan* to *Popular Mechanics.* For her, as well as for thousands of others, it all started with Betty Friedan's book: "I remember reading *The Feminine Mystique* when I was a senior in college, and it had a profound impact on how I wanted to live my life. It made me believe that I could be what I wanted to be. I didn't have to live a traditional life the way that my mom and her generation had lived, and I thought, 'This speaks to me.' There was nothing else like it at that particular time.

"So I think there was that sense of wanting it all, feeling as though if you worked really hard, it could happen. Now of course it doesn't happen for everybody. But I think there was that sense of 'This is a very different time—it's my time to seize the moment.' That certainly is, I think, very applicable to the women of my generation.

"When I was at *Ms. Magazine* in the early seventies, the word *feminism* was just becoming a part of the vocabulary, and most women had difficulty saying, 'I'm a feminist,' and yet if you read the definition of *feminist,* which was, essentially, equal opportunity for all, you'd say, 'Why wouldn't I believe in that?'

Rowan and Martin's Laugh-In *added some colorful phrases to our vernacular, including "One ringie-dingie," "Sock it to me," and the ever-popular, "Look that up in your Funk and Wagnalls!"*

129

"But I would say for my generation it was a rare time when I didn't believe I had to do even better than the men that I was working with because I knew I was always on the firing line, always having to prove that I was as good or better than they were."

"Ms.?" What the heck does *Ms.* mean?

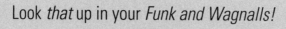

Look *that* up in your *Funk and Wagnalls!*

From Laugh-In

While the feminist movement has been hugely successful, it should not be inferred that this revolutionary change in America came about without a price being paid. Revolutions don't come cheap. There is always a cost both to the rebels and to those who are being rebelled against.

Love, Honor, and *What?*

Most of our mothers had vowed before God to "love, honor, *and obey*" their new husbands. Now at least half of us began to question and challenge yet another sacred icon of our fathers. "*Obey?* Who made up *that* rule? I didn't read *that* in *The Feminine Mystique!*"

And then, as boomers finally began to marry, came the death knell to the *Father Knows Best* model of the American family: "Fix your own dinner!"

Male boomers, even the most liberal of us, still had the June Cleaver model of femininity firmly ensconced in our brains, as well as visions of our own stay-at-home moms cooking and cleaning and raising the kids: "*Father Knows Best* to me was the sort of the archetypal image of what life was like growing up," Shelly Lazarus remembers. "That's where you look at it and you go, 'God, people, it used to *be* like that.' You know, the mother was always dressed for dinner, and she was always sort of fussing around, and

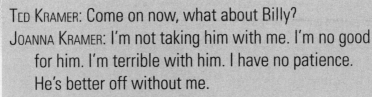

TED KRAMER: Come on now, what about Billy?
JOANNA KRAMER: I'm not taking him with me. I'm no good
    for him. I'm terrible with him. I have no patience.
    He's better off without me.
TED: Joanna, please.
JOANNA: And I don't love you anymore.

From Kramer vs. Kramer
Screenplay by Robert Benton

the father was always the source of all knowledge and the authority figure, and daughters were always worrying about boys and dates. It was so typical of a time, but it never looked as pretty as that. But I still remember those times."

So the Lucy Ricardo we all grew up loving was now educated, employed, and empowered. But she still had "some 'splainin' to do." For one thing, modern-day Lucys had to explain to their husbands and the fathers of their children precisely why it was that father did *not* necessarily know best, and a great many of us didn't want to hear it.

In 1975, the number of divorces in America passed the one million mark for the first time. By the end of the seventies, the United States had twice as many divorced persons in its borders than it had only ten years earlier. The generation that had grown up in an age when divorced people were pointed at, gossiped about, and had to stop going to church because of the social stigma attached to such a failure had now produced the highest divorce rate in history.

Marriage expert Dr. Steven Nock understands that everything changed in the seventies and that not even the institution of marriage could withstand such an onslaught: "There's a lot of debate about what was done to the baby boom generation to make them end up so screwy. After all, they are the generation that grew up in the most intensely familistic generation of the

131

twentieth century. And yet, they went on to produce the highest divorce rates and unmarried birth rates in history.

"One of the great failures of the baby boom is the way it chose to craft personal relationships. I think that the very, very high divorce rate that we produced will undoubtedly be regarded as a failure. We couldn't make it work—we couldn't make our marriages work the same way our parents had been able to.

"If you think about it, the baby boomers had no model to follow. Their fathers and mothers did not grow up in *households* where men and women were regarded as equals. They didn't grow up in an *economy* where men and women were regarded as equals, and they certainly didn't grow up in *schools* where men and women were regarded as equals. They didn't play *sports* where men and women had equal opportunities. But the baby boom came of age when all of those things were starting to happen.

"You introduce a seemingly simpleminded idea like equality between the sexes, and think of what that does to a generation that had never seen it before. I've never found it surprising that the marriages formed by these pioneers, who were facing equality between husbands and wives, were so fragile. They fell apart in the face of unprecedented challenges. Men, who had seen their fathers be traditional, male, wage-earner husbands and fathers, could not live that way and have a happy marriage. There was no other model for them."

Oliver Stone thinks Hollywood put unreasonable pressure on young men in those days with some pretty macho cinematic role models: "You know, also we had the man-woman culture. The man culture was based on John Wayne in *Sands of Iwo Jima* as a role model. Audie Murphy was a role model based on his great film, *To Hell and Back*. You know, to be a man was to be tough."

But John Wayne and Audie Murphy haven't held up so well as masculine role models for the boomer generation. Trend spotter Faith Popcorn tells us that the modern man is much less macho and much more sensitive: "I think a lot of men are self-defining. This is not my opinion; it comes from interviews. A good man will look very much like a good woman. He's a nurturer; he's a lover;

he's an artistic being; he makes the world, his world and other people's worlds, beautiful; he, hopefully, has something he loves to work at. He won't be defined by how mean he is or how strong he is physically or how many people he beats up every day or that kind of thing. He'll just be a good person. A good man will be a good person." Ah, the modern American SNAG* is born!

The traditional man-woman model was under attack in the workplace, in the kitchen, and in the bedroom as well. As the women's liberation movement caught fire, the sexual revolution was in its death throes. In the previous decade, we not only had the Pill, but also penicillin. Communicable diseases of the day, diseases that had been fatal for thousands of years, had finally been cured. *Playboy Magazine* and the lifestyles it promoted came into vogue. There was no longer a fear of pregnancy, no longer a fear of death, and no longer a *Fear of Flying*.

Erica Jong remembers that "for a little while people could hook up and fear no consequences, because of the Pill. Young people could hook up. But that period when people were really free to hook up was—maybe less than a decade. Because right after that, we got new sexually transmitted diseases. We got AIDS. We got genital warts and God knows what. You name it. So, it's a slim decade, and after that the backlash was bigger than the revolution."

"[People were] experimenting, exploring, trying things out," Dr. Dychtwald says. "They were experimenting with lots of partners. 'Open marriages.' It turned out to be completely unworkable, but it was a hypothesis born in an era where you couldn't get a disease and wouldn't get pregnant, so sex became fun."

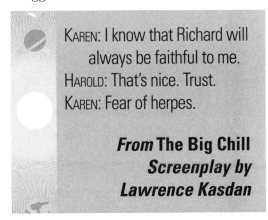

KAREN: I know that Richard will always be faithful to me.
HAROLD: That's nice. Trust.
KAREN: Fear of herpes.

From **The Big Chill**
Screenplay by
Lawrence Kasdan

Sensitive New-Age Guy. It's not *in your* Funk and Wagnalls.

But, of course, there were as many reasons for divorce as there were divorces. The bottom line is that the mores of our parents' generation, which vowed "till death do us part," and the cultural demand that couples who hated each other stay married "for the children's sake," was simply another rule that boomers elected to disregard, for better or for worse.

There were myriad new choices available in relationships, but Shelly Lazarus thinks it was all about newfound freedom: "Well, I actually think that it was an exercise of freedom that people didn't know they had before. You know, they felt comfortable enough and self-confident enough that they could say, 'This is not a good situation for me; I'm leaving because I can.' The opposite of that, to me, is if your relationship is strong and good and you prize it, you work at it, you don't take it for granted, because it's a positive choice that you make every day to continue on in the relationship."

In the early seventies, divorce still had a very serious social stigma attached to it. In the original pilot for *The Mary Tyler Moore Show,* Moore's character, Mary Richards, was to have been a divorced woman. "No!" screamed the network executives. "You can't do that! Everybody will think that Mary has *divorced* Rob Petrie." Rob, of course, was Mary's husband in the long-running and amazingly popular *Dick Van Dyke Show.* "Worse yet," the Cro-Magnon men at the networks shouted, "they will think that Mary Tyler Moore has *divorced* Dick Van Dyke! Make her a single girl, living alone. We can't have the audience believing that Mary has had—horrors—'a failed marriage.'"

Erica Jong hates the expression "failed marriage": "I don't think divorce is failure. Of course, how can I think divorce is a failure when I've been married four times? So maybe my own ox isn't being gored and so I think it's a good thing. Sure it would have been wonderful to have married the person I'm with now when we were eighteen and nineteen. Maybe we should've met at eighteen and nineteen. But you know what? If we had met at eighteen and nineteen, he would've been terrified of me, and I would've thought he was too nice to be interesting, because I was interested in bad boys at that moment in my life, and I had to cycle through all those bad boys before I could realize that a really nice guy was really lovable."

Dr. Nock has a very different perspective: "So marriage becomes optional and, not surprisingly, a lot of people find that divorce is now the answer to an unhappy relationship. . . . And one interpretation of that is that whatever the changes were that brought about these high divorce rates, the baby boomers began to work through them; their children came of age at a time when working moms were regarded as normal; when equality between the sexes was regarded as normal.

"So I believe that future generations, and, hopefully, our children, will look back upon the baby boomers as facing these enormous challenges, especially of gender equality and racial equality, and starting to make a solution to most of them."

But What about the Kids?

Baby boomers married later than their parents, bore children at an older age, had smaller families, and, from the moment their children were born, announced to the world that parenting would never be the same again.

Since the days of the caveman, men have gone off to work (woolly mammoth hunting, one might presume), and women have stayed home, gathered berries, and raised the kids. Tens of thousands of years of human tradition were about to be changed by a single generation of Americans.

In the late seventies and early eighties, the "Spock babies," who were so adored and pampered and spoiled by their own parents, had to figure out how to be parents themselves. The old rules, needless to say, no longer applied. June Cleaver now has a career, Ward helps with the dishes and changes diapers, and after school, Wally and the Beaver are on their own.

Many baby boom women went to work not because of need but because they wanted a life outside the home. The two-income family became commonplace. But just because you became a vice president of your company didn't mean that your husband no longer wanted a wife or your children a mother.

Faith Popcorn earns her living anticipating trends to help us sneak a glimpse into the future, but we asked her to look at the past and present of parenting: "I think women are saying, 'Oh, my God, all I do is work.' They work from 6 a.m. till 7 p.m., 8 p.m. They go home, they have a moment, maybe, with their families, and try and do something for the kids, and they work again. And so many of them describe life as 'I'm not doing a good job at the office, and I'm not doing a good job at home.' And you look at that fifties woman with that little apron and we laugh at her. . . . So I actually think, given the choice, they wouldn't want to go back to the fifties. But they're finding this is a little bit disillusioning as well."

Shelly Lazarus, president of Ogilvy and Mather Worldwide, knows a thing or two about commercials and remembers one in particular not very fondly: "There was one for Enjoli Fragrances, and it showed a woman who actually changed clothes over the course of a day from working, to being in the kitchen making dinner for her husband, to being sort of a siren at night. I can even remember her sort of flipping off her rubber gloves. And you look at it now and you say, 'What a lie—come on.' You said, 'If you looked at this woman, everybody else was inadequate, because she brilliantly led four lives over the course of thirty seconds!'

"I think when parents work outside the home, it does give children a different growing up experience. I think it's positive, but that might be a bit self-serving. I think that when I look at my own children . . . I think that the time that I had with them was so precious—it was very joyful, very meaningful, we looked forward

I can bring home the bacon . . .
Fry it up in a pan . . .
And never let you forget you're a man.
Commercial for Enjoli Fragrances

to it. It wasn't taken for granted. We used it well together. I think I set different expectations for both my sons and my daughter. I frankly can't imagine my sons marrying women who don't have a varied life. I'm not even saying an important professional life, but some life outside the home because that's just sort of what they saw. And I think that families with two parents working outside the home—it was a different growing up experience for the children. But I'm now old enough and my children are old enough that they seem to have come out just fine."

And what about the young girls today whose *grandmothers* were active participants in the sexual revolution? Specifically, what about young girls whose grandmothers stand up on stage every night in front of hundreds of people and talk about vaginas? What kind of parents were these veterans of the sexual revolution, and what kind of children have they raised?

Eve Ensler makes it a point to speak with people who come to her *Vagina Monologues* performances, particularly young women: "There are girls that I've interviewed who were brought up by women in the sixties, who absolutely love their bodies, who know their bodies, who feel comfortable with their bodies, who know they have agency over their bodies, who know they have the right to say no and yes, who know what feels good. And there've been people who went in the opposite direction, . . . who didn't want their daughters to be anything like they were, so they got more restrictive and more repressive and more conservative.

"I think of my granddaughter who's nine, and she's my heart. And she told her teachers that her 'Bubby' invented vaginas, and I thought, 'That's okay, that's okay.' You know, she's going to grow up, and she's going to feel good about her body, and she's going to feel good about herself, and she's already comfortable saying the word, and that made me really happy. That made me really happy!

"I don't know, though, my experience interviewing teenage girls is that it's very retroactive right now, that girls seem to be very performative. They're able to expose their bodies and show their bodies and objectify their bodies. But they're not really living 137 inside their bodies with real power and real agency over them, and that concerns me."

So far, we've only spoken about working mothers and liberated mothers and "Super Moms." Working fathers with working wives have to be "super" as well, and our fathers were no better role models for the modern marriage than were the "stay-at-home moms of yesteryear," as Oliver Stone is quick to point out: "My father, as many people of that generation—it sounds corny, but it's true—they just didn't touch you, they didn't feel, they didn't hug you the same way that we have the tendency to do today. So maybe we hug our children more. And we are more touchy-feely. They used to kid Bill Clinton about that, you know. That 'I feel your pain' kind of mentality, and I think it is a bit of a cliché. But we are reaching out to touch, and feel, and be, because we felt an absence of that in our lives or a denial of it by our parents."

For most of us boomer boys, especially leading-edge boomer boys like Mr. Stone, it has been a long, hard, steep learning curve. But, in a scant quarter-century or so, many if not most of us have finally caught on. According to Leonard Steinhorn, we may have finally figured out that husbandhood and fatherhood are both very good things: "I think baby boomers, men and women, have really gone through this voyage together. And thankfully, we had a women's movement that was able to point out the hypocrisies from the old era, that easily could have been ingrained in boomer culture, but weren't. And the interesting thing is that men have been moving, slowly and imperfectly, but moving, and in the direction of greater equality, in the home and in the workplace. . . . And so it's again not perfect, but, remember, in the 1950s and sixties, men were either not allowed to or didn't want to be in the delivery room when a child was born. Now, basically, all men are there when their children are born. Forty percent of the family and medical leave requests in the 1990s came from men. You have, increasingly, men saying in surveys that family is as important as work, and that they want jobs that provide them with the greatest amount of flexibility to be around their families. You have men coaching girls' soccer and girls' basketball and girls' softball, and encouraging their young daughters to pursue those sports without any roadblocks or without any obstacles. So in a funny way, a lot of men may resist here and there or may be stuck in the old ways to some extent, but they have changed as well.

"So I think women have probably taught men that you can't live by those old ways, those 1950s morals and values anymore, and you've got to change. And men, boomer men, to their credit, have been open and receptive to it, and that's a good thing."

Rob Reiner thinks that a growing economy and comfortable lifestyle also played a role in our metamorphosis: "We had basically what we needed on a material level. So our generation was looking to more emotional security, personal growth, psychological growth, those kinds of things, and we wanted those things for our children. Each generation wants more and better for their children. Our generation wanted their children to be more psychologically aware, more emotionally secure than the previous generation."

To a point, presidential press secretary Tony Snow agrees. If we don't have to worry about material things, we can devote more time to our kids, and to teaching them the things they need to learn: "The one thing that we have that our parents didn't have is kind of a notion that our kids materially are going to be okay. And I think a lot of baby boomers are trying to get beyond some of the immediate material wants and needs and trying to answer the two questions that kids and adults ask: 'What's it all about?' and 'What do I need to do?' If you can give people a sense of purpose in life and what the guidelines are, you've gone a long way toward doing what you can as a parent."

According to Erica Jong, making it okay for fathers to be daddies has also given our children an added advantage: "We made it mainstream for men to parent. We gave men a great gift. And now, we have a whole new generation of men who are close to their children and nobody says, 'You're a freak, you're a fairy, you're a fag.' That's a gift, and that's a gift of feminism.

"It's difficult, and we've put this huge burden on marriage. But are we demanding the right things of marriage? Absolutely.

Are we demanding that our spouse be as invested in the children and grandchildren as we are? Absolutely. Are we saying that men ought to change diapers and even like it? Yes. Are we saying that a woman ought to relinquish her possessiveness over her baby and not make fun of the guy and not say, 'You're changing the diaper wrong,' and not say, 'You don't do it like I do, therefore you can't do it.' We've got to let go. That's a big one. Women find it hard to let go. Men find it hard to let go. People find it hard to let go. But are we doing something good for marriage? Absolutely.

"I think we were terrific parents. I mean, actually we gave them unconditional love. We told them they were wonderful. We believed that they were wonderful. They always were wonderful. And except for a brief period in adolescence, when they want to kill us, they *are* wonderful. And you can live through that. I mean, if you're smart, you can live through the brief period in adolescence when they hate you. You just basically say, 'Okay, I know you hate me, and yes, I'll drive you to the mall.'"

Just like mothers and daughters many generations before and many more yet to come.

Parenthood seems to be one common bond that unites the diverse boomers. We can all brag about our kids, pass around photographs, sell cookies, and respect each other for doing so. Politics, religion, race, and all the other things that divide us are set aside and forgotten when little Billy scores his first soccer goal.

But as boomers move through the many challenges of parenting, there ultimately comes that dreaded moment when we open our mouths to speak to a child, and out comes the voice, the tone, and often the very words of our parents!

Neil Steinberg is one of the producer/directors of the PBS documentary for which this book is the companion. He is a long-time associate of Dr. Dychtwald and has had a distinguished and diversified career in motion picture and television production. But none of that is why he appears here and now. He appears here and now because he is a boomer—and a dad.

When I Was Your Age

Neil Steinberg
Producer/Director, *The Boomer Century 1946–2046*

"When I was your age . . ." As a child growing up in
Chicago, this was a familiar refrain in my home. The
speaker was my father, and his saying it was usually
precipitated by a request I made for money to see a
movie or by my reluctance to walk a mile to go visit a
friend. For when my father was a kid during the
Great Depression, everything was a nickel, and he
told me, "We couldn't afford even that!" And as far
as walking, in my father's stories all his childhood
destinations were five miles away, and it was always
snowing—apparently, even in the summer.

The phrase "When I was your age . . ." may
sound logical, but the concept is flawed. He is from
the newly dubbed Greatest Generation, and I'm a
baby boomer. Once upon a time, we both might have
been ten years old, but we grew up in completely
different worlds—shaped by different events—that
profoundly affected who we are. So in many ways,
we were never the same age. We are both a product
of our times, and the times defined us differently. I
protested the Vietnam War; he enlisted in the army
during World War II. Our attitudes toward family,
government, money, and work in general were
clearly shaped by the social and political environments of our respective youths.

About a year ago, Ken Dychtwald called and said
he would like to discuss a documentary project. Ken

and I first worked together about twenty years ago, and I've always had great respect for his intelligence and vision. He is also a true friend, which I believe is one of the most meaningful compliments you can give someone. The project he first described evolved into *The Boomer Century 1946–2046.* Along with my partner, Joel Westbrook, and a very talented production team, I've spent the last year exploring and trying to understand what it means to be a boomer.

I had thought my personality was shaped by my family, my friends, my DNA. However, there is another big piece of the puzzle. I lived through the Kennedy assassinations, Vietnam, and Watergate. I saw the first man walk on the moon. I was deeply affected by the movies *West Side Story, The Graduate,* and *Annie Hall.* Bruce Springsteen sang of teenage frustrations and hopes, and I was there.

Many of my contemporaries and I share a rebellious streak, a sense of idealism, a need for community, and the ability to reinvent ourselves. We still listen to the Beatles, desperately try to avoid a nine-to-five existence, and believe that equality for all is the noblest of human values. We belong to a generation and a time that shaped our views toward relationships, success, happiness, and even aging itself. We share a common history, and a common future.

What are the factors that shaped our formative years and how will they resonate throughout our lifetimes? The journey of this production for me became an exercise in connecting the dots. These dots form a path through my generation's collective past, present, and future. Some of the links between cause (world events) and effect (personality traits) were obvious, but some were more subtle.

An example of one of the more subtle links can be found in how our approach to parenthood, particularly fatherhood, has been redefined by our generation. Though my dad was incredibly supportive and even affectionate, this was atypical for his generation. I never questioned his love, but I have no doubt he couldn't name one of my teachers from elementary or high school. Not only couldn't he name them now, but he couldn't have named them even back then. That generation of fathers didn't love their kids less, just in a different style.

My generation of fathers, by and large, is extremely involved in our kids' lives. We hug them all the time, coach them in Little League, and we know their friends. And as far as knowing the names of my son's teachers—get serious—I even have all their e-mail addresses.

One of our interview guests made a statement that brought instant clarity to my understanding of this new generation of dads. As you just read, author Erica Jong said that the new role for men as involved fathers was a gift of feminism. It was a total "Aha!" moment for me. Dads are no longer viewed as unmanly or wimpy if they choose to cuddle with their kids or help them with their homework. That doesn't have to be the mother's role any longer. Fathers can now be an equal part of the child-rearing process, and that is feminism's gift to men—it was quite a gift.

For me it was a completely fresh way of understanding our generation's transformation of fatherhood. There is a reason why boomer dads are encouraged to behave differently. Ms. Jong connected the dots.

So just the other day, my twelve-year-old son and I were shopping for basketball shoes. Inside a sporting goods store, I stared at a wall that featured scores of basketball shoes in every conceivable style and color. Finally my son found a pair to his liking and handed me a shoe that was endorsed by his basketball idol. I looked at the price.

"What? One hundred and twenty-five dollars! Are you kidding? When I was your age . . ."

But navigating an entirely new family structure, like all new waters, created some casualties. Abandoned marriages and neglected children of that era cannot be denied, and presidential press secretary Tony Snow finds tragedy in that. And for those who long for a return to at least some small semblance of Ward, June, Wally, and the Beaver, Snow sees a glimmer of hope as well: "As a parent, I'll tell you, a lot of people miss the boat because there's nothing more wondrous than being a parent. And sometimes, for some folks who may want to try to tap-dance past that, they often end up waking up one day full of regret for what they missed— that there's nothing greater than the blessing of being able to be a parent and especially a married parent. And I think a lot of people may have learned that the hard way. And I wouldn't be surprised to see the institution make a comeback, because not only are the failures fairly powerful, but also the successes."

The presidential press secretary isn't "spinning" that opinion all alone. Dr. Steven Nock agrees: "There's an awful lot of backlash to the trends that began in the sixties. Not just the ideologies and beliefs and values of the sixties—the free love and challenging authority—but the demographic trends that were initiated in the sixties: the retreat from marriage, the high rates of divorce, the high rates of unmarried births, for example, on the one hand; the sense of personal entitlement and individualism on the other hand. These are legacies of the sixties that I do believe have fostered a lot of backlash. The fifties, the forties, even the early sixties, were homogeneous with respect to some things like religion and family to some extent. But certainly to people who are deeply religious today, the trends of the sixties and the seventies—the legalization of abortion, the widespread availability of sex, and unmarried births—undoubtedly seem decadent. And there is predictable backlash against that.

"Those who see the demographic trends ushered in by the baby boomers as socially problematic are now forging public policy in an attempt to reverse them: welfare reform, promoting marriage, discouraging unmarried births, and so forth. So I think that the political Right, as well as many people in the middle, look back on the sixties with admiration for some of the trends, but with alarm at most of the trends. They see especially the demography that the baby boomers ushered in as decadent and dangerous to the society. And for many, it is as simple as the denigration of marriage. But for most, it is something like marriage, the fertility issues, who has a baby, whether or not couples who are of the same sex can marry, and so forth. All these things are radical changes historically, and it's no wonder that change of that magnitude will produce confusion—it will produce resentment among some people, and it will surely produce a backlash."

But in the seventies that backlash was a millennium change away. Regardless of the stresses and strains on their personal lives, women entered the workforce by the millions—and against all odds. Shelly Lazarus thinks that this alone changed everything: "I'm sure that the biggest legacy of the baby boom generation will be the role that women assumed in this country, that they entered the workforce, and that they took an equal place beside men, everywhere."

In retrospect, Dr. D. Quinn Mills tells us that women have brought more than only their ethics, talent, and skill into the workplace: "A lot of the behavior which was more suited for barracks, actually, at the end of World War II than for a civilian workplace has disappeared. Women have, as a rule, a greater understanding and ability at interpersonal relations than many men do. And that shows up in the workplace. But it's a matter of degree; it's not really a matter in kind. I think they're very effective managers, very effective indeed. . . . Having the women working has allowed the economy to grow larger, and it has improved the quality of the workplace."

As huge an impact as boomers had by including our wives and sisters in the workplace, we brought with us other dynamic changes as well, many of which resulted from our proclivity to question authority. Old procedures, old standards, old methodologies, were all up for question—no matter how tried and true. "Because we've always done it that way" was no longer an acceptable answer.

▪ ▪

From Nine to Five to 24/7

> C. C. BAXTER: I work for an insurance company— Consolidated Life of New York. We're one of the top five companies in the country. Our home office has 31,259 employees, which is more than the entire population of, uhh . . . Natchez, Mississippi. I work on the nineteenth floor. Ordinary Policy Department, Premium Accounting Division, Section W, Desk Number 861.
>
> *From* **The Apartment**
> *Screenplay by*
> *Billy Wilder*

The boomers grew up believing that if you don't like something, you don't have to accept it," Dr. Ken Dychtwald says. "You can alter it, transform it, find a way around it. The boomers didn't like the oppressive corporate environment they found in the workplace, so they found ways to change it."

Leonard Steinhorn examines how the new economic realities of the seventies spurred the boomers to change the workplace: "In the 1970s, our economy started to decline, and people couldn't figure it out. Here we were, the wealthiest country in the world, but we had just lost a war; our economy was out of control—high interest rates, high inflation, increasing unemployment. Boomers began to look at what was happening to their parents. These were people who had given their lives to a company, and all of a sudden, they were being fired or laid off! And without a job!

"So the economy was transforming at that time, and I think the message that boomers got in those sort of economic troubles in the 1970s was that you couldn't be sure of anything economically, that maybe we were living sort of in an exceptional time, based on our victory in World War II and our complete international economic dominance at the time. And boomers also looked at the sort of encrusted hierarchies and companies like General Motors and Ford that couldn't come up with gas-efficient cars and kept putting out these ridiculous Gran Torinos every year that were gobbling up ten miles a gallon, that were so completely out of touch with the needs of a changing world. So they looked at American industry and said, 'This is hierarchical, it's stodgy, and they're not investing in the future, and they're not thinking about change.' So boomers understood increasingly that change was a part of their very nature; it was a constant in life. And boomers began to build a system which acknowledged that change."

Techno-boom

Boomers didn't invent the computer. We didn't land a man on the moon. Those credits go to the Greatest Generation. But we certainly picked up the high-tech ball and ran with it. Bill Gates et al. didn't start the fire, but they fanned the heck out of the flames, and virtually every part of our lives—social, economic, political—has been altered by it, and not only in America but throughout the world.

Our children (and their children) will roll their eyes and sigh heavily if they have to hear one more time about the days before the remote control, when Grandma and Grandpa had to stand up and walk across the room just to change channels from *Lawrence Welk* to *Perry Como*. They can't imagine the pre–Ted Turner days

Bill Gates didn't invent the computer, but he changed it, and, in so doing, he changed everything.

when we had only three or four TV channels to choose from. They seem totally unimpressed with the accomplishments of Neil Armstrong and would quickly get bored with Asteroids. They can surf the Net at a mile a minute but have never seen a typewriter. They have not made the journey from Pong to BlackBerry along with us, but even they are impressed when someone comes out with a cell phone that can take pictures and store a music library bigger than a bookcase full of our beloved LPs.

The digital age, most would agree, has brought positive changes to the world but may have enlarged the preexisting

> HAL: Let me put it this way, Mr. Amor. The 9000 series is the most reliable computer ever made. No 9000 computer has ever made a mistake or distorted information. We are all, by any practical definition of the words, foolproof and incapable of error.
>
> ***From* 2001: A Space Odyssey**
> ***Screenplay by Stanley Kubrick***
> ***and Arthur C. Clarke***

generation gap by marginalizing the value of experience. Grandpa's vast knowledge of how things used to get done is no longer of any value. Instead of teaching the younger generation how to use a slide rule, he has to ask his grandkids how to send an e-mail.

All things are relative to perception, and the generation that *did* have to stand up to change TV channels is more amazed with every passing day. Because we are boomers and change doesn't frighten us as it did our parents, we have welcomed the digital age, latched onto it, and pushed it forward.

"We now have the capacity to make our garage door open with a click of a button, and we have technology that can monitor our heart and stimulate it if it fails," Dr. Dychtwald says. "I can send an e-mail to a billion people all around the world, and it appears on their computer screens in a second, or I can make a cell phone call to China. As a result, so many parts of our lives are different. We have instantaneous information at our fingertips, whether it's for the purpose of sending a rocket ship to space or finding a criminal. It's genuinely remarkable.

"As the boomers entered the workforce in the seventies, this technological revolution was just beginning to replace manufacturing as the center of our economy. Boomers seized on this new technology to create the digital revolution."

High schools in the midsixties had typing classes. They were reserved almost exclusively for girls. Any boy who took typing might as well have signed up for home economics too and counted on getting beaten up in gym. But typewriters became "keyboards," and keyboards accessed information, and information is power. These days, if you don't type, well, "Welcome to McDonald's." High-tech (and hence "typing") was suddenly a very macho skill.

Leonard Steinhorn asserts that "technology requires independent thinking, creative thinking, a certain amount of individuality among the workers to be able to come up to the ideas. So you see all those stories about Apple Computer being built in a garage, and so the high-tech economy emerged, and new types of economic activity were going on. So boomers were really at the cutting edge and the leading edge of that.

"Would another generation have done just the same if the economic shifts were going on? Maybe, maybe not. We have no idea. We can't say. But boomers seized that and reshaped the economy, and we actually have seen a remarkable economic recovery in these last twenty-five years, from the decline that was hitting in the seventies to the reemergence of a new postindustrial economy that boomers have seized onto, pursued, led, organized, initiated, and created."

By the turn of the millennium and all the Y2K fuss (remember the Y2K fuss?), we had begun to take the technological revolution for granted. Harvard economist Dr. D. Quinn Mills keeps it in its proper perspective: "The electronic innovations that have been brought about mainly by baby boomers in the United States are probably the most important single set of mechanical and electronic—of scientific—innovations that we've ever seen in the world. They have only begun really to change the world. I think the generations that follow us will see much more impact than we have, although the impact that we and the baby boomers have seen is absolutely enormous."

Now we had a new tool that enabled us to question authority and challenge tradition even faster. We began to look at how things were being done and figured out ways to use computer technology to do them faster and better, and we built new businesses to accommodate those changes. Those of us who did those things are called "entrepreneurs."

Hey! I've Got an Idea!

Dr. Mills observes yet another very important characteristic that boomers seem to share: "Baby boomers have been broadly quite entrepreneurial. It's not the vast majority of the group, but it's a very large portion of them, much more than in any other country. America is almost unique in this, by the way—in all this entrepreneurship and building companies and venture capital and almost all of that. While it's not a creation of the baby boomers, it's something that they have built to much greater size and carried forward dramatically. I think the notion that 'it can be done' comes out of two things. One, it is a great deal of self-confidence. Well-educated people, healthy people, many of whom had good family upbringing, have a lot of self-confidence. They think they can do things. And the second thing is the sense that even if you fail at it once, it doesn't end your life. You don't get just one shot at life. If something doesn't go well, you can go do something else. And so it minimizes the risk and maximizes the opportunity."

But why boomers? How in the world did hippies evolve into entrepreneurs?

Emotional Intelligence author Dr. Daniel Goleman can opine on that: "Some boomers are very nontraditional and have been all their lives, and some are very traditional. Those boomers for whom the distrust of authority was really the most salient, which really affected them in their early years, brought a very healthy attitude that fostered huge creativity and innovation.

"There's been a direct line drawn sociologically and historically between Haight-Ashbury and Silicon Valley. They are only thirty miles apart, but in spirit, they're very much the same, because they were both groups that didn't respect the old rules and that were creating new ways, new means, and new methods, and I think the spirit of creativity and innovation and the entrepreneurial strengths of this generation relate to the fact that authority didn't have to be listened to. You could think for yourself."

Jeff Taylor had the idea of moving standard and well-established newspaper "help wanted" ads into the digital age and started a Web site. Not only was his idea nontraditional, he also gave it an amazingly nontraditional name—Monster.com: "If you look at classic job searching, it was done in the newspaper. It has really been the same for 150 years, no innovation whatsoever. So when I came along with the idea of putting the buyer and seller, or, in our case, the job seeker and the employer, together electronically, I used the old job posting and the old résumé. I just made the distribution mechanism more exciting. The result was Monster.com and we've changed the world. We're now in twenty-seven countries.

> My definition of an "entrepreneur" is when everybody around you thinks you are crazy, but you still think you have a good idea and you act on it.
>
> *Jeff Taylor*

"If you look at people's expectations, I think that there was a moment where you expected your company to take care of you. There was this kind of comfort zone. It didn't mean you didn't work hard, but you didn't have to think about outside influences that were going to affect your career. You just did your job.

"I think much more today, your job *is* your skills, and you take your skills from place to place. If you're not improving your skills, you're itchy and yearning to learn and go somewhere else. If your company's not paying attention and training you, then you're in a situation where you have a very bad mismatch, which is probably going to mean you're going to move on."

The television ads for Monster.com are compelling and unique. They feature children giving somewhat less than standard answers to the age-old question, What do you want to do when you grow up?

153

"When I grow up, I want to claw my way up into middle management," one child says. Others chime in with, "When I grow up, I want to file all day." "I want to be underappreciated." "I want to be paid less for doing the same job."

Taylor knows the true message of those powerful ads: "The reality is, having kids talk about what their future outcomes might be ended up being incredibly powerful, and the message from Monster was 'If you're not happy, do something about it.'"

The kids in those commercials are a metaphorical flashback to their boomer parents thirty years ago. We weren't happy in the old corporate environment, and we did something about it. We weren't happy with nine to five, Monday through Friday. We weren't happy with missing the kid's kindergarten graduation. We weren't happy with living in the suburbs and driving to work in the city. So we used the technology to open the door for such things as long-distance telecommuting, and we created the "virtual" workplace.

Casual Friday? Lose the Bathrobe

Dress codes and baby boomers? Grab your *Funk and Wagnalls* and look up *oxymoron*.

"Boomers wanted a more relaxed workplace," Dr. Mills says, "with less command and control, with less military-type autocracy, and I think we've largely gotten that."

Glass-ceiling crasher Shelly Lazarus has witnessed the evolution of and revolution within the workplace: "In the1950s people were all taught they had to conform to what the organization needed. . . . I think the organization is now going to have to conform to the individual. So at Ogilvy, we treat each individual as this precious resource that we have, and we encourage people to speak up, and we say, 'What do you need in your life that will make working at Ogilvy a productive part of it, will make you want to come to work for us every morning and have you come with enthusiasm?' So it's sort of ultimate flexibility. . . . We have an approach and an attitude that says we can be as flexible as each person needs us to be to continue to be productively employed here.

"We had a creative person working for us in the New York office who lived on his ranch in Penelope, Texas. And he became more and more valuable to us, and it was clear how talented he was. And so we wanted to employ him full-time. . . . So we said, 'Okay, David, come on board as a full-time employee,' and he said, 'Sure, as long as I can continue to live in Penelope, Texas.'

"Now most companies would say, 'Well, that's absurd. I mean how can you live in Penelope, Texas, and come to work every morning in New York?' And when he actually started to tell me that there were twenty-six flights each day between Dallas and New York, both ways, and that it would be a snap for him to come to New York when he had to, I mean now he gave me the choice. Was I going to have David on his terms, or was I not going to have David? Given that choice, it's a no-brainer. You know, you take David on his terms."

"David" is not nearly alone in the world of telecommuting. Home PCs, the Internet, cell phones, e-mail, text messaging, and BlackBerries have made the four-walled office all but a rusting relic of the ancient past. The book you are reading was written in Marietta, Georgia, edited in Sperryville, Virginia, and published in New York, New York—and nobody cared what the author was wearing.

It's not only about the virtual work*place*. It's about virtual work *time* as well. Boomers are experiencing a shift in the time-space continuum. Everything in our lives continues to move faster and faster. What used to be nine to five, Monday through Friday, is now 24/7, 365. When our fathers worked in factories, they had to clock in at eight in the morning, otherwise the entire assembly line might shut down. Time was precise and strict and that's all there was to it. This fixation with time dominoed into every aspect of our lives. Up at 6:00. Breakfast at 6:30. Work by 8:00. Home by 6:00. Dinner by 7:00, and, of course, *Leave It to Beaver* at 8:00. These days, our work hours are longer but less rigid. Our meals are taken on the run, and, of course, TiVo allows us to watch whatever we want, whenever we want.

Not only are we no longer slaves to our watches, we have also emancipated ourselves from the dress codes that encumbered our fathers. From tie-dyed T-shirts and peace-symbol necklaces to gray flannel suits and red-striped ties is a leap that Carl Lewis couldn't accomplish, and neither could the boomers. It has taken decades, but "business attire" has changed. Pantsuits for women and golf shirts for men are perfectly acceptable. Some corporations pay health club memberships for their employees. Family Leave is the law, and there is something that Archie Bunker would never understand in a gazillion-million years—paternity leave.

There is something else that would have left Archie scratching his head. It's called work-life balance, and at times, to guilt-stricken parents, it often feels like trying to balance a brick on a feather.

Ms. Lazarus understands that boomers are seeking a balance between their work and home lives: "Boomers come in to the working parts of their lives with a view that work is only one part of life. We worked really hard, and then we looked for balance. I think they're coming into work demanding balance from the start. Maybe it's because they watched their parents being so involved with the professional parts of their lives. But I think from the start, boomers demand a wonderful balanced life. And so I just think it's a different perspective. I think it's pretty healthy.

"But unless you love passionately what you do professionally, you'll almost never find balance. I always believed, and I now know, that you will adore and love and be consumed by your children. You know this will be the remarkable love of your life. So to balance that, you've got to find a calling, a career, a line of work that is equally compelling—that you love as much—because if you don't, you're going to resent every single moment that you spend away from the thing that you really do love. And I think if you look at most women who've been successful, who've been able to hold down big jobs, it's because they love them."

While Cathleen Black has made her way to the top in the magazine publishing industry, she understands that the desire for work-life balance can cripple ambition in some: "Some talented people may say, 'I don't want that top job because I'm earning a significant amount of money here, and perhaps my mate, my partner, my husband, is also earning here; this is a pretty nice lifestyle.' I'm not saying that they're not as ambitious, but perhaps they're redefining how they want to live their lives."

Dr. Mills agrees that achieving the elusive work-life balance is among the greatest challenges faced by virtually all boomers: "Baby boomers, as a broad group, I think give family life and work life a rough equality in the way they approach life generally. I think many of them would say that their family is the most important priority that they have, and *then* work. It's been difficult. I think that one of the great struggles that the baby boomer generation has is to find an appropriate balance in life between the family and the workplace. While there are exceptions, employers by and large have not made it easier—they've made it very difficult. And, in fact, Americans work more today than they did ten or twenty years ago, and baby boomers did not want that to happen. That's been because of international competitive pressures. And the baby boomers running big companies today, somewhat surprisingly to me, don't really make that balance easier. They don't really make it easier for people to spend time with their family. So I think that's been a continual struggle that is not resolved. I think the baby boom generation in the next decade or two will pass out of the workplace without ever really having resolved that."

Dr. Mills may have just made one of the understatements of the generation. If we are, in fact, seeking a balance between work and family, in this area at least we may be abysmal failures.

Dr. Dychtwald contends that Americans these days are simply working too hard: "Americans don't get anywhere near as much time off as most Europeans. Italy and Germany pretty much shut down during August. In France, there's a mandated thirty-five-hour workweek, and workers spend 30 percent less time at the office than do Americans: Fifty-eight percent of [American] managers plan to stay in touch with their workplaces while on vacation, and only 31 percent take more than a week off at a time. 157

On average, Americans take off only ten days a year with pay versus thirty in Germany and Spain. Italians average an astounding forty-two vacation days a year."

So much for work-life balance.

Are we sacrificing family and leisure time because we love our jobs? Are we working ten or twelve hours a day to provide the very best for our children? Or are we doing it because we are scared to death of being laid off, outsourced, globalized, or any of those things our fathers would have called "fired"?

Of course there's another option. Maybe we're doing it simply because we are on an obsessive quest to obtain the most extravagant possible trappings of success. Those who believe that we are driven to accumulate BMWs, country club memberships, and McMansions have, rightly or wrongly, branded us with an unflattering moniker that seems to have stuck. We have evolved from "boomer babies" to "flower children" to something else altogether.

chapter 8

The Me Generation

I n 1971, Janis Joplin, the diva of our generation, gave us what she described as "a song of great social and political import," in which she prayed to God to buy her a color TV, a night on the town, and, of course, a Mercedes-Benz. Apparently our materialism was already beginning to show, and what was soon to be known as the me generation now had its very own anthem.

First, the origin of the phrase, "the me generation." Apparently it has its genesis in a 1976 collection of essays by Tom Wolfe titled *Mauve Gloves and Madmen, Clutter and Vine.* The culprit essay is "The Me Decade and the Third Great Awakening." In it Wolfe observes that truck drivers in the seventies made enough money actually to have some leisure time and enjoy some of life's luxuries, like "wall-to-wall carpet you could lose a shoe in." Even this early in the seventies, Wolfe had already observed the increasing divorce rate and made note of the historical fact that "the right to shuck overripe wives and take on fresh ones was once seen as the prerogative of kings only, and even then it was scandalous." He wrote about the EST (electroconvulsive shock therapy) treatments

In Oliver Stone's Wall Street, *Gordon Gekko, portrayed by Michael Douglas, epitomized the me generation and coined a slogan for self-absorbed boomers when he said, "Greed, for lack of a better word, is good."*

and primal scream treatments and luxury bath treatments that had become popular in those days, and observed that "the word *proletarian* can no longer be used in this country with a straight face."* And so the "me decade" was born.

How the me decade evolved into the me generation appears to be anybody's guess, but the difference between the two applies only to duration. The perception persists that we boomers are here on this earth primarily to serve and glorify ourselves and to acquire as much stuff as we possibly can. Even bumper stickers announce to anyone trailing behind us (in a smaller, older, and less prestigious car) that "he who dies with the most toys wins."

Oliver Stone manufactured a caricature of the me generation

---

*Tom Wolfe, Mauve Gloves and Madmen, Clutter and Vine *(New York: Farrar, Straus and Giroux, 1976).*

in his movie *Wall Street* in the form of one Gordon Gekko, a corporate raider who has set out to amass an obscenely gigantic personal fortune—everybody else be damned. "I thought when I made *Wall Street* in the 1980s that Gordon Gekko was the bad guy," Stone remembers, "but I was shocked to see—they *loved* him. They were worshiping money. We lost something. Something happened between 1978 and the Reagan revolution. Something happened."

> Gordon Gekko: The point is, ladies and gentlemen, that greed, for lack of a better word, is good.
> *From* **Wall Street**
> **Screenplay by Stanley Weiser**
> **and Oliver Stone**

Our historian, Dr. Zeitz, asserts that "the boomers were the first generation that was brought up fully on this kind of ethos of consumer prosperity. They were brought up in an era when everything is possible and so much of citizenship in the 1940s and fifties and early sixties was bound up with the ability to consume. In 1959, when Richard Nixon met Khrushchev in Moscow and had a famous showdown with him at a GE Kitchen Exposition, the so-called kitchen debate, much of what the two argued about was which country manufactured the best kitchen gadgets, and this said a lot about the way the Americans understood democracy in the 1950s. They understood it as entailing certain rights to comfort.

"It was the freedom from want that Franklin Roosevelt talked about in 1941, and the boomers have never forgotten that freedom from want, and they've driven it to new extremes, and they've insisted that the kind of material prosperity they grew up with in the 1950s is something they can continue to enjoy even in the face of diminishing circumstances. And so it's this generation that has created such a surge in household debt and national debt. This has had obviously important repercussions, and it will continue to have important repercussions for what their children inherit and what their grandchildren inherit, the kind of country they live in."

161

Dr. Mills admits to being disappointed in the boomers' seemingly perpetual quest for "stuff": "Baby boomers got a lot more materialistic than I had thought they would. You can't look at an American city and its suburbs without seeing these very large houses that are now being built and purchased by the baby boomers. We were conflicted in our own mind. We compared and contrasted, if you will, idealism with materialism. But a person can be idealistic *and* materialistic; a person can be highly idealistic and like the comforts of life and be very active in trying to obtain those comforts. That doesn't make a person necessarily less idealistic in a whole variety of ways, and boomers continue to have the basic kind of idealism—the optimistic approach to life."

Does this incredibly uncomfortable shoe of greed fit? Must we wear it? Will we go to our collective graves being remembered only as the generation that had more stuff than any generation before us? Is there really nothing more to us than that? Are we really just a bunch of self-centered, narcissistic, money-grubbing, me, me, me brats who never grew up? Are we, really?

Dr. Dychtwald argues the point: "So were the boomers very self-centered when they were teenagers and then in their twenties? Yes, because that's the stage of life we were in. But if you look at all the studies of this generation now, they're ten times more inclined to put their children and families first, ahead of their own priorities. Our generation is not really looking to be Gordon Gekko. They're trying to get through the day and enjoy time with the people they love and go fishing once or twice before the year's out. They're decent and hardworking. They've become the backbone of the country.

"This is the generation that's paying more taxes than any generation in history. It's got the highest volunteer rate of any adult segment of the population. A third of boomers—twenty-five million men and women—now volunteer. We make the greatest amount of charitable contributions of any age group. Everybody's trying to do what they can do, and, frankly, are not terribly driven by being rich, famous, or powerful. Yet, for some reason, they got branded the me generation, and it's stuck. I look at every study of this generation, and nothing ever comes out to match that."

Emotional Intelligence author Daniel Goleman adds that even if the me generation accusation may have been accurate at one time, it is a look back at what we were. A closer look at what we *are* may absolve us: "To think of the boomers as the me generation is to miss the boat, because things have shifted a lot since this self-focus. Boomers have had kids, are parents, are grandparents now, and boomers are, in my experience, largely looking for ways to give back and to help and to be there for others rather than for themselves."

Reverend Carole O'Connell is the senior minister emerita (that's a fancy term for a highly respected retired woman) of the largest Unity Church in the Southeast. Unity is a part of the "New Thought" movement, which offers a nondenominational philosophy that encourages meditation and self-awareness. She is the author of a book with a very "me-estic" title, *The Power of Choice: Ten Steps to a Joyous Life,* and she doesn't think that "me-ism" and materialism are necessarily the same thing: "You can't make a difference or be a force for change in your family, or your community, or for the world at large—those things that exist outside of you—until you have first established within yourself a 'sense of self.' We can't accept others until we are able to accept ourselves just as we are. In order to accept ourselves, we must become self-reflective and introspective, and if that is 'me-ism' then so be it. If that is me-ism, then me-ism is good.

"Self-judgment leads to the projection of judgment onto others. Self-acceptance leads to acceptance of others. And the one thing that is the hardest to accept is that *all* judgment is *self-*judgment. Once we are able to accept ourselves, it becomes much easier to accept others—to accept other attitudes, other races, other lifestyles, and, maybe most importantly, other religions. Only when we learn to look at ourselves without judgment can we look at others without judgment. If everyone accepted this, there would be no more religious wars because there would be no judgment of others.

"So, if the boomers are taking time out for themselves, to look within themselves, what they will ultimately discover is that we are all one—and that can't possibly be a bad thing."

The me generation accusation is really just one of many assaults against us. Because we are so numerous, and because we have demanded the spotlight for so many decades, and because we are responsible for so many changes in the world, we have become a cultural lightning rod that beckons unhappy demigods to hurl bolts of discontent in our direction. Anybody who wants to rant about anything can find a boomer to serve as an apt example of whatever it is that frightens him or threatens him or angers him the most at the moment.

Leonard Steinhorn contends that those who are most critical of the boomers are the social conservatives "who are angry that their authority is no longer the only authority in society. They have had a hard time accepting the pluralism that is sort of endemic in baby boom culture. So what happens is that some of the greatest accusations you get against boomers have been thrown by a number of the sort of conservatives, social conservatives, who really love to dwell on all of the boomers buying Savannah dill bread or drinking lattes. It's as if drinking a latte undermines everything else you stand for.

"Their goal, in effect, is to so trivialize boomers, to say this is such a frivolous generation, such a silly generation. It's a generation that's so narcissistic that all of these social changes are also silly and frivolous and narcissistic, and let's go back to the old ways in the 1950s where we knew where we really stood in this society. And I think what's happened is that boomers have become a sort of a proxy in the culture wars. And when you see baby boomers being lambasted and pilloried, especially in the conservative press these days, what you see is it as a substitute for anger that the world has passed many of these folks by."

Marc Freedman is founder and president of Civic Ventures and founder of the Experience Corps. He is the author of *Prime Time: How Baby Boomers Will Revolutionize Retirement and Transform America.* Naturally, he has a positive view of boomers and thinks referring to us as the me generation is a bit of a bad rap: "I think that the me generation label misrepresents what the boomers were all about in the middle years. I think they were focused on raising their kids, on getting by. They were working longer hours than any previous generation had; 162 more hours a year between 1972 and the late nineties. So people were shortening thirteen months of work into twelve. And that's an enormous burden. So what appeared on the outside as self-centered behavior is really, in many cases, survival."

Survival? Perhaps in some cases. Perhaps in many cases. But seldom survival in a literal sense. Not survival in a Rwandan sense. "Need" is a subjective thing after all. Using a *Funk and Wagnalls* definition of the word may lead us to believe that food, water, and shelter are the only things that legitimately fall within that category. It's that survival thing again. But we "need" a car. We "need" a cell phone. We "need" a king-sized bed with a top-of-the-line, super-firm Beautyrest mattress. And we're going to fulfill those "needs" even if we have to go into debt to do it.

In our time boomers have added many words to the American lexicon. What began in the sixties with *groovy* and *far out* morphed in the eighties into *conspicuous consumption* and *charge it.*

Dr. Dychtwald suggests that attitudes about money are yet another gap that exists between us and our parents: "Perhaps there is no greater contrast between our generation and our parents' than our attitudes toward money. Our moms and dads had been traumatized by the Depression in their youth and were basically told that you shouldn't spend what you don't have, and you should 'save it for a rainy day.' That was a phrase that had a lot of weight in their lives. You should be able to live within your means.

"We grew up, not in the shadow of the Depression, but in the enthusiasm of the time of middle-class prosperity. We grew up believing that there was *not going to be* a rainy day.

"In 1960, Americans carried less than one credit card per person and collectively owed $56 million in credit card debt. Today the average baby boomer carries between five and ten credit cards, and the outstanding credit card debt in America totals one and a half *trillion* dollars. So it's multiplied ten thousand fold."

Whoa! "Charge it!"

Our children, Generation X, may get some of the credit for the United States becoming a "debtor nation," because not only did we want to "have it all," we wanted our children to have it all as well, and they were not going to be content with our old canvas-topped Chuck Taylors that cost about twelve bucks a pair. Oh, no. They had to have the hundred-dollar Nikes.

"Charge it."

Of course our parents had to "keep up with the Joneses" in the sixties, and the eighties were not much different. The only difference was that "the Joneses" of the eighties had more to keep up with. "Charge it."

And so the United States became not only a debtor nation, but a nation *of* debtors as well. According to Dr. Zeitz, "In 1946, when the boom began, average debt was about 22 percent of household income. Today it's about 120 percent of household income, and the boomer generation has presided over that tremendous surge."

The very word *debt* carries with it some seriously negative connotations. The *NBC Nightly News* and *The Oprah Winfrey Show* pound us with stories about people who are "hopelessly in debt." Not an evening goes by without a commercial sponsored by a charitable (or not) organization promising to help us "get out of debt" and urging us to destroy our credit cards. According to some economists and analysts, however, the larger picture is not so gloomy.

Debt—For Lack of a Better Word—Is Good

According to Dr. Mills, "[Debt] improved the economy considerably. One of the things that baby boomers do because they are better educated is they carry a lot of debt. They know a number of things about that; they're able to manage it in a way that their parents were not. Their parents were frightened by the Great Depression; baby boomers are not. And so they've spent a lot. They've built the economy in that way. So that, I think, is very important."

Dr. Jeremy Siegel is currently the Russell E. Palmer Professor of Finance at the Wharton School of the University of Pennsylvania, and he too believes that while we have run up some debt, for the most part we have done so responsibly: "One thing we've always been ahead in is how to get credit if people want to buy. I mean, we were the first country to really have the thirty-year mortgages. We're the first country to really have consumer credit that we find today. I think, in a way, it's an engine that fueled the economy.

"In fact, people are taking money out of their houses with home-equity loans; we have a fancy name for it. It's called 'mortgage-equity withdrawals.'"

While he describes the total dollars involved in these loans as "absolutely astounding," he doesn't believe that it is entirely a bad thing: "People say we're using our homes as ATM machines. The truth of that matter is that few people are abusing that. Overall, there's been a build up of equity in the home. Overall, it has been responsible."

Dr. Lester Thurow is a Rhodes Scholar, a Harvard PhD, and former dean of the Sloan School of Management at the Massachusetts Institute of Technology, and he begs to differ: "The stupidest thing we ever did as a society was let a lot of people take home-equity loans. My parents retired; their only asset was their house. They sold it, and they lived on the proceeds for the rest of their lives. Most of the baby boom generation will die *not* owning their house, because they equity out everything as it comes. So, there's no house to save them in their old age."

Debt is so widespread and accepted these days that there is little social stigma attached to it. According to Dr. Dychtwald, "You're not ostracized if you're in debt. Our presidents do it, our companies do it, our parents do it, we do it, everybody does it. I don't know anybody who didn't get invited to a party because they had a couple of credit cards maxed out."

Okay, so we've got some disagreement between the respected scholars on our panel. We've got some household debt; we don't pay off the full balance on our credit cards every month; and we refinance our mortgages and take out home-equity loans from time to time, and we may or may not be doing it "responsibly."

So, how much *do* we have in savings, dear?

No Gold Watch for *You!*

"There have been important transformations in the workforce that the boomers haven't necessarily driven, but they've had to contend with and deal with and adjust to," says Dr. Joshua Zeitz. "For instance, in the late 1940s, when the boomers' parents came of age, most large American corporations offered their workers generous packages of employment incentives, including private health insurance, vacations with pay, pension plans with guaranteed benefits, and rights involving seniority. Their parents' generation are the first Americans to enjoy generous new health care plans that largely came out of the so-called Treaty of Detroit that the United Auto Workers forged with General Motors in the late 1940s.

"These health care plans became the industry standard not only in the automotive industry, but in most large American corporations. Large companies said that they would assume the responsibility for health insurance if they could keep the government out of it. And this was in large part a ploy to keep Harry Truman's administration from delivering on its promise to provide national health care. The boomers to some degree enjoyed that arrangement at least as far as health care was concerned throughout the 1980s and early 1990s, but it's increasingly not so. And these kinds of benefits have been slowly eroded in the 1980s and 1990s. just as the boomers were really reaching the peak of their influence on the economy. And the reason that these benefits were eroded has largely to do with globalization and the demands that it's placed on American corporations.

"That having been said, baby boomers have had to adjust to a world in which employment is much less stable and carries far fewer benefits than what their parents experienced in the 1940s and fifties, and that's placed tremendous strains on their own resources.

And in all fairness to the boomers, they've had to deal with problems that their parents simply couldn't have anticipated."

According to Dr. Dychtwald, perhaps the most significant of those new-economy problems is the incredibly stressful insecurity in the job market: "It used to be that the only time companies would fire people was if they were struggling to survive. Now companies fire people when they're doing great, just because they want to improve their profit margin by 2 percent. So they'll lay off five thousand people. There's no loyalty at all." Exit, pensions and corporate-paid health insurance; enter, 401(k)s and HMOs. For better or for worse, you're on your own, boomers.

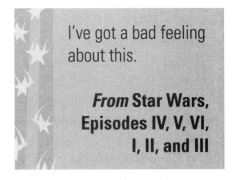

I've got a bad feeling about this.

From Star Wars, Episodes IV, V, VI, I, II, and III

Finance guru Dr. Jeremy Siegel thinks we brought a lot of this on ourselves: "I think that a lot of the initial impetus actually came from the boomers themselves to change the pension benefits. It used to be that the company, or the university in my case, would provide you with a monthly stipend once you retired. What happened was, when the stock market was doing so very, very well, a number of advisers were coming to people and saying, 'You know what? If instead of giving it to the company to provide that, if you start investing on your own, we can do better for you.' And so, a lot of people said, 'Gee, I want to control my own money, you know, so that if I leave, I still have the money.' And so I personally think it was a movement by the baby boomers to get control of their money and, hopefully, better returns.

"I think what made that change was the fading memories of that 1929 stock crash. I know when I was growing up and I was a young boy interested in the market in the fifties, I knew a lot of people who lost everything in the crash of '29. It was so fresh in their memory. As time went on and everyone said, 'Hey, we've got protections in our economy, greater stability, the government steps in here or there. We're not going to have a repeat of the thirties, so it's safer for me to move into stocks. And when I see the returns on stocks, and the long-run accumulation possibilities, why not own a share of America?'

"Maybe only 10 or 15 percent of the population in 1929 owned stock. Today, over half the households own stock, and that's a huge difference."

To many, 401(k)s looked like what gamblers call "free money," and in the boom years of the nineties it was. The problem is, of course (gamblers take heed), that there's no such thing as "free money." Pensions were, in fact, closer to that elusive dream than are 401(k)s.

To make the point, Dr. Siegel doesn't have to look back very far in time: "From March 2000 through October of 2002, I'm talking about 2.5 years, we had a 50 percent decline in stocks—and tech stocks were down 70, 80, 90 percent and more."

As though he has to remind us.

But the end of pension-driven, long-term employment suited most of us just fine. For independent-minded, free-spirited, self-confident, antiauthoritarian boomers, the opportunity to reinvent ourselves from time to time was a good thing.

Tony Snow theorizes that baby boomers have "a sense of excitement about life that distinguishes us a little bit from other generations, because we have behind us medical advances the previous generations didn't have, the kind of affluence they didn't have, the career prospects they didn't have. I don't know about you, but I've been through about six different careers, and I'll go through one or two more before I'm done. And so you've got a certain sense of experimentation and variety in our lives that nobody else has had before."

The Bureau of Labor Statistics reported in 2006 that the trailing boomers born between 1957 and 1964 had held an average of 10.5 jobs between the ages of eighteen and forty.* That's a far cry from a thirty-year career at the Ford Motor Company. Boomers are simply not going to stay still for that long. We've got to move on to something new. We've got to keep the learning curve pointed ever upward. And while it may well be that we simply get bored quickly,

*www.bls.gov/news.release/pdf/nlsoy.pdf.

economist Lester Thurow says it's all about the money: "Boomers are doing exactly what the baseball stars are doing—moving to the teams who pay the higher prices." So we tell 10.5 bosses to "take this job and shove it" before we even hit the big four-oh.

But there's still that "lifetime security and a gold watch" thing that, on occasion, seems pretty darned enticing, especially to those of us who lost our derrieres in the dot-com bust or were loyal employees of Enron. Like everything else, 401(k) plans can have an upside, and, according to Dr. Dychtwald, a serious potential downside to our financial futures as well, if we fail to manage our accounts properly: "In the last decade or two, so many of the benefit programs have shifted from being corporate commitments to 'You're on your own.' It's the dark side of self-reliance. Self-reliance is 'Instead of my employer looking out for my pension, I'll need to take care of it myself.' But there's a serious problem. Many boomers are not maxing out their 401(k)s. Many are not saving. And now there is such a thing as 401(k) 'leakage.' If you have a 401(k) plan with an employer, and you change jobs, you get to look at how much you have, and you can either roll it over, or you can cut into it. [Cutting into it is] called leakage, and there's a great deal of leakage right now.

"So, you say, 'Well, I've got twenty-two thousand saved up—I can use a trip to Club Med. Or maybe I'll buy a new car.' Far too many boomers don't have a responsible mentality regarding long-term savings and planning, and that's going to knock a lot of us out. So our employers are not going to be there for us. It's also possible that government entitlements may grow more shaky. We don't have a sufficient savings mentality. We don't have enough fear about poverty. And a lot of us are going to fall into quicksand."

If that forecast isn't gloomy enough for you, Dr. Fernando Torres-Gil, one of the nation's foremost experts on public policy and aging, has even worse news: "If you look at the average amount of money in 401(k) plans for a fifty-five-year-old, that amount of money is maybe no more than $60,000. Now to earn at least $25,000 a year guaranteed income, you need at least $300,000 to $350,000 in your 401(k) plan, assuming you don't have a defined benefit plan through your employer. And so we're finding that with the demise of defined benefit plans, the demise of retiree health care coverage, the fiscal problems that Medicare or Medicaid are facing, and the potential fiscal gap in Social Security—yes, there could be potentially a large proportion of baby boomers in their old age who need help. Where they get it, how they demand it, will be the big question mark in the politics of aging as baby boomers grow old."

So, How Far Have We Come?

If Rip Van Winkle had dozed off at his desk (Desk Number 861) in 1970 and awakened in 2005—oh, my! When he began his nap, the last movie he would have seen may have been either *M*A*S*H* or *Patton*. He may or may not have been ticked at Yoko Ono for breaking up the Beatles. He might have read in his morning paper that a new Gallup Poll listed the most admired American men as President Richard Nixon, evangelist Billy Graham, and Vice President Spiro T. Agnew, in that order. But most significant, just prior to nodding off, he would have been in a building full of white men wearing gray suits and red ties. He would have been under the autocratic control of, well, other white men wearing suits and ties. His company, in all likelihood, would have been involved in manufacturing something—widgets perhaps. He would have had a telephone, but it would have been wired from his desk to the wall. He might have summoned his secretary from time to time to "take a letter" in shorthand that she then would have passed along to the "girls" in the secretarial pool, who, if they were lucky, had a self-correcting IBM Selectric typewriter (the kind with the interchangeable little balls inside that allowed her to select between two different font styles) and a well-worn sheet of carbon paper for copies. Of course, the "girls" in the pool did all the typing because the white men in the office didn't know how. There might have been a countdown calendar on his desk showing how many days he had left before the pension kicked in. His wife, the "little lady," "the old ball and chain," would have been waiting for him in a clean home with a hot dinner.

Dr. Condoleezza Rice was not the first female Secretary of State (Madeleine Albright was), nor was she the first African American with the title (that was Colin Powell). She was, however, the first African-American female to hold the office, and, as such, she represents simultaneous victory for both the civil rights movement and the feminist movement of the 1960s.

Imagine his surprise when he awoke in 2005.

The Oscars that year went to *Crash* for best picture, *Brokeback Mountain* for best-adapted screenplay, and for best original song? "It's Hard Out Here for a Pimp."

At the office, the white men were still there, but the suits and ties were gone. They had become sissified somehow, because not only did they know how to *type*, but typing was virtually the only thing they did. The first woman he told to "take a letter" would have either laughed at him, slapped him across the face, or filed a sexual discrimination lawsuit against him. She even might have been his boss!

He would have looked around him to see a building full of women. Women wearing pants! Literally and figuratively. And, oh my God—horrors, horrors, *horrors!* Many of the women would have been *black!* His fellow employees were no longer chained to their phones—in fact, they were *wearing* them. Oh, and by the way, his company no longer makes widgets. In fact, it no longer makes anything!

173

"We have half the number of factory workers as we had twenty-five years ago. That trend's going to continue," Dr. Jeremy Siegel says. "There's absolutely no way that we are going to maintain our manufacturing base when we've got two to three billion people elsewhere in the world, and you could build factories anywhere now, that are willing to work at 10 percent of the price that American labor is willing to."

Oh, and another thing, Mr. Van Winkle, about that pension . . .

During his nap, boomers had staged a victorious assault on virtually every institution and tradition our friend Rip had ever known.

Leonard Steinhorn says that there is little in this world more "American" than assaults on institutions and traditions: "America was born challenging tradition and promoting individual freedom, and boomers have rescued it from the jaws of lockstep conformity and willful authority. In the choices we have and the way we lead our lives, the baby boom era has made it acceptable to do our own thing. And we're a more free, equal, expressive, and democratic country because of it."*

It is now a good time for us to step back and take a look at all that we boomers have accomplished, with our proclivities to question authority, to challenge the status quo, and to think for ourselves, and to consider how we might continue to use these talents and tendencies to make the world in which we live an even better place for generations to come. With our stable of extraordinary scholars and accomplished professionals, we have a deep well to dip into for an abundance of incredible insight on these weighty matters. We have elected, instead, to hand the microphone to a man who has to his credit only very strong opinions. He is precisely what we need at this point in our journey. He is a stand-up comic!

Ladies and gentlemen, *mesdames et messieurs, Damen und Herren,* Mr. Lewis Black!

---

*Leonard Steinhorn, The Greater Generation *(New York: St. Martin's, 2006), 139–40.*

My Generation
Lewis Black

I love my generation, but let's face it—we certainly didn't live up to our potential. Whatever collective vision we had, the future certainly went right in the Dumpster. The sixties may have informed us, but it didn't transform us. The joyous experience of "we" turned right into a generation of "me," and there's been no looking back. The sixties were over before they even started.

For God's sake, we haven't even been able to legalize marijuana, even though many of our generation are still puffing away on it. Not even for medical purposes! Are you kidding me? And that was on the top of the "to do" list.

If our generation has done anything while it's been in charge, it is just to take things from bad to worse. We've provided very little leadership of any kind. Under our guidance, the United States has become less a land of opportunity and more a country of "he who dies with the most things wins."

We have given the world two presidents, Bill Clinton and George Bush. Wow, that should give you pause. Bill learned nothing from the sexual revolution, if there even was one, but we will save that argument for another time. I sure missed out. He couldn't figure out the definition of the word *is*. He just straight-up lied, in the grand tradition of our presidency. And as for George Bush Jr., he makes his father look like Churchill. He and his cohorts seem to pine for World War II. What the hell are they thinking?

Along the way, we have completely forgotten how to educate our children. For the past fifteen years or so, 45 percent of the high school students in New York City haven't graduated, and that's not seen as some sort of an emergency. What's it take to get our attention? So many of us brilliantly make our schools worse by sending our kids to private schools. Three-year-old kids are interviewed . . . interviewed . . . interviewed by prospective schools, and no one sees that as utter madness. And all of this for the privilege of spending twenty grand a year to send the three-year-old to school. How much paste can a child eat?

The one thing we did get right was our push to make women equal to men. It was called women's liberation. And I know it was right because it scared the hell out of a lot of folks. You mean "no" actually means "no?"

The problems we face are endless, and we've only seemed to make them worse.

Health care is at an all-time low. It's cheaper to fly to New Delhi to have a gallbladder operation than to have it at the hospital in your hometown. Prescription drug prices soar like the price of oil.

We have talked about the energy crisis for thirty years and haven't done a thing. No solar energy, just iPods as far as the eye can see. If we could download the sun, we'd have solar energy.

We are mired in a war in Iraq that makes the Vietnam conflict seem almost bucolic in comparison, and we can barely lift our voices above a whisper, except to yell at the college students that they should be protesting more.

We let idiots talk about a culture of life and yet won't let stem cell research take place, 'cause they mistakenly believe the frozen embryos are alive. Which is nuts! Frozen means too cold to do anything. I've adopted three. They are in my freezer. I am taking them as a tax write-off.

We leave generations to come to pay the debt for our follies. And with all this on our plate, we take the time to freak out about gay marriage, even though we allow gays to adopt. One might think we are insane.

So, I feel better now, and that's what counts really, isn't it, when all is said and done? We are a generation that just wanted to feel better, and dreams are just dreams. It's hard to make a dream real, especially while sitting in the hot tub, sipping port, and staring at the stars wondering where our youth went.

The ball game's not over, and even though it might be the seventh-inning stretch, let's hope we come on strong in the late innings.

Hm?

A late-inning rally! We can do this! We can come back! We've got the skills—we've got the talent! And, with our gigantic numbers, we've got an incredible amount of political clout.

Or not.

Boomers Come in Two Colors, Red and Blue

As we approach "our golden years," by now we boomers should have banded together, put our decadeslong differences behind

> William Jefferson Clinton has undermined the integrity of his office, has brought disrepute on the Presidency, has betrayed his trust as President, and has acted in a manner subversive of the rule of law and justice, to the manifest injury of the people of the United States.
>
> ***From Articles of Impeachment***

us, and formed an alliance of incredible political power. We should speak with one voice on the issues that will soon affect us all.

We will deal later with those hugely important issues: Social Security, Medicare, and "retirement" (whatever and whenever the heck retirement is). But right now, let's deal exclusively with the politics part.

There are nearly seventy-eight million of us. We compose 26.75 percent of the population. We control 2.1 *trillion* dollars in spending power.* That's trillion, with a *t*. So we are an incredibly powerful voting block, right?

Ah, well, no. Not so much.

The fact is that the things that divided us back in the sixties, when many of us were demonstrating against the war while others were volunteering to go over there and fight it, are still very much with us.

According to CNN exit polls in the 1996 presidential election, while President Bill Clinton won a plurality of voters between ages forty-five and sixty, 51 percent of us voted against him, with 9 percent voting for Ross Perot. In 2004 (when that statistic is much more in alignment with boomers), we were 30 percent of the total number of voters nationwide, and we voted to reelect President George W. Bush by giving him 51 percent of our votes.†

---

*Mature Market Institute of the Metropolitan Life Insurance Company, http://www.metlife.com/WPSAssets/18827370211149688405V1FBoomerProfile6206.pdf.

†CNN.com/ELECTION/1996 and cnn.com/ELECTION/2004.

Our first boomer president. A far cry from Truman or Nixon playing the piano.

179

Our second boomer president was George W. Bush, the antithesis to Clinton. Proof once again that boomers have a difficult time agreeing on anything.

There could be no better example of the "diversity within our cohort" than a quick examination of our first two boomer presidents themselves. Julian Bond takes a look: "There are some similarities. They both have this war experience. It's a different experience for these two men, but they both have it. They had to contend with what they were going to do about military service, and they handled that in different ways. They both come out of a youthful tradition of good times and fun, and they handled that in different ways. They are both, I think, in their own way, into the popular culture of their times. Clinton, the saxophone player. George Bush today, the iPod user. So there are all these parallels in their lives, and in some ways they are the same man. It is in their political outlook that they are very different. But in many other ways, they are the same man."

And yet, so very different. As a demographic cohort, we are 51 percent one way, and 49 percent the other. We are cut in two, right down the middle, just like the rest of the nation. Boomers in Congress stand on opposite sides of the aisle and call each other names and cancel out each other's votes. Only in years of dramatic change nationally do boomers break out of this 51/49 split. In the 2006 midterm elections, when Democrats won back control of the U.S. House of Representatives for the first time in twelve years, 53 percent of boomers (aged forty-five to sixty) voted for a Democrat for Congress and 46 percent voted for a Republican.*

In the view of many of us not trapped "inside the Beltway," not held captive by the "election cycle," not lorded over by autocratic ideologues called "whips," American politics has not only become dysfunctional, it has become dangerously counterproductive, especially for the tens of millions of boomer Americans who are approaching retirement age.

Bill Novelli is the CEO of AARP, and as the official head lobbyist for the aging, he knows a thing or two about politics and doesn't care for what he sees: "I don't know. The kind of government we've got now is not a very happy picture. If you go up and look around Congress, you'll see intense partisanship. In fact, you can read about it in the newspapers every day. I don't think it's necessarily liberalism or conservatism. It is just basically two parties clashing and trying to be in the majority.

"I think boomers can make a difference. I think what we need is for the voters to unelect some people. And if voters say, 'Look, we've got to stop this partisanship; we've got to do the people's business,' I think it can make a difference."

"So far, it appears that baby boomers, as they get older, are following the pattern of their parents and grandparents in terms of voting," according to Dr. Torres-Gil. "That is to say, as they get older, they're more likely to be registered to vote and to actually vote. If that pattern continues, then they may well become the hundred-ton gorilla in American politics.

"The partisanship and the negativity we see in American political life today, I don't believe, is about baby boomers. I think it's

---

CNN.com/ELECTION/2006.

just the nature of politics in the United States today. Either you're on one side or the other, and there's less willingness to compromise, to achieve a consensus, to be a moderate. It is not about generations. It is just about American politics gone astray. But it will hurt baby boomers, unless we somehow alleviate or minimize that partisanship. It will hurt baby boomers as they grow older, because . . . to assure any kind of quality of old age for baby boomers as we hope to retire and live longer will require a series of compromises—compromises to restore fiscal integrity to Social Security, compromises to address the serious problems that Medicare is facing, compromises to deal with the large number of Americans without health or long-term-care coverage, compromises to deal with the serious financial problems in pension and retirement plans.

"Unless we have moderation in American politics, we will not have the compromises and the consensus to deal with the very real issues and needs that baby boomers are going to have. So baby boomers didn't cause the partisanship, but they will pay a price if that partisanship continues."

Tony Snow, the White House insider on our panel, knows full well what's going on in politics today, and he doesn't like it any better than we do: "I think what has happened is that there has been a dramatization of political conflict because of twenty-four-hour television and so on, and so people sometimes give an impression of being more uncivil than they actually are. And I think quite often that serves to incite people on the outside. I've seen that a bunch of times. I do think that there is a political divide, but also if things stay too nasty too long it bores you. Then it's like watching an angry couple argue. You don't want to watch that. It's horrible. And I think what people want to see is the ability for politicians who disagree to shake hands and say, 'Well, that's okay, we like each other.' That's the ideal, and that's where I think we need to end up again."

From time to time it is best to stand aside and allow one of our experts to rant. This is one of those times. Mr. Gergen, you have the floor!

On Boomer Partisanship

David Gergen
Commentator, and director of the Center for
Public Leadership, John F. Kennedy School of
Government, Harvard University

"In the World War II generation, you're a strong Republican or you're a strong Democrat, but first and foremost you're a strong American. In the baby boom generation, you're a strong Republican or you're a strong Democrat. And, oh, by the way, when you think about it, remember, you are also an American. It's a very different sense of how one governs, how one leads, what one thinks about the country, because it's no longer a sense of 'we're all in this together.'

"You know there's a famous relationship between Ronald Reagan and Tip O'Neill: one a strong Republican, the other a strong Democrat. And they could fight like hell all day, but five o'clock at night they could put down their differences and lift up a glass of scotch and have a good time. . . . When Tip O'Neill reached his seventieth birthday, Reagan had him down to the White House for a birthday lunch and all his friends in from the Hill. And after it was over, Reagan got up and gave a toast, and he said, 'Tip, if I had a ticket to heaven, and you didn't have one too, well, I'd give my ticket back and go to hell with you.'

"And if you read Tip O'Neill's memoirs, you'll find that one of the finest tributes to anybody is actually to Jerry Ford for the transition day. He said it was a matter of awe and dignity, and he said, the country, every once in a while, we get ourselves in a real bad ditch and then we have always been blessed that a Lincoln would come along or a Roosevelt would come along. In this case when we needed him, there was Jerry Ford.

"Now, that was a Democrat writing about a Republican. You just don't find that today. . . . The first time I ever went to see George H. W. Bush was in his home in Kennebunkport. He had a Democratic congressman staying with him for the weekend. I was very impressed by that. They were friends, and it showed a kind of approach to politics I think is lacking today in the baby boom generation. . . .

"If you look at the collective efforts of the baby boom population in government, they've been disappointing. They've fallen short of what they might have been, of the promise we thought was out there. I'm sure President Clinton is disappointed in himself, because he was a man of such enormous talent. And yet he got caught up in things in Washington we all know about, and I'm sure he feels, 'Golly, I wish I could have just gotten a little higher up than I did.' I'm sure that's in part what the Hillary Clinton movement is about—finish the job. And George W. Bush, with 'compassionate conservatism.' Well, we've seen a lot of conservatism.

"We're not facing up to the big problems of our time. With the World War II generation, you felt that they were looking after their children and their grandchildren. They were attending to the problems of the future. And with the baby boom generation, you feel like they're *not* attending to the problems of the future. Whether it's in changing the schools fast enough, or climate change, or energy, or the debts that are building up, or the health care that's running up to bigger and bigger costs. There's a great sense of drift now, and my sense is we're drifting to our waterfall and that our kids are going to pay a big price for this—our grandkids are going to pay a big price for this—unless we in this generation grow up. Unless we really say, 'Okay, this has been a lot of fun, but now we've really got to fix some things.' And I don't care whether you're a Democrat or a Republican, let's get together and let's get some big solutions on the table and let's do it.

"I worry a lot that the baby boom generation, the generation that's in power now, is not paying sufficient heed to the gathering storms that are coming our way. Katrina showed us what can happen when you're not prepared for a big storm. And we weren't. And we now have many more bigger and more important storms than Katrina just over the horizon and coming our way."

Of course the metaphorical storm of which the distinguished gentleman from North Carolina speaks is the tidal wave of boomers that is about to crash onto our Social Security shores with a vengeance.

Empowerment or Entitlement?

It is another of those differences between the Greatest Generation and the boomers that our parents tend to approach retirement as a kind of payback for their years of service and hard work. According to Dr. Dychtwald, "The current elder generation doesn't necessarily approach their later life experience from a place of empowerment. It's more a place of entitlement. They believe they've made their contribution. They've made their sacrifices, and now it's their time to enjoy their remaining years, to have a relatively unobtrusive existence, and to receive the benefits to which they're entitled.

"Are boomers going to accept that view of aging as the status quo, or are they going to take their rebellious nature and change it? To what extent will the boomers have the capacity and the firepower to rewrite the language, the rules, the marketing, the media, the messaging, to create a version of aging that more suits their needs and reflects their actual feelings, and makes it a more hopeful and desirable stage of life?"

Magazine publisher Cathleen Black understands that the older *we* get, the older "old" is: "I find that when I think of *old*, I've added three decades to it. . . . So many people today are saying a person turning sixty, when he or she looks in the mirror, sees a fifty-year-old. A fifty-year-old sees a forty-year-old. But I believe there is some validity to that, because we are healthier, we care more about our health, we care more about what we're eating, we care about exercise."

But no amount of exercise can stop the clock from ticking or the calendar from turning. The Census Bureau estimates that by 2035, seventy million Americans will be over the age of sixty-five, sixty million of whom will be aging boomers.

That's right, sixty-five years old! Time to pack it in and move to Florida—heaven's waiting room—and tell our doctors to bill Uncle Sam. *The Life of Riley.* We can't wait to get to our long-awaited lives of leisure. Chuck the cell phone and the BlackBerry. We're looking forward to three full decades of contract bridge and shuffleboard and the eagerly anticipated annual visits from the grandkids. The big six-five. The age at which our burdens are shed, our responsibilities passed on to others, and the workaday productive years of our lives are finally over.

chapter 9

Over? Did You Say *Over?*

BLUTO: Over? Did you say *over?*
    Nothing is over until *we decide* it is!
    Was it over when the Germans bombed
    Pearl Harbor? *Hell no!*
OTTER: Germans?
BOON: Forget it, he's on a roll.
BLUTO: . . . And it ain't over now!

From **Animal House**
Screenplay by Douglas Kenney,
Harold Ramis, and Chris Miller

hat in the world would make anyone think that the boomer generation would suddenly start following the rules just because we're getting a Social Security check? We've been breaking the rules since we were eighteen years old, and we're sure as heck not going to stop now. We stopped a war. We stood up to Jim Crow. We reinvented the whole gosh darned world! We refused to accept our father's version of home, of country, of work, so why on God's green earth would we accept his version of—go ahead, go on, *say* it . . .

187

Old age?

Good question. We won't.

But if we are going to change this particular American institution, we must first end our nation's obsession with youth, an obsession that, forty or so years ago, we helped to create.

"We are a celebrity society," Dr. Dychtwald observes. "In some cultures, it's the philosophers, it's the religious leaders who society emulates. In ours, it's the movie stars. It's unbelievable to me. I walk through the airports, and I see all the magazines, and I can easily see how another culture would see us as this degenerate society, because we tend to praise and glorify people because they made a movie!"

Alice, it appears, has been watching too much television. In

> "But then," thought Alice, "shall I never get any older than I am now? That'll be a comfort one way—never to be an old woman. But then—*always* to have *lessons* to learn!"
>
> *From* **Alice in Wonderland**
> **By Lewis Carroll**

Alice's mind, all people worthy of emulation are beautiful and vibrant and young. Who ever sees anybody on TV or in the movies or in magazine ads who is beautiful and vibrant and *old*?

One of the hottest stars of the newest century, one of those most likely to be on the cover of a dozen magazines each and every week, for example, is Jennifer Aniston, who came to the nation's attention when she starred in an immensely popular sitcom called *Friends,* in which older people were rarely ever seen. The characters in *Friends* on occasion had to deal with their parents, who were, frankly, boomer buffoons.

So where are the sexy, beautiful, and vibrant *old* people—or even the sexy, beautiful, and vibrant *aging* people? Are there any?

Well, okay, there's that Sean Connery guy who was voted the

In 1963 John Glenn was the first American to orbit the earth, sending the world a message: America was determined not to lose the space race. Thirty-six years later, at the ripe young age of seventy-seven, he orbited the earth again, sending another message: you don't become irrelevant at age sixty-five.

"Sexiest Man Alive" when he was in his sixties—not in *the* sixties, in *his* sixties. John Glenn blasted off into space (again) when he was seventy-seven! Godspeed, John Glenn! Sophia Loren can still turn a head or two, and Dolly Parton, well, talk about vibrant!

But it's still Jennifer Aniston, "Jen and Ben," and "Bradjolina" who grace the covers of our magazines and grab the A-block lead on the endless array of youth-worshiping entertainment programs. In its first season, the hugely successful *American Idol* talent show wouldn't even accept applications from anyone over twenty-eight years old!

Former President Jimmy Carter finds the results of this obsession with youth to be almost sinister, as this endless barrage of images of the young and beautiful creates not only favoritism toward youth, but a prejudicial attitude against age, a prejudice "which is similar to racism or sexism," made even more disturbing by the fact that it "also exists among those of us who are either within this group or rapidly approaching it."*

The boomers—the richest, most numerous, most dynamic generation in the history of the world—have apparently now become the "Rodney Dangerfield" generation. We've become the "I Don't Get No Respect" generation.

Historically and in most of the world's cultures, Dr. Dychtwald says, the greatest respect is reserved for the oldest among them: "Before we created twentieth-century models of life, it was believed that people lived a long life if they were selected by God. That was the prevailing notion. So an older person was wiser, more powerful, and more enlightened—so everybody *wanted* to look old. The style in colonial times was to look as old as you could. People wore white powdered wigs. The look of old was 'in.' If you look at the painting of the signing of the Declaration of Independence, everybody's got their white wigs on. That all switched during the Industrial Era, the Roaring Twenties.

"The Industrial Age brought with it the concept of modernization, which is the idea that 'new' is better than old. 'Young' is better

---

*Jimmy Carter, The Virtues of Aging (New York: Ballantine, 1998), 8.

Mitch Robbins: Value this time in your life, kids, because this is the time in your life when you still have your choices, and it goes by so quickly. When you're a teenager you think you can do anything, and you do. Your twenties are a blur. Your thirties, you raise your family, you make a little money, and you think to yourself, "What happened to my twenties?" Your forties, you grow a little potbelly; you grow another chin. The music starts to get too loud, and one of your old girlfriends from high school becomes a grandmother. Your fifties, you have a minor surgery. You'll call it a procedure, but it's a surgery. Your sixties, you have a major surgery; the music is still loud but it doesn't matter because you can't hear it anyway. Seventies, you and the wife retire to Fort Lauderdale; you start eating dinner at two, lunch around ten, breakfast the night before. And you spend most of your time wandering around malls looking for the ultimate in soft yogurt and muttering, "How come the kids don't call?" By your eighties, you've had a major stroke, and you end up babbling to some Jamaican nurse who your wife can't stand but who you call "Mama." Any questions?

From City Slickers
Screenplay by Billy Crystal,
Lowell Ganz, and Babaloo Mandel

than old. New ideas, new technology, new hairstyles, new fashion styles are better. The Industrial Age brought with it a belief that old ways, old thinking, old technologies were what were holding us back, and that the new people, new ideas, unencumbered with history, were the future. The Roaring Twenties were the epitome of that, and the 'cult of youth' began where all of a sudden young was 'in' and 'hip.'

"It's not aging that troubles our generation, it's the version of aging we see around us. When you're with an uncle and he's not doing anything with his life and he feels like he has sort of checked out, or he's doing the same thing for twenty years in a row, you say to yourself, 'If that's aging, I don't want it.' But then you meet someone else that's the same age who's not that way, and it occurs to you that your 'old' uncle is not an absolute conclusion of growing older—it's simply a version of aging—like a fashion or a style or a choice that's become popular.

"But we can learn from our own history and from other cultures how to see older people in a more favorable light, to see that older people are more spiritual. Maybe they're more enlightened. Maybe they're more thoughtful. Maybe they're deeper, richer. People who have sixty or eighty or ninety years of life behind them often have more wisdom, more experience, more respect than any human being in the history of the world. To not have that be a contributory dimension of society is, I think, one of the biggest errors in a youth-oriented civilization."

According to studies performed by the National Institute of Aging, it now appears that negative stereotypes about aging can have more than just an impact on how others view "seniors" in our society. They also influence how elders view themselves and can even adversely affect health and longevity. Images of the elderly as "senile," "frail," or "confused," the studies seem to indicate, can become almost debilitating self-fulfilling prophecies. In reporting on these results, the *New York Times* says, "Rigorous studies are now showing that seeing, or hearing, gloomy nostrums about what it is like to be old can make people walk more slowly, hear and remember less well, and even affect their cardiovascular system."*

---

*Gina Kolata, "Old but Not Frail," New York Times, *October 5, 2006.*

Former President Carter studied the phenomenon of disrespect of the elderly when researching *The Virtues of Aging:* "The status of the elderly reached a low point during the Great Depression, when poverty was prevalent and jobs were scarce. When I was a child during that era, the value of members of a household was measured by their ability to work and earn income, which many of the older generation were unable to do.

"These nonproductive 'elderly,' some still in their fifties or sixties, were often a hardship, even an embarrassment, for a family. I remember the disgraceful status of 'old folks' homes', or 'po' farms.'"*

And who are the culprits who have forced on us this "youth cult" that is so prevalent? Well, ah, er—to a certain extent, we are.

When Tony the Tiger told us that Frosted Flakes were "Grrrreat!" we believed him. The private, secret message that our Captain Midnight decoder rings deciphered for us was "Drink Ovaltine." And we did, by the tens of millions of gallons. And later on, unfortunately, when the glowing box told us to "smoke Marlboros," we did that too.

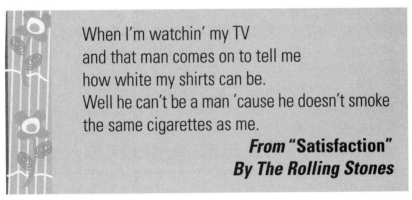

When I'm watchin' my TV
and that man comes on to tell me
how white my shirts can be.
Well he can't be a man 'cause he doesn't smoke
the same cigarettes as me.
From "Satisfaction"
By The Rolling Stones

But as the boomers grew out of the golden demographic of ages eighteen to thirty-nine, Madison Avenue stayed behind and continued showing us images of beautiful, vibrant young people who were apparently *made* beautiful, vibrant, and young by drinking Pepsi-Cola.

We have brought together a distinguished panel, and it may be time to allow them to discuss this issue in depth.

---

*Jimmy Carter, The Virtues of Aging *(New York: Ballantine, 1998), 12.

IN DEPTH

A Discussion on Marketing and the American Culture of Youth

Erica Jong

"This pretending to be young is a bigger deal in America than it is elsewhere. We imagine sexuality and youth as being inseparable. This is a very American thing. You can be Catherine Deneuve and be sexy. You're allowed to find a woman of sixty beautiful in France. You're allowed to find a woman of sixty beautiful in Italy. You're allowed to find a woman of sixty beautiful in Serbia, for goodness sakes. But not in the U.S. of A.!"

Eve Ensler

"I think what we have is a malignant self-hatred that possesses and absolutely contaminates most of us. It is induced obviously by this consumer state capitalist machine, which keeps showing us *who* we're supposed to look like, *what* we're supposed to look like, and those images are unbelievably powerful.

"Ninety-five percent of the world is round and dark, okay? That's how most of us look—round and dark. There may be six people on the planet who are blonde and skinny, and they live in Iceland. Do you know what I mean? And if you go and you see those people and then you think all of us on this planet who are round and dark are trying to look like these six people in Iceland, you realize how absurd it is. Yet, in those images, their teeth sparkle, they look happy, they look rich, they look like they own the world, they look like they're 'inside,' they're included, they're in that exclusive upper-royal celebrity class, which has become our royalty, which makes all the rest of us feel like we're nothing, and no one, and outside.

"You can talk to women who are living in poverty, and what they tell you is that if they only lost weight, things would be better. They can't even feed their children. They can't feed themselves, but if they only lost weight, things would get better. That's how strong this imagery is. . . .

"I think we live in a culture that is all about youth. It's 'the younger you are, the better you are, the gooder you are,' because obviously youth can be manipulated, right? Particularly as women. If you look young, you *look* like you can be manipulated. When you get older, you look like you have substance, and you *are* somebody, and you have an opinion, and you actually don't take any prisoners anymore. You have a point of view. So I think what women are taught is that if they look younger, people won't be scared of them. You know, they won't look like they actually know something. They won't look like they're wise. They won't look like they have power. And I think that's a huge piece of it. And I think we still live in a culture that doesn't see age as beauty. That doesn't think that aging women are beautiful."

But let us set aside Ms. Ensler's "consumer state capitalist machine" for just a moment and talk specifically about baby boomers and about how we're being shunted aside by marketers, publishers, and television executives. According to the AARP, "Despite representing nearly 50 percent of total consumer spending, companies have often failed to recognize the preferences, desires, and needs of the 50+ population. But now, as the baby boomer generation enters the second half of their lives (one every eight seconds), companies across every industry are beginning to take notice."*

---

http://www.aarp.org/about_aarp/focalyst.html.

Joel Westbrook

"By the time I got to the point in my career where I could actually influence what was going on television, the advertising people had decided that my watching wasn't important. I would sit in meetings with marketing pinheads and sales weasels who didn't care if I watched my own shows since I was no longer in the eighteen to forty-eight age group and, to make matters worse, I wasn't even female. These were the same types who changed the *Learning* in 'The Learning Channel' and the *Fried* in 'Kentucky Fried Chicken' to the letters *L* and *F* because the actual words didn't 'test well' with Gen Xers.

"Finally the size of our generation is overwhelming that school of thought, and advertisers are realizing that we have money and buy things. I guess that's a good thing."

Shelly Lazarus

"You want to hit trendsetters, you want to hit influencers, and for so many categories of products and services the influencers are young people, because they do set direction. And so I don't think it is a question of boomers or the different generations, I think it is a question of wanting to associate with young, attractive people. I don't think it makes all that much business sense very often, but it is true."

But there are nearly *seventy-eight million* of us and we've got money. We control more than 70 percent of all wealth and account for more than 50 percent of all consumer spending. And even if we didn't have money, well, that never stopped us from buying stuff before! We may not have invented consumption, but we have certainly made it conspicuous!

Dr. Joshua Zeitz

"There's this wonderful kind of event last year when the Rolling Stones played their North American concert, and all of these generation Xers, people of my generation, were looking on with shock and horror at their sixty-year-old parents trying to slip into designer jeans and dance to the Rolling Stones. And it was really terribly embarrassing, but what's happening is that you see the boomers continuing to be an important part of the consumer market.

"A magazine that I've written for, *American Heritage* magazine, which is avowedly a journal dedicated to American history and the study of it, has recently retooled itself to look at the baby boom generation in history. In part, that's because they've been such an important influence on America in the twentieth century, but also because advertisers are interested in reaching a boomer market. And they understand that boomers are affluent, that they have a history of borrowing, that they were raised in a culture that put a high premium on material comfort, and that they're simply not going anywhere. And while advertisers have traditionally been really interested in reaching that key demographic between the teenage years and the late thirties, they're now realizing that the boomers themselves can afford to buy more high-end products and that they're continuing to put themselves in debt if they have to do so to procure these items. So the boomers are incredibly important to America's consumer market."

Shelly Lazarus

"I think advertisers are waking up to the fact that just targeting youth is not going to give you a big enough market."

Okay. So why are we still seeing Jennifer Aniston wannabes in every commercial? Apparently, according to Ms. Lazarus, it has something to do with psychographics.

It is time to return, once again, to our trusted *Funk and Wagnalls*, where we will discover that *psychographics* has nothing to do with pictures of Norman Bates.

"I think everyone is getting more sophisticated in figuring out how to target other segments of the population. But we went through a period, though, where it all was very self-conscious. You could just see advertising calling out, 'Hey, old person with gray hair who is retired to Florida,' and it just didn't work. It was just that kind of flat-footed, self-conscious 'I know who the target is, and I'm going to call you out specifically.'

"So, I think over the years we've gotten much more adept at figuring out the psychographics of people. You don't necessarily have to *show* the people in the advertising who you are targeting, but you *do* have to figure out what's important to those people, what they are thinking about, what their issues are. And so I think we are in a much healthier place in terms of figuring out how to fashion advertising messages that will be meaningful to different groups of people. The boomers to us are only a part of the demographic landscape, because they are so diverse.

"You can target the most narrow groups of people today because of all the media options. So we're sort of in a world where mass is rejected. So even generationally, that's much too broad a definition for advertising. We can get it so much tighter for clients now, and part of what we have to do is to understand who the customers are in the most likely group of prospects. And so it's got to be a much more narrow definition than just an age cohort."

But changes, many believe, are afoot.

Ms. Lazarus's firm represents the Unilever Corporation—makers of (among thousands of other things) Dove Beauty

Bars—and, as such, it is responsible for one of the most interesting and "age-friendly" advertising campaigns in history. Age-friendly because it shows aging and older women "just as they are." This is not a series of focused, local cable television commercials. It is a worldwide, multimedia, multigenerational campaign set out to revolutionize the way women of all nations, ages, and body shapes perceive themselves and the way they are perceived by others.

Dove's Web site tells guests, "For too long, beauty has been defined by narrow, stifling stereotypes. Women have told us it's time to change all that. Dove agrees. We believe real beauty comes in many shapes, sizes, and ages. That is why Dove is launching the Campaign for Real Beauty. Dove's global Campaign for Real Beauty aims to change the status quo and offer in its place a broader, healthier, more democratic view of beauty. A view of beauty that all women can own and enjoy every day."*

Take *that* "consumer state capitalist machine"!

The site includes the results of an international survey that says 90 percent of all women aged fifteen to sixty-four years old worldwide want to change at least one aspect of their physical appearance (with body weight ranking the highest) and 67 percent of all women fifteen to sixty-four withdraw from life-engaging activities (like giving an opinion, going to school, going to the doctor) due to feeling badly about their looks.

Of course, it's about selling soap (whoops, sorry, *moisturizing bars*), but it is also about self-image and all of those things Eve Ensler was talking about, and, according to Ms. Lazarus, it seems to be taking off: "I think Dove actually is almost a movement. Dove has always been about real women, but this went a little further and said, 'Come on now, real women are *real* women!' And what makes them interesting and beautiful are things that are unusual. It is freckles and lines and ages, you know, this is what makes women beautiful and interesting. And what has really amazed us

---

http://www.campaignforrealbeauty.com.

is the way it seems to have captured the imagination of the world, because we are running it all over the world now, and wherever we run this point of view—it's not even advertising, because it's much broader than that—wherever we run this point of view, women seem to stand up and just applaud and go, 'Thank you for showing real women in their most beautiful natural state.' So I think it goes beyond Dove. I think we've hit a nerve here."

Perhaps. We can all hope. But Unilever and a handful of other companies have only just begun to chip away at a cultural phenomenon that has permeated our consciousness since Grandma was a Charleston-dancing flapper. The old view of what *old* means is a cultural perception that aging boomers have already set out to change.

The Ponce de León Generation

The fact remains that all of America has bought into the youth culture big time, even the boomers who have graduated from it.

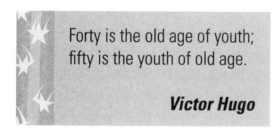

Forty is the old age of youth; fifty is the youth of old age.

Victor Hugo

We spend billions on moisturizers, skin toners, and "exfoliating masks" with "thermal fusion." Slap "anti-aging" on the label, and you've got yourself a surefire winner. And while it may be a deep, dark secret at the office, they even make these products for *men!* (Hey, they wouldn't make 'em if nobody was buying 'em.)

And then, of course, there's Botox. According to *BusinessWeek* magazine, the boomers and other Peter Pan wannabes will pay over $7.5 billion for "antiaging cosmetic treatments" in 2007. There are fifteen thousand "antiaging" doctors practicing in the United States.* In 2004 MarketResearch.com did a study of "Facial

*http://www.businessweek.com/magazine/content/06_12/b3976001.htm.

Cosmetic Surgery and Rejuvenation Markets." To anyone interested in purchasing the four hundred-plus-page report (downloadable for $3,500), they announce that "new technologies and alternatives to traditional cosmetic surgery have opened up a huge new market for antiaging products. Cosmetic facial rejuvenation is no longer the purview of plastic surgeons, but represents a booming cash business for a large number of dermatologists and other practitioners. Botox, dermal fillers, resurfacing modalities, lasers, and other alternatives are creating a dynamic and growing marketplace and finding millions of eager patients."*

It might be successfully argued that these people are not really "patients" at all. Our trusty *Funk and Wagnalls* would tell us that in order to be the "patient" of a doctor, one must first be ill. These "millions of eager patients" might be more properly defined as "consumers," "clients," or simply as "customers." And we haven't even begun to discuss tummy tucks, nose jobs, face-lifts, breast enhancements, and other procedures that involve scalpels or broken bones.

Leading-edge boomer Dolly Parton makes no bones about it: "I've had lots of work done," she says. "I'll have some more done when I need it. I always said, 'If I see something sagging, bagging, and dragging, I'm going to nip it, tuck it, and suck it.' Whatever needs to be done."†

She's had "work done." Cosmetic surgery is the only medical procedure that has its very own euphemism. There remains a stigma attached to cosmetic surgery because in most cases it is about vanity and vanity alone. Vanity (or pride) is frequently listed as the very first of the "Seven Deadly Sins"; wrath and greed are fifth and sixth—hence the euphemism.

Dr. Ken Dychtwald explains: "The world of plastic and reconstructive surgery was initially created to help people with deformities and people who had been through mutilating accidents. That was the purpose of the field, for somebody who had a car accident

*http://www.marketresearch.com/map/prod/849260.html.
†*"Dolly Parton: Nobody's Fool,"* CBS Sunday Morning, *July 25, 2004, http://www.cbsnews.com/stories/2004/02/27/sunday/main602806.shtml.

or was in a fire. Look at the field now. It's divided in half. You've got the reconstructive people whose business is to heal the sick and to fix the wounded. That's healing medicine. Then you've got the plastic and cosmetic people—many of whom started out in that field and broke off—who are now in the business of creating human enhancement. People show up with their credit cards and say, 'I want to look like this; I want a different nose; I want bigger breasts,' and they'll do it for you."

We all know that for people like Ms. Parton who are in the entertainment industry, where a line or a wrinkle is grounds for dismissal, cosmetic surgery is certainly not considered voluntary. But, as with everything else in this world, there are people who take things to the extreme.

Michael Jackson is a boomer too.

But let us not focus on boomer celebrities. What about John and Jane Boomer who have two jobs, two kids, two cars, and, in many cases, some sort of overwhelming emotional need to have "work done"?

Dychtwald finds that disturbing: "What you've got is this enormous craving in the youth-oriented society for people to make themselves young. My preference would be that we *felt* healthy rather than we *looked* twenty."

Dr. Andrew Weil is perhaps the nation's foremost expert on natural and preventive medicine, and he too has a serious problem with this antiaging craze and our fixation on maintaining a youthful appearance: "I'm alarmed at the rise of antiaging medicine in the society and the extent to which antiaging philosophy dominates our thinking about aging. My feeling is that aging is universal and natural. Everything ages. Aging seems to be written into the laws of the universe. And if you make your goal antiaging, I think you're in a very wrong relationship with nature. So, instead, I urge people to think about healthy aging or graceful aging. And the first step of that is learning how to reduce the risk and delay the onset of age-related disease. So the goal would be to live as long and well as possible, then have a rapid drop-off at the end. I think that's realistic. If people want to improve their appearance or do cosmetics or cosmetic procedures because it makes them feel better about themselves, that's not my business, but I worry about these things when they're done to deny the reality of aging. Because I think the denial of aging really takes us away from one of the important goals of later life, which is to really focus on change, aging, mortality, and to come to terms with those. You know, we're just youth obsessed. So, given that youth obsession, I think it's understandable that so many people want to try to pretend that they're going to stay young forever.

"It's an interesting observation that we judge people by youthfulness, and my hope is that the baby boomers are going to change that. I think when they get to be really old, where they can't escape the fact that they're old, they might be able to change these attitudes in our culture, and I certainly hope they will."

And most of us hope that right along with you, Dr. Weil, at least the older of us do. But you know what? You know what we *really* hope for even more than a radical shift in the deeply engrained attitudes and perceptions of an entire culture? What we really want is eternal youth. While we might prefer to *talk* with Madeleine Albright, we'd still rather *look* at Jennifer Aniston. We look at Jennifer Aniston because we *like* to look at Jennifer Aniston. Truth be known, a large minority of us would like to look *like* Jennifer Aniston, and to the other 52 percent of us, well, Jennifer Aniston is just really, really pretty.

If only there were a fountain of youth. If only there were some way to beat back the ravages of time. If only there were a *pill* you could take.

They're working on it.

Of Youth, Vigor, and Tiny Little Worms

In his book, *Age Power*, Dr. Dychtwald goes into some detail about the miracles of modern science, present and future, all designed to maintain youth and vigor and to ward off the deterioration of the flesh. He talks about nutraceuticals. Do not look up that word in your *Funk and Wagnalls*. It's probably not in there yet. Nutraceuticals are macro- and micronutrients that are magically made into food and drinks to fight aging, promote energy, sexuality, and a host of other really good things. He talks about cosmeceutical therapies made of pharmaceuticals, herbs, minerals, and vitamins that promote "youthful skin." He talks about a host of brain enhancement treatments to make us smarter and about futuristic bioimplants that will deliver antiaging nutrients and hormones on an as-needed basis.

For those of us who forty years ago tried mind-altering, psychedelic chemicals and basically did everything but drink the bong water, nothing is "experimental." Dr. Dychtwald contends that we'll try anything: "People are willing to take a drug to make them sleep better, another drug to make them happier, another drug because 'I've got a restless leg,' another drug to give them an erection. Once you get a taste for the solution being made available through some sort of substance . . . Can I imagine people in the future taking pills to make their bodies seem younger? Absolutely! When hormones come on the market that make your body feel like it's forty-five again, they're going to sell a billion of them!"

Of course, some of these things are in the future, but some are available now. While Ponce de León has long since gone to meet his maker (he got old and died, apparently), his quest survives. But his successors don't wear body armor and trudge through the swamps of Florida. They wear white lab coats and study the effects of such things as human growth hormones, and some dive deeply into the genetic composition of microscopically tiny worms. People in the antiaging field actually prefer to refer to it as "age management." They are attempting to "treat" aging as a disease.

Some of their treatments are based on sound science and are basically the lifestyle changes we've all heard so much about. These people are the ones responsible for the trendy diets we have become so obsessed with, and for regimens of exercise and vitamin supplementation. Some, on the other hand, are not quite so widely accepted.

The guru of the "age management" profession is Dr. Alan Mintz, founder of the Cenegenics Medical Institute in Las Vegas. Sixty-seven years old in 2006, Mintz is a longtime bodybuilder and fitness expert. He offers his clients all of those good things mentioned above—exercise, nutrition, and vitamin supplementation—*and* injections of the same kind of stuff that got baseball superstars Jose Canseco, Mark McGwire, and Barry Bonds in so much trouble with Major League Baseball and the United States Congress: human growth hormones. He obviously believes it to be safe—he does it himself. In a 2006 interview with *60 Minutes* he told Steve Kroft: "What happens to forty-year-old men is not unlike what's happening to forty-five-year-old women—energy, body composition, libido, even a slowing of mental processes. Hormonal decline is at least a part of it. So, on my own volition but with another doctor monitoring me, I put myself on a stimulating hormone to increase my testosterone production. Not testosterone, but a hormone that mimics a pituitary hormone that says, 'Put out more testosterone.' Lo and behold, life changed: Within three or four months, body composition improved, energy and mental outlook, libido—and life was very, very good again.

"I think what most people want is to affect the signs and symptoms of aging. So we focus on the quality-of-life issues. How can we be healthier longer? Be proactive about disease; don't let it happen. Stop it before it begins."*

Cenegenics Medical Institute has thirteen hundred physicians "in the family" and claims to have about twelve thousand–plus patients worldwide. Dr. Mintz and other proponents of such procedures argue that the injections increase muscle mass and decrease fat. They erase wrinkles and increase bone strength, energy level, and sexual function. Apparently, they also add one hundred feet

---

*"Aging in the 21st Century," 60 Minutes, April 23, 2006, http://www.cbsnews.com/stories/2006/04/19/60minutes/main1512855.shtml.

to the distance a baseball will travel when hit by a recipient of such "enhancements."

Critics claim that the injections can have dangerous side effects, including diabetes, arthritis, and carpal tunnel syndrome. They *may* also increase the risk of certain cancers, although there are no data showing what the long-term risks could be.

"You have got to give this industry its due," Dr. Dychtwald says. "It's got traction. Physicians all over the world are saying, I'll tell you what, we're learning a lot about the body. We can alter the aging process, or we can alter your body's relationship to disease. We can give you an injection of hormones; we can stimulate you with vitamins. And coming down the pipe may be the ability to reprogram your genetic story so that not only can you live healthy, we may even be able keep you young for many decades."

STUDENT: Isn't it true that Darwin preserved a piece of vermicelli in a glass case until, by some extraordinary means, it actually began to move with voluntary motion?

DR. FRANKENSTEIN: Are you speaking of the worm or the spaghetti?

STUDENT: Why, the worm, sir.

DR. FRANKENSTEIN: Yes, I did read something of that incident when I was a student, but you have to remember that a worm—with very few exceptions—is not a human being.

From **Young Frankenstein**
Screenplay by Gene Wilder
"Loosely" based on
a book by Mary Shelley

And what, one may ask, does all of this have to do with *worms?*

Microbiologist and geneticist Dr. Cynthia Kenyon of the University of California at San Francisco has been internationally recognized for her groundbreaking work in the analysis of the molecular causes of aging and life span control. Dr. Kenyon studied under 2002 Nobel laureate Dr. Sidney Brenner and is one of the first scientists to adopt the short-lived, small soil nematode *Caenorhabditis elegans* as a study system, and now uses it to study aging and longevity. In 1993, by altering a single gene called daf-2, which makes a protein similar to the human insulin receptor, she doubled the life span (and the duration of youth) of these incredibly tiny worms.

By manipulating its genes, Dr. Cynthia Kenyon at the University of California at San Francisco has been able to double the life span and youthfulness of microscopic worms known as C. elegans. *Might it work for humans as well? Stay tuned.*

Genetics and Longer Life

Dr. Cynthia Kenyon

"The kinds of things that are in the works now, in addition to more and better treatments for diseases, are the possibility of actually changing the rate at which you age, and possibly increasing the period at which you stay youthful, and ultimately affecting your life span as well. And this is a new idea.

"If you look in the animal kingdom, different animals have very different life spans. A rat, for example, lives about three years, but an Eastern Gray Squirrel can live twenty-five years. These animals look the same, they're very similar, but they're different because their genes are different. So that tells you right away that genes have a big effect on life span. And so we've evolved to have very long life spans, probably because of the way we live, the way we organize our societies.

"In my lab, I study these tiny little round worms that are microscopic, and they live in the soil, but they're real little animals. They have a nervous system; they have all the different tissues; they like certain things and dislike others; but they live only three weeks, and their strategy basically is to turn any food into worms as soon as possible. So basically it takes them three days to reach adulthood, and then in the next three days, they have three hundred progeny. So they're compounding at a rate of 300 percent every three days and that is huge. So that's a successful strategy for the worm. If you're going to have three hundred brand-new worms every three days, why bother to build a worm that can last a very long time? You don't need to. You've got brand-new worms. But we don't do that. We don't have that strategy. Our strategy is to learn. We teach each other things; we learn about our environment; we actually control resources; and we deploy them in ways that benefit our groups—and that requires time and experience. And so I think our strategy is basically different, and I think it's very interesting. Our life spans are much longer than they would have to be for us just to have children and get the children out of the house. They're much longer than they need to be for that.

"So, you ask yourself, why do people have such long postreproductive life spans? I think there are a couple of reasons for that. One is that it may be beneficial to have grandparents around to help take care of the grandchildren, to free up the parents, and another is that there is actually wisdom with age, and that's valuable.

"One of the really remarkable things that scientists have learned in the last few decades is that the basic biological processes that take place in a simple animal like these little worms are very, very similar at the molecular level to processes that take place in humans. So, for example, the mechanisms that cause individual cells to divide or that stop them from dividing inappropriately are identical in a worm and a human. And now the research from our lab and other labs is showing that there are actually genes that control life span, and if you tweak those genes and change them, then you can extend life span, and not just life span, you can extend a period of youthfulness.

"So different species of animals have really different life spans. For example, a mouse lives two years but a bat can live fifty years. So I thought, maybe there are some control genes that actually determine the rate of aging, and maybe these genes are more active or less active in the mouse versus the bat, and that's why the life span is so different. And these genes are not functioning in a haphazard or passive way— they're actually actively controlling the rate of aging. And so if that's the case, then if you change one of these genes you ought to be able to increase life span.

"So we started with these tiny little worms that we call *C. elegans*. They're microscopic; you can barely see them. They only have one thousand cells in their body, and they age and die really quickly. Their whole life span is just about two or three weeks, which is good for studies of aging, because you can do an experiment and then you can do another and another. So what we did was we changed the genes of the worm at random, and then we looked among the descendants for individuals that live longer. And we found that if we change a certain gene, a gene called daf-2, that the worms lived twice as long as normal. So basically, what we have now is a sort of a 'race' of worms that's exactly like the normal worms except one gene has been changed, and these animals and all their descendants age twice as slowly and live twice as long.

"So the question is, how far are we from something that could produce this extension of youthfulness in people? People who work on other animals are very eager to make the same kinds of changes in the same genes in those animals and see if that also increases life span. And in the case of this daf-2 gene, it does. Flies live longer when you change the daf-2 gene of the flies, and mice live longer when you change either the receptor for insulin or the insulin/IGF-1 gene.

"I think it's possible that we could extend our life span. We have our little worms that live twice as long as normal, and looking at one of these worms is like looking at a person who is ninety and thinking that they're forty-five. You know, it's really remarkable, the difference."

So, let's get to it! Will there ever be an antiaging pill? And, if so, *when?*

"There's no question that we can isolate and manipulate these genes that affect longevity drastically in other species," healthy-living specialist Dr. Andrew Weil confirms, but with a very large caveat: "Whether we can do this in humans, I don't know. . . . But if we are ever able to do this, is it a good thing? Assuming you could do that, how long would you want to live? I mean, how long would you want to live until you get bored with it?"

That is one question. Others most certainly will revolve around the morality and the ethics and the economics of the very existence of such a pill.

Dr. Fernando Torres-Gil is one of the nation's foremost experts on public policy, which would be drastically challenged should a "longer life pill" actually become available: "We as a generation in this country are enjoying dramatic advancements in biomedical discoveries, in pharmaceutical drugs that are like magic bullets— in R and D and all the technological innovations that allow us to repair body parts, to deal with diseases to live longer and healthier. Right now, unfortunately, those great advances are affordable to those who have the money and the [health] coverage, and not available fully for those who don't have health insurance. And that is a great divide right now in these wonderful, magical advances. I think one of the great needs for baby boomers as they get older and attempt to leave a legacy is to push, once and for all, for some type of universal health care. Unless we have universal health care, where all of us benefit from these dramatic advances, then we will see a strict difference between the haves who enjoy them, and the have-nots who are just struggling and not benefiting from these wonderful biomedical advances."

Dr. Kenyon herself recognizes the unanswered questions looming ahead of us: "There are two things I want to emphasize. One is that I don't want it to sound as though I am saying that we're definitely going to live forever or even for two hundred years. That is not clear. We may not be able to do that. Also I don't want it to be portrayed that I think there won't be any problems and that there won't be something that would be a matter of concern to society.

"What would it look like for insurance companies and for pension benefits? Suppose there is a pill that allows you to stay young longer. Well, some people will take the pill, and some may not take the pill. So at age sixty-five, it's already the case that some people are more useful than others. But there could be an even bigger difference. There could be people who are sixty-five, who look forty, and are as talented as they were at forty. So there's no way the taxpayers are going to pay for them to retire. It's just not going to happen. So I think age will stop being the indicator but rather some kind of means testing—I don't know what it would be—a mental acuity test or a physical capacity test. I don't know what it would be, but it would be something having to do with how youthful you are rather than how many years you've been alive.

"There is a concern that a pill like this might be priced very high so it would be a drug for the affluent and only the rich people could live longer. That's the kind of thing I think society would step in and think about. . . . Insurance companies might want people to be taking it so that they could delay these age-related diseases and stay healthy longer. So there might be pressure from lots of quarters to spread it around.

"One thing that's important to realize is that if there is a pill for life span extension, it won't be *approved* for life span extension. The FDA trials would take forever, and they'd be too expensive. You couldn't do it. They would be approved because they are efficacious for diseases."

So what is the future of "age management," and, perhaps more important, what will be the social, political, and ethical questions that are already being raised?

Dr. Ken Dychtwald is a highly respected gerontologist and has devoted his entire career to the study of these very questions: "Whatever your views on today's antiaging medicine, it is clear that the developing science of longevity is only in its infancy. Within the foreseeable future, it's possible that researchers will be able to prescribe for each individual an optimal blend of vitamins and hormones to keep them healthier and younger for longer periods of time. And there are even more miraculous possibilities just over the horizon.

"And then you have the farther end of the antiaging continuum where you literally manipulate the aging clock itself, which is not

Former President Jimmy Carter and his wife, Rosalynn, are perhaps our best models of vibrant aging.

about cosmetic surgery and it's not about some vitamins. It's about getting down into the genetic information where the clock of decline is programmed, *and changing it!* There's no question in my mind, it's going to occur in our lifetimes. No question in my mind.

"And that breaks all the rules. It breaks all the rules. It will create more political and religious drama than you can even imagine. What else? What happens to the world where the rich class, the Gordon Gekkos of the world, get to live to two hundred? Who decides who gets those treatments and who doesn't, and how do you get on the list? Who decides that?"

But where is the rule that says we have to have gene therapy and human growth hormone injections and all of that chemical rigmarole to stay youthful? Who made up that rule, and who says we have to play by it? Some of us, it seems, are doing just fine without it.

> So then, when are we old?
> The correct answer is that each of us is old when we *think* we are—when we accept an attitude of dormancy, dependency on others, a substantial limitation of our physical and mental activity, and restrictions on the number of other people with whom we interact.
>
> **Former President Jimmy Carter**
> **From The Virtues of Aging**

"One of the things that we see today, which I think is heartening," Dr. Weil affirms, "is that people are aging differently from their parents. You know, you commonly hear it said today that people in their seventies look like they're in their sixties, and people in their eighties look like they're in their seventies. I see that all the time. And first of all, this says something about the relative influence of genes versus lifestyle. Whatever genetics you have, the expression of those genes is always modified by lifestyle. I think people today have better information available to them, and better products, better services, and greater motivation to implement these strategies."

Bill Novelli is the CEO of AARP, and he understands that there are virtually *no* rules that boomers won't at least attempt to defy: "Boomers act young, I think, for two reasons. One is because they *are* younger. If you look at the average boomer today, that person is healthier than his parents were at that age. But there's another reason too, which is, boomers are boomers, and they just want to defy gravity and defy aging for as long as possible."

Ah, gravity and aging. Two more rules we have simply chosen to challenge as we move from adulthood into middlescence.

"Into *what*?" you ask.

Into middlescence.

part three

When

I'm
Sixty-four

chapter 10

"Middlescence"

J oel Westbrook plays "hardball" in our nation's capital, but Chris Matthews has nothing to do with it. Westbrook literally "plays hardball," as in horsehide balls, aluminum bats, ninety-foot base paths, and "high heat." Okay, maybe not "heat" exactly.

> Since baseball time is measured only in outs, all you have to do is succeed utterly; keep hitting, keep the rally alive, and you have defeated time. You remain forever young.
>
> **Roger Angell**

In and around Washington, DC, and Baltimore, there exists a baseball league for "seniors." That's right, baseball, not softball. It calls itself the "Ponce de León League: Baseball's Fountain of Youth." They have six hundred players divided into two divisions: one for those thirty to forty-eight years old and another for those forty-nine and older. While it is the player's option to slide or not to slide, as a concession to brittle bones collisions are prohibited. Other than that, they play by the same rules used by Westbrook's beloved Atlanta Braves.

While Westbrook is our Emmy Award–winning documentarian, resident expert on broadcast media, and the producer of the PBS program for which this book is the companion, he also drives for two hours or more thirty weekends a year to step back in time and play the childhood game that he still loves best.

217

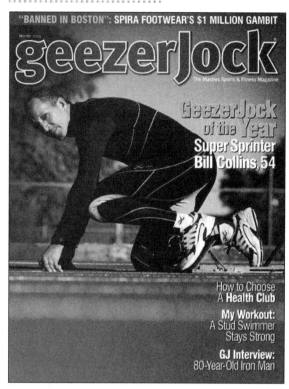

More than 1.5 million men and women over the age of forty play organized league softball. There are even senior women's hockey leagues. Baby boomers, apparently, do not intend to spend twenty years in a rocking chair.

"I never got through playing baseball," Westbrook laments. "I made my team in college but broke my foot and couldn't play my freshman year. I then grew a beard and became too 'hippie' for the coach, so I never finished.

"For my fiftieth birthday my wife sent me to the Atlanta Braves Fantasy Camp, and I remembered how much I loved baseball. Then I saw an ad for the Ponce de León League, joined up, and now it's the one thing I most look forward to every week.

"I went two-for-four last week and it *hurt* my .545 average. Foot speed is an issue in our league—there are a lot of places a ball can fall. My son says it looks like baseball being played under water."

The Men's Senior Baseball League reports thirty-two hundred teams nationwide, with forty-five thousand players. Senior Softball-USA, which claims to be the country's largest seniors athletic association, tells us that 1.5 million men and women over forty play organized league softball. There is even an "over sixty-five" league.

While obviously not a boomer, President Carter sets the bar high as a role model for retirement. A Nobel Peace Prize may be slightly out of reach for most of us, but we can remain physically active and volunteer to help others.

One person who loves to play over sixty-five softball is former President Jimmy Carter. He was seventy-two when he wrote *The Virtues of Aging* and boasted of pitching seven innings for his Plains, Georgia, softball team: "I kept from being too proud by reading about other older athletes. A recent front page article in the *New York Times* described a softball league in Sun City, Florida, where the pitcher was eighty and had to take eleven pills a day to control his arthritis. Recently they forced the retirement of one of their ninety-year-old teammates because the ball, which he could no longer see, frequently hit him."*

---

*Jimmy Carter, The Virtues of Aging (*New York: Ballantine, 1998*), 78.

There are even senior *hockey* leagues. There are even senior *women's* hockey leagues! (Although one must assume a general reluctance to hip check.)

"Sexy?" Not really.

"Old?" Not quite.

Anne Abernathy is known to the world as "Granny Luge." At fifty-two years old she had to withdraw from the 2006 Olympic Winter Games because she broke her wrist in a practice run. She is the only woman ever to compete in six Olympic Winter Games.

Two more members of our expert panel continue to dabble in rock 'n' roll bands. Episcopal Bishop John Chane had some success in his youth as a musician and looks forward to the occasional reunions of his old group, "The Chane Gang," and presidential press secretary (and accomplished flutist) Tony Snow takes time off to "jam" with friends whenever he can.

"There's no law against having fun in this society," says the boomers' chief defender, Leonard Steinhorn. "I think when people want to have fun and express themselves—and if you're fifty-five, and you want to play baseball or basketball—enjoy it, love it, appreciate it, live your life to the fullest. That's what it's all about.

"Unfortunately, there was always this message in the old era, that when you got older, you had to stop having fun, that you had to act like an adult or an image of an adult, and only be solemn and sober and have no fun. Well, you can be a responsible adult and still have fun. They are not mutually exclusive. So again, this is a problem with the media. The media will seize on sixty-year-olds playing hardball and say, 'Ah, look at these folks! They can't let go of their youth.' Again, that's another element of the media narrative which distorts the baby boom experience. Why not have fun? There is no law against it. Everybody should be able to do it. And let go people. Just let them have a good time!"

But the point is this: What we are looking at in the coming years "ain't your average middle-age crisis." Nor is it going to be your father's style of "retirement." In fact, the way we are spending the years between forty and "retirement" is so unique to boomers that Ken Dychtwald has invented a name for it. He calls it "middlescence": "Childhood, adolescence, adulthood. We have seen how the boomers redefined these life stages. And we have seen the enormous social, economic, and political impact they have had on the country. Work, marriage, parenthood, money—these were all issues of our middle years. In 1996 the first of our generation hit

fifty, the big five-oh, the traditional marker of middle age. A generation that didn't trust anyone over thirty was now turning gray. But turning fifty did not have the same meaning for boomers as it did for previous generations.

"What this generation is doing now and will do in the future is even more remarkable. Today, we are witnessing the birth of an entirely new life stage rising up between traditional adulthood and tradition-

> Men and women approaching retirement age should be recycled for public service work, and their companies should foot the bill. We can no longer afford to scrap-pile people.
>
> **Mahatma Gandhi**

al old age. I've called it 'middlescence.' Like adolescence, the period between childhood and adulthood that was introduced in the last century, this new *middle*scence, is a time of growth and discovery, of rebirth and reinvention, and a major detour on the path to old age."

The great question is, will there be a role for us to play during our middlescence, or will we simply be 'put out to pasture' like a triple crown–winning Thoroughbred whose heart still wants to race, but whose body won't let him? The question was first put to us years ago by those "Fab Four" metaphysicians known as the Beatles.

Will You Still Need Me?

Here we have begun to reach the heart of Dr. Dychtwald's primary area of study. He is a psychologist and gerontologist, yes. But he is 221 also a bit of a futurist, and he travels around the country anticipating what our gigantic generation will do, will accomplish, and will suffer in the decades to come.

"We will have more time to goof off," he tells us, "to read some good books, learn to paint, enjoy a fine dinner with close friends, make love, go sailing, or just kick back and enjoy a beautiful sunrise than during any previous period of our lives. We will have the mental perspective, the financial wherewithal, and the emotional depth to finally create a better work-play balance. We may have a few more wrinkles, but with them comes the realization that material ambition does not equal personal fulfillment."*

"We have grown up equating retirement with old age. But with the oldest of our generation starting to celebrate sixty, that's beginning to change. We aren't looking to be old or to wind down. We're looking to begin a whole new life when we reach our fifties and sixties. Having a positive outlook and understanding that life's next chapter is just that, not the beginning of the end of life, are vital to making it fun and fulfilling.†

"What I think is interesting about baby boomers is we never think we're going to grow up," Presidential Press Secretary Tony Snow asserts. "I mean, there's a Peter Pan aspect to this generation. A century ago, people our age were *dead*. The average person our age had been dead for three years. That's an amazing thing. Here we have a president who at the age of sixty has a standing heart rate that's about the same that Bjorn Borg had when he was winning the Wimbledon.

"Right now, you're just starting to get warmed up. And I think that what you have is a sense of a kind of vigor. Keep your mind on John Kennedy in his early forties, who was seen as the benchmark for vigor for presidents and yet in some ways these guys [Bill Clinton and George W. Bush] have been every bit as active as Kennedy ever was."

---

*Ken Dychtwald and Daniel J. Kadlec, The Power Years (New York: Wiley, 2005), 29.
†Ibid., 23.

So where are we going to channel all of that energy?

AARP CEO Bill Novelli thinks we're going to reach our creative potential at about the same age that our parents began counting down the days until "gold watch and golf" time: "There are more people who are starting their own businesses in this country who are *over* fifty than under fifty. Boomers do innovate. When I went to college, the word *entrepreneurship* never appeared. But boomers are entrepreneurial, and when they think about their so-called retirement, they're thinking about work; they're thinking about education; they're thinking about travel—all kinds of interesting things that will make them different in some ways."

As founder of the Experience Corps, the country's largest national service program for Americans over fifty-five, Marc Freedman obviously agrees that the boomers are not going to fade softly into the night. We are not counting the days until retirement. We're active, healthy, and expect to live to ninety and beyond—and a quarter century is a heck of a long bridge game.

According to Freedman, "The vast majority of boomers are going to work in this stage of life when previous generations went to the sidelines. The notion of phased retirement, a 'bridge' job, a way to make ends meet between the end of real work and the beginning of real leisure, is going to work for some segment of the population. But for a lot of other people, rather than phasing out or fading out they're zeroing in on the things that they care the most about and trying to turn their work into something that advances those causes. They're creating essentially a new career stage. . . . Many are going to move from the focus on money to one on meaning. But meaning that's not just personal fulfillment but that has an opportunity to make a difference for people around them. I think they're going to launch second careers in areas like teaching, nonprofit management, health care, and many are going to be social entrepreneurs in this phase. So they're really defining not only a new stage of life but a new stage of work, and a stage of work that's got a different focus than the work they did in the middle years."

Unfortunately, because most Americans continue desperately to cling to the stereotypes of "senior citizens" rolling carts loaded with magazines from hospital room to hospital room, or serving apple juice to kindergartners after school, carrying out these kinds of dramatic aspirations may be tough. According to Faith Popcorn, the marketing expert the *New York Times* has called "the trend oracle," "Boomers are redefining middle age because they are really trying to stay—to *be*—young. What's driving them to be young is not the same thing that drove the fifties housewife. What's driving them to be young is the fact that they know they're going to have to live and live healthy, because they're going to have to work, because they're going to need money. So, what's driving them to be young is to be more acceptable to the job workforce."

Sociologist Dr. Steven Nock posits that a youthful appearance may not be enough to guarantee boomers a place in the workforce of the near future: "I think that one of the great challenges for us as a society is to determine how to use the talent of this enormous generation as they leave employment. How can we integrate them into society as volunteers and activists? They are a generation accustomed to these things. They've been activists, and they've been professionals, and they've been healthy, and they will remain that way. But at the moment, we don't really have a society that is welcoming to seventy-year-old unemployed people. The opportunities for individuals like that are just now emerging, and I think that the baby boom, like it always has, will face this challenge, and struggle, and make many mistakes in trying to figure out how to find a viable life after work."

Marc Freedman founded Civic Ventures for the very purpose of placing seniors in positions where they can be helpful to their communities and can continue to have a sense of self-worth. But before any of his ideas can work, society must change its view of what aging Americans are capable of doing. Freedman says, "In the nonprofit world, we keep trying to shunt people into roles that were comfortable for people thirty or forty years ago, but which hold no chance of capturing the imagination of the current generation.

"I think of a physician that I interviewed in Palm Beach, Florida, who had been chair of a medical school department in Philadelphia, who had been one of the leading researchers in her field, retired for six months, and was bored and living in Florida. Ultimately she approached the local hospital and said she was going to provide her expertise in services, free of charge, and they were delighted. They called her back the next day, offering her a job *refilling water pitchers*. And that notion of being disregarded, of being misunderstood, diminished, is something that's making a lot of people angry."

Daniel Kadlec is a columnist for *Time* magazine and the coauthor (along with Dr. Dychtwald) of *The Power Years*. In a *Time* essay titled "The Right Way to Volunteer," he tells readers that "the days of envelope stuffing may be numbered." He accuses established nonprofits of clinging to "their old ways of asking volunteers to do little more than stuff envelopes and make fund-raising calls. . . . That is a waste of talent and desire."

Boomers volunteer at a rate of 33 percent, and we are still in our working years! The Greatest Generation (sixty-five and older) volunteers at a rate of 24 percent, but it should be noted that many of them are well beyond the age of ability. The point Kadlec makes is exemplified by the fact that, like the Palm Beach doctor mentioned above, many of us show up to volunteer, get insulted, and never go back. As shallow a pursuit as golf may be, it is infinitely preferable to filling water pitchers, stuffing envelopes, and begging for money from a total stranger on the telephone. "Nearly thirty-eight million Americans who volunteered with a nonprofit in the past," Kadlec says, "didn't show up last year [2005]."*

It is the assessment of Dr. D. Quinn Mills, our human resources expert, that, while golf is great, it's not thirty years great: "There still is a traditional concept of retirement. There still are massive numbers of people leaving jobs, moving to Florida, to Arizona, to Las Vegas, to Southern California, and playing golf, playing bridge, enjoying their grandchildren in the traditional retirement way.

Daniel Kadlec, "The Right Way to Volunteer," Time, September 4, 2006. 225

But when one looks ahead with an expectation of twenty or thirty years of that, as many people do now, so that you're talking about as long as your career, it's not obvious to me that that's a good way to live, or that many people are going to want to do it.

"So, what's the alternative? The alternative is to develop another major part of one's life, whether it is moving to big cities and

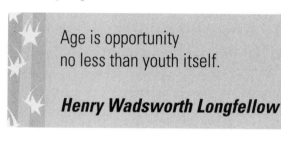

Age is opportunity
no less than youth itself.

Henry Wadsworth Longfellow

enjoying that when I've lived elsewhere; whether it is another career in a different industry, in a different kind of activity; whether it's a major social contribution, teaching, consulting, any of a number of things. And I see boomers kind of splitting into two groups, one of which is doing the traditional retirement thing, the other of which is doing the nontraditional thing. My own guess is the nontraditional, as it develops, as people learn how to do it, as mechanisms and support systems and businesses develop to make it possible, it will be much more important."

One of those farsighted companies that is taking the lead in setting up "mechanisms and support systems" for boomers to step into middlescence is, believe it or not, stodgy old conservative IBM. That's right. Big Blue is leading the way. Of course, it was the Blue boomers themselves that came up with the idea. There we go again, challenging the status quo again, thinking outside the box again, changing the rules again.

IBM's "mature" engineers and others suggested that the company look into ways to ease this difficult transition time, to "create a pathway" leading from one career to another. So the company has established a pilot program that seems to be a win-win-win proposition. It is called the Transition to Teaching Program, and it's headed up by a man extraordinarily qualified and downright exuberant about its potential.

Fellow boomer Stanley Litow is the president of the IBM Foundation and IBM's vice president for global community relations.

He is also a past deputy chancellor of schools for New York City, the nation's largest school system, serving 1.3 million children. It may seem to be an odd leap from teaching executive to the high-powered world of high tech, but IBM's primary philanthropic focus has been on education for quite some time. Since 1994, IBM has been involved in school reform through its Reinventing Education program, the company's flagship charitable contribution arm, with an investment of $75 million worldwide. More than one hundred thousand teachers have been trained by forty-four thousand employees who have donated nearly two million hours of service to local schools.

So now, here's one of the world's largest companies with an understanding of what Litow calls "the crisis in our schools—the crisis in teacher quality": "According to the U.S. Department of Labor, jobs requiring science, engineering, and technical training will increase 51 percent by 2008. This increase could lead to six million job openings for scientists, engineers, and technicians. In order to prepare today's young people for these careers, more than 260,000 new math and science teachers are needed by the 2008–2009 school year.

"In conversations with our employees, a number of them told us that they want to make a contribution after leaving IBM. They have no interest in the old view of 'retirement.'"*

Hmm. IBM has hundreds of the world's best mathematicians and computer scientists with decades of professional experience. These people are approaching the end of their "first" careers and are wondering what's next. IBM has the supply—our schools have the demand.

So what Mr. Litow is doing is building a bridge from IBM to high schools in a few markets where the corporation has large numbers of employees. IBMers who sign up (the pilot program has one hundred signees) can "flex" their work schedules to take teacher certification classes. They will be given a stipend and a leave of absence from IBM to do their student teaching, and,

---

*Stanley Litow, personal interview with the author, November 2006.

hopefully, will move from the corporate world directly into the classroom. A win for IBM, a win for our children, and a win for boomers who are looking to move from success to significance in their middlescence.

It is certainly a win for Kathy Kelly, a thirty-year IBM veteran who "raised her hand on day one." In an amazing kind of time warp, while Kathy is "twenty-one plus" years old, she came to work for IBM on the day Neil Armstrong first set foot on the moon. "In college, my goal in life was to teach math. I've been talking about it for a while and had a friend who was egging me on. With IBM's help, I applied to Pace University's Come Teach with Us Academy. Of course, IBM is big on flex time anyway, and my management team was very supportive, and I never had to miss a class." Kathy will get her "classroom experience" with the help of IBM and begin teaching at Fox Lane High School in Bedford, New York, in fall 2007. Simply by telling her students her history, they will come to know that "there are real-life environments where you can use math and science."

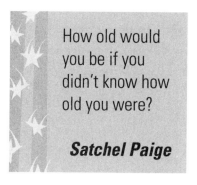

How old would you be if you didn't know how old you were?

Satchel Paige

According to Litow, there will be another winner as well: "This program will be at the heart of future innovation in the United States, which will be hugely important in the new global economy."

The Monsanto Company has what it calls the Retiree Resource Corps, which brings former employees back into the fold on a part-time or as-needed basis. These are called "Boomerang" jobs. These people cost 10 to 15 percent less than temporary workers; they don't require any training, so they hit the ground running; they already have their pensions; and they don't require expensive benefits like health care insurance. Win-win.

Jeff Taylor, who gave computer-savvy boomers a place to go to find work in the middle of our careers with Monster.com, has started a new Web-based company designed specifically to help us find a way to spend the rest of our lives. It is called Eons, and it is his intention to help us revolutionize both our middlescence and our "retirement," no matter where the vague line that separates the two might fall. He has, by the way, given us yet another moniker. In Jeff Taylor's world, we are now the "Eons" generation.

"What will you do with your time?" Taylor asks. "How will you challenge and how will you inspire yourself? What I would like to do with boomers and seniors is see if I can inspire a whole generation to live the biggest life possible. By perspective, if you're fifty-two, you could have forty-eight years to go. This is the longest, most unstructured period of your life. What are you going to do?

"One of the things we all know is if you make a list and you put a date on it, the rest of it will take care of itself. So I'm asking everyone, have you top-ten'd yourself? Have you top-ten'd your life? What are the most important things, your dreams, your adventures, things that you'd like to accomplish that will make you a bigger, better, stronger person? Do you want to improve playing the piano? Do you want to go to Tuscany? Do you want to go explore India? Do you want to learn a new language? These are the things that are going to change who you are, give you a bigger life, get you engaged, meeting new people, accomplishing things that you'll talk to your friends about.

"I think that boomers are not going to lie down; we're not going to dry up like a raisin. We're going to pump up our life. That's what I think the Eons generation is going to be all about."

Far out.

Beyond IBM, Eons, and a few other forward-thinking corporations, there are also new nonprofit corporations being formed to help boomers find a path to their bridge careers. Panelist Marc Freedman founded the Experience Corps because he feels he spotted both a need and a solution. Experience Corps provides service opportunities for Americans over fifty-five. It works to solve serious social problems, beginning with literacy. In 2006, more than eighteen hundred corps members in fourteen cities served as tutors and mentors to children in urban public schools and after-school programs, where they helped teach children to read and develop the confidence and skills to succeed in school and in life.

Freedman hypothesizes that "the changes that are happening now are of historic proportions. We've got this population explosion of boomers who are flooding into that period of traditional retirement age. That's a big change as a society, and yet in the realm of public policy we've mostly been tinkering with the policies that we invented for a different generation of older adults. And I think we need to think big in the way that we did with the GI Bill when we had millions of people crossing a geographic divide—coming back from military life and moving into civilian life.

"Well, now we've got tens of millions of people who're crossing over a divide between stages of life, and they're pioneers on this frontier. We need to think in the same dramatic sweeping proportions. How can we keep them engaged? How can we use all that human capital investment that they've made and that society's made in them?

"That period between midfifties and mideighties, I think, is going to be a period of great productivity. And I think [for] many people, it'll be the time when they do their most important work."

Another such company is a New York firm called ReServe: Next Steps for Older Adults. Their mission is to connect "educated older adults with *stipend-paying* jobs that challenge them to use their lifetime skills for the public good."

This is not volunteer placement. These mature adults will be given a job with greatly flexible work hours *and* a stipend. "When money changes hands," ReServe says, "both sides feel a deeper commitment to the work."

In just over a year of operations, ReServe, working in cooperation with various other nonprofit organizations, has found positions for resource coordinators, writers, marketing associates, after-school teachers, IT experts, graphic designers, social workers, and librarians.*

Dr. Zeitz points out that "the boomers who have a longer life span and live more healthfully and have been raised more health-

---

http://www.reserveinc.org/news.htm.

fully than the generations that came before them can continue to work well into their seventies and even into their eighties."

When Franklin Roosevelt bought into Otto von Bismarck's concept of sixty-five years old being the age at which a worker was "no longer useful," the economy of the day demanded muscular work. Today we need brains, experience, and ideas. Unlike muscles, brains, experience, and ideas don't wither at age sixty-five. And as we leave the workforce, the work*load* will stay the same. As the old song says, "something's gotta give."

Business management expert Dr. D. Quinn Mills assesses the ramifications for our country's economy should tens of millions of us leave the workforce and never return: "If boomers really retired, large numbers of them—meaning out of the workplace, not just out of one company and into another, but if they really withdraw from the major contributions that they've been making in the society—there will be a huge brain drain. And it's not just that there are fewer numbers of people in the generations that follow coming into the workplace; it's that, by and large, they're not as well educated. On paper, they appear to have the college degrees, et cetera, but the quality of American education, the actual experience and ability of people to do things, like to read effectively and to write and express themselves well, has been strongly declining. . . . They've been very well entertained and they've lived very well, but they have not applied themselves.

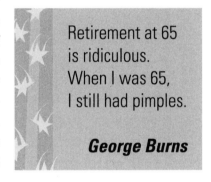

Retirement at 65 is ridiculous. When I was 65, I still had pimples.

George Burns

"So brain drain is twofold: it's numbers, and it's quality and knowledge and experience—and it will be significant."

There may be a few negative repercussions created by boomers staying in the workforce longer. For example, how will it affect the Gen Xers who are impatiently waiting for us to get the hell out of the way so that they can get their promotions into the premium jobs, the high-level management jobs, the "big bucks" jobs that boomers are hanging on to for dear life? It's called "clogging up the pipeline."

"The generations that are following the boomers in the workplace are smaller," Dr. Mills notes. "That means that they have not been able to move quickly up the ladders of promotion. The baby boomers were able to move in and grow in organizations behind a smaller generation ahead of them."

Almost universally our experts agree that, in addition to greater flexibility, what boomers will want most during middlescence is a feeling of worth, of giving back, of making a contribution. Eve Ensler wants that contribution to be on the grandest possible scale: "I think we probably have a ten-year window right now, the ten years before we have blown the environment and we have created so much anger and rage in the world that, you know, there are too many people who are blowing up too many people. I say to women now when I tour, 'Put your self-hatred on hold for ten years, get out there, and devote yourself to stopping the annihilation of the planet, to ending racism, to stopping sexism, to beginning to really shift things around, and then you can go back and get your self-hatred and worry about your hips later on.' But right now, *right now,* we are being called on as human beings to be bolder and to be more daring and to be more outrageous than we've ever been before. And if we don't heed that call, I don't know that the future is going to be so good."

Perhaps not on Ms. Ensler's scale or on Ms. Ensler's issues, but apparently boomers are ready to heed the call to public service. Civic Ventures founder Marc Freedman is encouraged by his company's recent research: "We did a survey last summer of the leading edge of boomers to find out if there's any relationship between the kind of work boomers are hoping to do and what we need them to do as a society, and the encouraging news is that half the people were interested in another phase of work in areas like education, health care, the nonprofit sector, where a vast labor shortage is materializing in the society. We're already seeing a desperate need for teachers, for nurses, for nonprofit leaders. And 20 percent of the people surveyed, 20 percent of the leading-edge people said one of their top priorities was to work in these areas where there's not only a need for human beings and human talent, but there's a great social benefit at play as well.

"The well-to-do segment of the population is going to be able to pursue renewal. They're going to be able to do work that's meaningful. And yet the vast majority of people are going to be struggling to find jobs at McDonald's and Wal-Mart. And I think we have a responsibility as a society to help people to continue to develop their skills, to have opportunities, through public investment, to make a meaningful contribution."

While numerous pundits love to pontificate about how boomers will not be able to afford a thirty-year retirement, Dr. Dychtwald adds a variable to that formula: the American economy won't be able to afford it either. "Because the economy will want to simultaneously prevent a brain drain and declining consumption by keeping all of us earning and spending longer, it will become easier to stay at work or start a new career. The vacuum of workers maturing means that older adults will be in demand and more able to choose our own schedules and still remain valuable. With the rise of flextime and part-time schedules and contract and project jobs and job sharing, there are a growing number of exciting paths for us to explore.

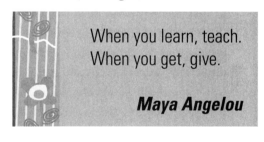

When you learn, teach.
When you get, give.

Maya Angelou

"If you look at the number of people flooding into adult education programs, if you look at the number of older adults pouring onto the Web, and the number of people who are trying to improve themselves, it's a revolution. I have to tell you it's a revolution. It's not just the rich people; it's not just at your gym; it's not just in that classroom; but it's everywhere. People are beginning to think, 'This can't be all there is. I still have decades in front of me. I want to make something of myself.'"

We all know an "empty nester" or two who has returned to school at whatever level, from bachelor's to PhD. Whether in "brick and mortar" institutions or by taking online courses, boomers are lining up to hit the books.

While the University of Phoenix and a number of other reputable institutions are offering legitimate courses online, some scholars are concerned by the growth of some rather questionable Internet companies and the quality of education they provide.

Dr. D. Quinn Mills looks at the potential for lifetime education: "I think we will still have traditional campuses in higher education, even with all of the modern communication technologies, but what should happen if things go well, to my mind at least, is that it will open up education in a real way to adults. What this is going to do for us is really open up lifetime learning. And in the United States, what's happening is that we are beginning to package a lot of learning as entertainment. The problem we're having is that much of what is packaged as entertainment and pretends to be nonfiction isn't, and so people are picking up large amounts of misinformation in entertainment forms and believing it to be information. Some of the bestsellers do that, and we have to come to grips with that in some way. We have to be able to tell what is represented by someone as 'true' versus what is pretended by an author to be true for the purposes of entertainment. Once we've done that, all this technology gives us an opportunity to do education on a much different, wider, and more effective basis."

Returning to school while in your sixties probably doesn't mean beginning a twelve-year quest to earn a PhD in astrophysics. It's probably more about keeping your mind active and learning new things and meeting new people and even keeping in touch with Generations X and Y. A continuing education bulletin might include courses in fly-fishing, yoga, or even the meaning of life, which may just be more challenging than astrophysics.

"What may start out as retirement really turns out to be more of a sabbatical," Marc Freedman says. "It's a transition rather than a destination. And then what people are facing is a period that could be as long as midlife in duration, where they're neither young nor old, not retired, not likely to be for some time. And I think they're going to shape that phase of life.

"The period between the end of midlife and the onset of true old age has been stretched and stretched and stretched. At one point, it was just a brief hiatus between the end of work and the end of life. Now it's decades in duration. And that period remains to be shaped, and the boomers are the group that's going to shape that stage.

"It's a combination of economic forces and psychological forces. The need on one hand to continue to supplement their income, but on the other hand to have a reason to get up in the morning—a sense of purpose, a feeling that your life still matters.

"Previous generations aspired to the liberation from labor, the freedom from work. This group is aspiring to the freedom *to* work, and not just the freedom from age discrimination, but the freedom to

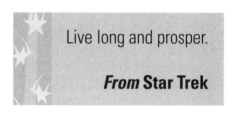

Live long and prosper.

From **Star Trek**

do work that is closer to their passions, to their heart, that gives them a sense of satisfaction that oftentimes is elusive in midlife work.

"Boomers are in a unique position. I don't think there's ever been a generation before that's reached this point in their lives, where they've had enough experience to know what they cared about, what they wanted, and enough time to do something with that experience. Just as people got to that point of really being a grown-up, their energy was waning. They were being shoved out the door. So now you've got a generation with that kind of insight, but also the time and opportunity to act on it."

When faced with the *r* word, *retirement,* our panel of experts all have generally the same reaction. "*Me?* Retire? *Never!*"

When Will *You* Retire?

So when can we at last officially "retire"?

Well, retirement begins at age sixty-five. Right?

Wrong.

Dr. Ken Dychtwald reminds us that "sixty-five was established as the marker of retirement over a century ago by Germany's Chancellor Otto von Bismarck when he was preparing his country's first pension plan. At that time, average life expectancy in Germany was forty-five."

Economist Dr. Lester Thurow puts that into a modern-day perspective for us: "It's like us saying you will get a public pension, but nineteen years *after* general life expectancy. So if general life expectancy is seventy-six, you will get your pension at ninety-five.

"My father retired at sixty-five. He died at ninety-five. He had a thirty-year vacation. Can you afford a thirty-year vacation? The answer is no."

Dr. Dychtwald concurs: "When Franklin Roosevelt created Social Security in 1935, he followed Bismarck's lead. Although the average American could expect to live only sixty-three years by then, sixty-five still seemed old to government planners. Despite increasing life expectancy, nearly every modernized nation has maintained sixty-five as the standard age of retirement and eligibility for old-age entitlements.

"Maybe our parents' version of retirement was fine if we were talking about a couple of years, but there is no way the boomers are going to lay in their hammocks for thirty or forty years or watch forty-three hours of TV a week, as the average retiree did this year. If the history of this generation has taught us anything, it is that boomers will redefine retirement.

"More than 50 percent of newly retired workers currently receive benefits at age sixty-two, and more than two-thirds retire before age sixty-five! While 62 percent of U.S. corporations currently offer early retirement plans, only 4 percent offer inducements for older workers to extend their working years.

"This approach makes no sense for the future. Let's not lose sight of the fact that retirement is a relatively new 'experimental' life stage that was initially envisioned to last three to five years, not twenty!"

But, if all goes well, we will keep working for a while and at our own pace, and, finally and at long last, we will achieve that desperately sought-after work-life balance that has eluded us for these many decades.

The preceding pages have dealt exclusively with the "work" half of that equation. Now what about the "life" part? Where are we going to live? Who are we going to live *with*? What are we going to do? And will God play a role? God, or religion, or spirituality, or whatever we're calling it these days?

Wait! God May Not Be Dead After All!

The Dalai Lama is a rock star in America. He does multicity tours and sells out everywhere he goes. Barbara Walters gushed over him and asked him on TV if she could kiss him.

Dr. Wayne Dyer is a staple on PBS and his book *There's a Spiritual Solution to Every Problem* is only one of the hundreds of bestsellers out there from people like Deepak Chopra and Alan Cohen, who teach that spirituality may differ from religion, and that spirituality may be right.

JERRY LANDERS: If you're God, how can You permit all the suffering that goes on in the world?
GOD: I don't permit the suffering—you do.

From Oh God!
Screenplay by Larry Gelbart,
based on the book by Avery Corman

Are boomers, then, taking their proclivity to question authority to its ultimate conclusion? Are we questioning the ultimate authority?

Thom S. Rainer is president and CEO of LifeWay Christian Resources in Nashville, Tennessee. He was founding dean of the Billy Graham School of Missions, Evangelism, and Church Growth at the Southern Baptist Theological Seminary. In a 2006 online article, he addressed the impact the aging boomers may have (or may not have) on the evangelical movement.

According to Rainer, "About two-thirds of the seventy-six million boomers are unchurched, which means they attend church no more than twice a year." He sees this as an opportunity: "Our early research indicates that many of these boomers are becoming profoundly nostalgic. Among the unchurched boomers, we found that a significant number would return to church if it resembled the church of their childhood."* (Really? The church, huh? We remember church.) And he may be right. There may be some nostalgia for the church "of our childhood," but maybe not so much for the church itself.

Episcopal Bishop John Chane speculates that the nostalgia may be more for the picnics and the camping trips—more for the warm and welcoming familial community that the church once provided: "The logical community is the community of the church because that's a given community. It may be small. In some cases you might have eight hundred or nine hundred people in that community. Other times it might even be smaller than that. But it's a community. But it's a place where in a sense you would live out the same values, simple values that you kind of lived out when you were growing up in a defined, civil community. And so that's the greatness of it. Psychiatrists tell you, mental health is very much dependent on the support of other persons and the nature of living in a community and friendships. People who you can share your stories with, let your hair down with, instead of sitting at a computer and logging in every night to some unknown soul. Hey, you've got mail.

"Today the big megachurches are really small communities. So that's where you have everything from bowling to you name it. Whatever went on in the community, secular community, that I can remember, is now offered by great megachurches, *along with* the worship that's very important in the lives of people. And my own denomination is built on small churches. We're a small church denomination. We're not a megachurch, but it's based on

---

Thom S. Rainer, "The Church in 2001: Catching the Age Wave," http://www.lifeway.com.

the concept of community, *albeit* a Christian community, and the healing nature of what it means to live in community, and that is what's missing in this country."

But for many boomers the "church of their childhood"—the actual damning, threatening, condemning, patriarchal, judgmental church—may not be all that nostalgic. We may have been reminded of that when, in 2006, the First Baptist Church of Watertown, New York, made headlines when it dismissed a woman who had been teaching Sunday school there for fifty-four years. The letter of dismissal quoted the First Epistle to Timothy: "I do not permit a woman to teach or to have authority over a man; she must be silent."

But that is one church and surely an anomaly. Not really. In 2000, the Southern Baptist convention modernized its approach to women in the pulpit. They changed their faith and message statement from this: "Southern Baptists, by practice as well as conviction, believe leadership is male," to the far more inclusive: "While both men and women are gifted for service in the church, the office of pastor is limited to men as qualified by Scripture."*

Not exactly a marketing campaign aimed at baby boomers.

The Gospel according to John (Lennon) told us that "Jesus was all right but his disciples were thick and ordinary." Remember that teenager quoted in *Time* magazine? "I love God, but I

Imagine there's no heaven.
It's easy if you try.
No hell below us.
Above us only sky.

From "Imagine"
By John Lennon

hate the church," she said. It is not very likely that that young lady—probably well into her middlescence by now—is a member in good standing of the First Baptist Church of Watertown, New York.

---

*http://www.wayoflife.org/fbns/southernbaptistconvention.htm.

Leonard Steinhorn suggests that "[boomers] grew up determined to create a more expressive culture than the one they were bequeathed, a culture that would value individualism over traditionalism, spirituality over religiosity.

"They began writing their own wedding vows in the sixties, refusing to say 'man and wife' and weaving in spiritual themes that drew as much from Eastern religion and Native American custom as from the Judeo-Christian tradition.

"Funeral services that were once scripted and structured around religion are increasingly giving way to more eclectic and nontraditional ceremonies that reflect individual character rather than religious ritual. The very fact that boomers are willing to transform and take on even such cherished and time-honored rituals indicates how deeply individuality and personal freedom have taken root in this generation."*

Rev. Carole O'Connell is ordained by the Unity Association of Churches, a small but growing "nondenomination" that is what Mr. Steinhorn would refer to as "New Age." "Unitics," as members of this nondenomination call themselves, call it "New Thought, even though the teachings have been around for several millennia."

According to Rev. O'Connell, "Most people find New Thought churches in their forties and fifties. I would guess that at this moment in time, a large majority of Unity members are boomers. When they first show up, most have left their childhood church many years ago and haven't attended church in many years. They have no connection with theology whatsoever. They went to college in their teens and twenties and were introduced to the fact that there are thousands of other religions out there, many of which claim to be 'the one and only true religion.'

"Boomers are more mobile than any previous generation. They went away to school; they travel in their jobs. Women especially used to be isolated, geographically and intellectually. And the boomers went out into the world and met new people and saw

---

Leonard Steinhorn, The Greater Generation *(New York: St. Martin's, 2006), 159.*

new things, and suddenly the rule 'Methodist born, Methodist died' no longer applied.

"The media has continued to show them all the different people with different beliefs, and they see all the religious wars going on.

"They grew up threatened with hell if they didn't follow the rules. We all know how boomers feel about rules. So they began asking, why can't I respect people who believe differently? How can God send all of the 'other' people to hell, just because they call Him by a different name?' It insulted their intelligence. So they simply retreated into themselves, set spirituality aside, and quit going to church. They settled into life, not struggling to survive, not constantly in crisis, and when they got comfortable, they started asking questions. And by now they have children, and they began looking for a place to take their kids to give them a sense of spiritual understanding, but they still weren't comfortable with the old childhood religion. They were looking for a God of love, and that generally isn't found in traditional religion.

"Many people who come to Unity have already been introduced to yoga and meditation and metaphysics in some form or another, and New Thought is a natural progression from that. Typical of boomers, they want to develop their own belief system, but they still have that need to fill the hole in their soul. So they come to a Unity church or a Science of Mind church, and they are told that God is not some anthropomorphic being 'up there' somewhere. They meet people who are comfortable referring to God not only as 'He,' but also 'She,' or even 'It.' God envisioned as a being, especially as a 'male' being, a father-image being, has control over us and makes decisions for us and we become puppets. And that God judges us and condemns us and tells us we are not worthy—not worthy of joy, not worthy of health, not worthy of prosperity, and baby boomers especially don't want to hear that! They want to hear that God is love, that God loves us all just the way we are—black or white, gay or straight, male or female, Christian, Muslim, or Jew. That's what boomers want to hear."

241

But aren't we supposed to believe in the Bible as the absolute, literal Word of God? Won't we go to hell if we don't? Won't we go to hell if we don't go to church? Isn't that what's expected of us?

Maybe in the old days, Leonard Steinhorn says: "In the 1950s, we were pretty much a society that universally accepted the Bible as the literal word of God. You're *expected* to go to church on Sunday. In fact, it was a social obligation. I think boomers began to break away from that because they saw that religion and spirituality shouldn't be a social obligation. It shouldn't be enforced by some authority telling you what to do. This is a personal relationship that you have with your own spirituality. So, as boomers have done with so many other parts of our culture, we've individualized the religious experience.

"Some people have broken off altogether and not associated themselves with any formal religion. In fact, the media never report this, but the fastest growing religious groups in the United States are those without any religious identity. So, what you have is an extraordinary outburst of religious freedom, of spiritual freedom, and so we may be less devout than years before, but we're equally as spiritual. We just have more freedom to express it in our own ways."

Bishop Chane observes that "young professionals who had been involved in megachurches found rigid interpretation of the Scriptures to be stifling. Stifling in the sense that the world that we know today cannot be justified or interpreted from the theological point of view that would be defined as Biblical literalism. There is now an apparent move toward more open discussion of Biblical interpretation.

"We live in a time of great Biblical illiteracy. People who haven't *studied* the Bible are taking passages from Leviticus and Deuteronomy—Sodom and Gomorrah—and using that story to form an uninformed point of view to define the immorality of homosexuality. But in reality, the story, if one studies it, is about the inability to engage in radical hospitality. . . . One has to remember that the Christian perspective is the revelation of the 'New Covenant'—the moral stripe at the core of Christianity—'Love the Lord your God with all your heart, soul, and mind, and love your neighbor as yourself.' That is the profound moral thread of Christianity."

"To boomers, God was far from dead, but he wasn't always found in a church," Leonard Steinhorn says. "Indeed to many boomers in the sixties and seventies, the church and its rules not only were extraneous but actually obstacles in their spiritual quest."

But according to Dr. Dychtwald, a "spiritual quest" can take many forms: "The war in Vietnam and the turmoil and disillusionment of the sixties and early seventies forced many of us to reexamine our values. If we couldn't trust authorities, whom could we trust? Raised from childhood to think for ourselves and make our own choices, we decided to listen to our own inner voices. 'Know yourself' became the new mantra, self-discovery the goal.

"Many in our generation turned to psychotherapy, meditation, Eastern religions, and encounter groups as a path to self-empowerment. The ability to rely on yourself, to trust your own instincts and judgment, became another distinguishing trait of the generation.

"The most important challenges we will face in our later years may not be material, but psychological and spiritual. Will the last third of our lives be our most satisfying years? Will we discover new purpose? Fulfill long-held dreams? Or will we retreat and retire?"

Good question, Dr. D. Our after-work life quest may be for spiritual enlightenment, but it may also be for nothing more than a nice, feisty eight-pound bass.

Gone Fishin'?

Are we going to "retreat and retire"? Are we going to vanish into "age-restricted," gated communities and never be heard from again?

Do they still build moats?

There are thousands of traditional "adult communities" out there just waiting—deposit slips in hand—for the boomer genera- **243** tion to come knocking on their doors. But will we? Of course not. But the old traditional models are long since gone. That is, the typical "old folks home" of the fifties that horrendously resembled a hospital ward is gone. The industry evolved from that into several different models.

Continuing care is one example. This is a system that allows one to enter as an independent "elder" and, frankly, to leave in a box. It's graduated care. From independent living in a cottage or an apartment, to assisted living, to skilled care, to an Alzheimer's unit, and from there to the Great Beyond. A large fee is paid up front and a monthly fee is then locked in, no matter how much care you need.

Then there are the "resort communities." THW Design claims to have begun the craze in 1990 with the construction of Cypress at Hilton Head. Their communities are little short of age-restricted country-club living. They offer pools, computer labs, tennis, fitness centers, and most, of course, offer golf. They call them "vital life communities." A long way from an "old folks home." But even "vital life communities" have become traditional these days.

There are also hundreds of nontraditional options, some of which are pretty darned exotic. You can purchase an apartment on a cruise liner. Some of these state rooms have a balcony with an ocean view and can run up to three thousand square feet! You can go to sleep in Italy and wake up in Greece!

Some people are house swapping for a year at a time and get to live for a while in a new town or a new *country*. In fact, a few American expatriates have moved to retirement conclaves in Mexico or Costa Rica or Belize where they can often live in semi-luxury for half the price.

But most of us, it seems, have families we still want to be near, and an emotional or even a biological need to nest. We are living the American Dream of home ownership and have no desire to awaken from it.

The questions then become, "where will these homes be? What will they look like, and who will be our neighbors? Do we want to move into a glorified 'old folks home' where everybody around us is just like us—the same age, the same race, the same economic status?"

Lynn Humer, who you will learn more about later, was a rebellious member of the Greatest Generation, and when her family pressured her to move out of her home and into "assisted living" when well into her eighties, she announced to them all, "I don't want to live with a bunch of old people!" That sounds like a very boomer thing to say. In fact, to withdraw into a homogeneous, gated, age-restricted community seems to be an incredibly unboomerish thing to do. It sounds like a retreat to the fifties. But nonetheless, it seems to be where many of us are heading.

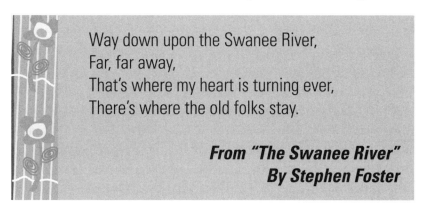

Way down upon the Swanee River,
Far, far away,
That's where my heart is turning ever,
There's where the old folks stay.

From "The Swanee River"
By Stephen Foster

While the Stephen Foster lyrics have been "politically corrected" (translated from the original's genuinely offensive Negro dialect into English), it is nonetheless appropriate that "The Swanee River (Old Folks at Home)" is the official state song of Florida, which for decades has been, in fact, "where the old folks stay." There is little indication that this is something that will change drastically as the boomers search for the perfect preheaven haven.

The Del Webb Company is perhaps the nation's leading developer of adult communities. As of 2006, they had built more than 450,000 homes in sixteen states, with more to come.

In 2005, Del Webb contracted with the Harris Corporation to do an extensive poll of baby boomers regarding our outlook for the future, and (obviously) our vision of what a retirement community might look like. The results of that survey indicate that the "old folks" will continue their migration to sunny climes, with 29 percent of us listing Florida as the "most favored state," and with Arizona finishing a close second with 25 percent. According to the U.S. Census Bureau, in July 2004, 17 percent of Florida's population was sixty-five years old or older.*

It should be noted, however, that Florida is also among the leaders of "*least* favored states," trailing only Alaska (weather and inaccessibility) and California (expense). There are, according to the study, 10 percent of us won't even consider moving to the Sunshine State.

So 54 percent of us are considering the traditional route of selling the house, moving to either Florida or Arizona, and perhaps even hanging out the "gone fishin'" sign. That leaves 46 percent of us who are considering "something different." Forty-six percent of seventy-eight million is 35,880,000. That is equivalent to the entire population of California.†

There will also be no small proportion of boomer men who will be excluded from age-restricted communities because they divorced at forty, took on a second wife twenty years younger at fifty, and had children at fifty-five. When they reach age sixty-five, their wives will be forty-five and their children will be ten.

No age-restricted community for you!

Magazine publisher Cathleen Black makes it her business to understand trends so that the magazines she publishes can focus more specifically on the interests and needs of her subscribers: "A couple of months ago, I read a very interesting piece that talked about all these Northeastern people who had gone to Florida or South Carolina or North Carolina and were, in fact, returning, because they were tired of being in a community with only people just like themselves. They wanted the diversity of a city that they had left. They'd learned that it was far more problematical for

---

*http://library.corporate-ir.net/library/14/147/147717/items/191323/
2005%20Baby%20Boomer%20Survey.pdf.

†U.S. Census report, July 2005.

their kids to come and visit them for their holidays or vacations or whatever, and so they wanted to be closer to their families."

Marc Freedman also studies trends and needs to know where boomers are headed and what real estate choices may be open to them in the future: "I think one of the big issues for society over the next twenty or thirty years is whether boomers are going to give in to a trend to cut ourselves off, to protect ourselves, to play it safe. Whether we're going to retreat to gated communities, where we only encounter people who are like us, or whether we reach beyond ourselves and try to become part of something larger, and try to connect with people who're different than we are in a society that's much more diverse than it's ever been before.

"Many people are out there building bridges. Not only for themselves but for their peers. They're bridging generations, bridging ethnic boundaries, bridging education levels, and I think that they hold the hope of society that makes a lot more sense. But I think if we do end up giving in to the cocooning impulse, well, it might be easier over the short term, but it's a social disaster over the longer term.

"There are a lot of people who are worrying that if the boomers do withdraw and there are no longer strong ties between the generations, and the boomers have unprecedented voting power, that we're going to become a land of gleaming hospitals and decaying schools, which would be tragic. And I think that there's another vision that's equally possible, which is that people's impulse to continue to be productive, to be part of something larger, to have a sense of meaning, will lead them to connect with future generations in ways that will not only allow them to transfer their own knowledge and expertise, but will create a constituency for the future. For posterity."

Regarding "gated communities," the Del Webb/Harris survey says that 59 percent of us do want gates, but 79 percent of us want full-maintenance lawn care.

As for the intergenerational diversity issue, there may be some hope. After all, we've questioned the status quo of every other institution we've ever passed through and changed almost every- 247 thing else we've ever touched. Dr. Dychtwald thinks that change, even monumental change, is not as threatening a prospect for us as it was for our parents: "If you've never encountered change, it's disruptive; it's unnerving; it can make you crazy. On the other hand, if you've done it again and again and had some cool things emerge from it, then, to some extent, you're locked and loaded. You may like it. It can be a turn-on."

Joel Westbrook remembers a lesson learned from his forward-thinking father: "I went with my father to visit his brother in an age-restricted community one time, and as we were leaving my dad asked me, 'Who would want to live anywhere where there aren't any children?'"

Leading-edge boomers all remember the communes of the sixties and the seventies. They were places where like-minded hippies gathered together, lived together, smoked pot together, listened to "In-A-Gadda-Da-Vida" together, and did all sorts of God-only-knows-what together.

That's *not* what we're talking about.

But Dr. Weil has noticed that the word *commune* is sneaking slowly back into our vocabulary: "Maybe we will see a revival of communes as the baby boomers get up into these age ranges, but a new kind of commune. Call them senior *intentional* communities. We don't want to be in what I've heard somebody call 'cattle holding pens.' We'd like to have a say in how we design our living spaces in our communities, and we would like to be with people who we *want* to be with."

In Eve Ensler's opinion, this could be a good thing: "I've always dreamed that we would live in extended communities, you know. My fantasy of being older, to be honest with you, is living with a whole group of women in some wonderful way and with a couple of great men. But just living in an extended community where we have our separate rules, where we get to communicate and exchange ideas and build movements and fantasize about how we're going to keep changing the world."

If the word *commune* is off-putting, let's erase it and start over. How does "intergenerational theme community" sound?

It sounds pretty interesting to Dr. Dychtwald: "The communities of our future will be carefully thought through for the perfect mix of companionship, stimulation, and convenience.

"Why couldn't we build a community and fill it with people that we care about and respect and look after? This intergenerational family may not necessarily be our own kids or grandchildren, because they may live all over the world, but it would be a new family. A family of choice. Conceivably, it could have four generations in it, all coming together on the basis of common interests and needs.

"In the past, as people aged, they often sold their homes and moved into age-segregated retirement communities, which separated them from their extended families and limited their involvement in the larger community. But today, more and more boomers are seeking other options, with the perfect mix of companionship, stimulation, and convenience. Some will be vast complexes set up by developers for hundreds of people with an interest in gardening, fitness, Zen, or the arts. Others will consist of just three or four friends who want to live with people they love being with.

"Sunset Hall in Los Angeles bills itself as 'a home for freethinking elders,' and ElderSpirit is a residence for artists in Manhattan."

Dr. Goleman agrees that who we retire with is going to be yet another choice we are going to make differently from our elders: "What I can see happening is that boomers will be more conscious about forming caring social networks, particularly as we become older and older and approach death. And I think that it's a very, very positive thing to do. We're going to break out of the old traditional models, and we'll create families of choice, people that we want to be with, we feel good being with, we care about, and we'll start taking care of each other at every level."

"We're going to be combining families, and families are going to be having many different faces," says the trend guru Faith Popcorn. "There might be a family of friends. There might be a family of like-types—we call these PLUs, people like us. It's called *ego*-nomics. People like us are clanning." **249**

Perhaps the most exciting example of "people like us" clanning is a trend that beckons us back to our youth, to our glory days, to the very place where many of us burned our draft cards or our bras or the ROTC building, locked ourselves in the president's office, and met and married our very first spouse. My, how we long for those good old days. My, how our hearts yearn for a return to those joyful days and the ivy-covered walls of our beloved alma maters.

Several major universities have constructed or become affiliated with retirement communities on, adjacent to, or within walking distance from their campuses, where alumni can return to recapture that spark of youth and to be a part, once again, of "the college life," in that most unique and almost oxymoronic of all environs, where intellectual stimulation meets small-town charm. We can don again the blue and white at Penn State or the azure and maize at Ann Arbor and cheer on a new generation of "Conqu'ring Heroes." We can patronize the off-campus coffee shops and hobnob with respected professors and exuberant students. We can audit classes (some of which are designed just for us) or attend poetry readings or plays or concerts or maybe even meet and marry our third and final spouse.

Go Blue!

For those for whom a small college town is not appealing, there are always the gigantic urban areas, many of which are making an attempt to reacquire a middle-class tax base lost to decades of "white flight."

Dr. Dychtwald sees the advantages of boomers moving back "downtown": "Our cities boast vast tracts of defunct industrial complexes, boarded-up storefronts, and underutilized residential neighborhoods. Homebuilders have in recent years begun to pick up the pace and are reclaiming urban tracts and turning them into desirable neighborhoods for empty nesters looking for some city action. Why not move to the city? The mass transit means we won't have to drive. Theaters, restaurants, museums, lectures, exhibits, and new friends are only blocks away."

Atlanta is one of those cities, and a concerted effort is being made to lure boomers into it. Like so many other major U.S. cities,

Atlanta has had a dual population for decades—a lot of very poor and a few very rich. This makes for a horrendously unbalanced tax base. Middle-income residents are at a premium, and Atlanta is trying to entice them downtown.

With the support and encouragement of Mayor Shirley Franklin, the Atlanta Development Authority (ADA) has what they call "housing allocation districts," and if you want to build there they will arrange tax-increment financing through bond monies or loans from the Urban Residential Finance Authority.

"The Reynolds on Peachtree," "Park View at Coventry Station," and "Atlantic Station" are some of Atlanta's up-and-running urban residential projects. While you can spend a fortune for some of these units, in order to qualify for government incentives, 20 percent of the units must be "affordable."

Sonya Moste is the director of marketing for the ADA and says that "a wide range of incomes helps to create a vibrant community." Win-win? "Sell your big ol' house in the 'burbs," she says, "and move downtown. You can sell one of your cars too, since you can walk to the grocery store."

Whether we live in a commune, on a cruise ship, near a college campus, or in any of the more traditional types of retirement communities, we all have to go home at night. After a day at work or volunteering or playing golf for that matter, those of us who are fortunate enough still to have a spouse, a soulmate, or a partner to come home to are eventually going to turn off the lights and go to bed.

So what then? Can we still . . . "do it"?

Will You Still Be Sending Me a Valentine?

Yes, we can. A journey that began with cannabis had led us to Cialis. So yes, by golly, we still can.

According to *Medical News Today,* erectile dysfunction (don't worry, it happens to everybody) affects an estimated 152 million men and their partners worldwide. The three leading ED drugs rang cash registers to the tune of $2.5 billion in global sales in 2004. The makers 251 of Viagra alone spent more than $400 million to advertise their product on television, at baseball parks, and on the hoods of race cars. The people who market these products have selected the most virile looking and athletic spokesmen the advertising world has to offer.

Do you remember Shelly Lazarus's marketing maxim from a previous chapter? "You don't necessarily have to *show* the people in the advertising who you are targeting—but you *do* have to figure out what's important to those people, what they are thinking about, what their issues are."

While the Viagra campaign may be an example of that, it is not illogical to consider the possibility that these particular pharmaceuticals may be being used by persons whose claims of impotency have been significantly exaggerated. But it is safe to assume that the marketers of these particular products have been able to figure out, probably with very little research, "what's important to those people, *what they are thinking about*," and "what their issues are."

For the aging boomer generation, lack of intimacy, for whatever reason, is soon to become a significant issue if it hasn't already, and for those who suffer from it, it is not a laughing matter.

"Our later years can also be a time to rekindle old relationships and forge new ones," Dr. Dychtwald observes. "During our hectic working and parenting years, we often lacked the time to devote to nurturing relationships—even to those closest to us. Old age presents new opportunities to reconnect with those we love.

"Old age also inevitably involves loss—loss of close friends, loss of loved ones. In the past, if you lost a spouse after sixty, little thought was given to finding a new soul mate. But with longer lifetimes, that might leave thirty more years for you to live alone. Today more and more men and women are finding new love and sex after sixty."

Dr. Steven Nock of the University of Virginia's Marriage Matters project agrees: "There's no reason to think that sex will recede in importance in the minds of the baby boomers. It will probably recede in the bodies of the baby boomers, as it does in all older people, but sex will remain an essential part of their sense of self. And I think that we will begin to see additional efforts to prolong sexual activity among older adults. It began with the erectile dysfunction drugs and products such as Viagra and so on, and I think that we will soon see comparable products for women, postmenopausal women, and more and more research and effort and money being put into the preservation of sexual activity. It is, after all, for the baby boom, what defines a big part of their relationships."

Sorry, Gen X. Sorry, Gen Y. Try not to "go visual" on this, but Grandma and Grandpa are going to keep "doing it" for as long as God and science allow.

Nonetheless, there will come a time, we all suspect, when middlescence will end and old age will begin. Most sociologists differentiate between "young-old" and "old-old," but that's yet another nebulous line we are all (we hope) destined to cross.

In *The Virtues of Aging*, Jimmy Carter recalled when he and Rosalynn found that line not to be all that vague: "Still feeling young and vigorous in our fifties and sixties [after leaving the White House], we didn't think much about facing another transition in our lives.

"But as we entered our seventies and eighties, there was another potential threat to our happiness: the forced realization that both of us fit almost any definition of 'old age.' I guess it is unpleasant for any of us to face our inevitable gray or thinning hair and the tendency for our waistline to spread, especially when advancing years correspond to a reduced income. This brings a challenging but inevitable transition in our lives—from what we have been to a new type of existence as 'senior citizens.'"*

In fact, there may be a specific moment in time, an instant at which each of us will be told, in no uncertain terms, that we are now officially "old." We will probably be told this by someone we love and who loves and cares for us deeply—or a judge.

Anyone who has ever had to take the car keys away from an "old-old" parent knows that it can be perceived as retribution for being old, and that the punishment for that crime is "cruel and unusual." It is roughly the equivalent of "life in prison."

*Jimmy Carter, The Virtues of Aging (New York: Ballantine, 1998), 8.

"Our communities or cities are automobile cultures," AARP CEO Bill Novelli points out. "So you can't walk to church; you can't walk to the drug store; and you can't walk to the doctor. And when people can no longer drive, what happens is social isolation sets in."

"The baby boom generation is a suburban generation," Dr. Nock adds. "They grew up in the suburbs; they now live in the suburbs. They are an automobile-oriented generation. They depend upon their vehicles to get everywhere. They no longer build sidewalks in new suburban developments. People no longer walk. This is a generation that depends more upon automobiles than anyone before. And this is a huge generation that will no longer be able to drive in ten or fifteen years. So for me, the question about how the baby boomers will age has a lot to do with transportation and mobility. I think that the values and beliefs of the baby boom will remain intact, because most generations do hold on to their basic core beliefs as they age. But the lifestyle that the baby boomers have become accustomed to, especially the free and easy mobility of commuting from the suburbs into the city and back and forth, is going to be a real challenge as people move from the young-old to the old-old and approach frailty, where they are no longer so able to drive.

"And when they can no longer drive and when they can no longer get around, the question is, *where* will they age? Not so much *how* will they age?

"How we'll deal with that, I think, is a great question, and I don't think there's really much attention given to it. So, on the one hand, the baby boomers may be imagining that they will remain young longer, and I think they will. I think young-old baby boomers won't become old-old until their mid- to late seventies, unlike their parents who were in their mid- to late sixties. So probably add a decade before the baby boomers start thinking of themselves as old, but it will happen."

Which, of course, brings us to the second great question posed to us by the Fab Four metaphysicians.

chapter 11

Will You Still Feed Me?

MILES MONROE: I don't know what the hell I'm doing here. I'm 237 years old. I should be collecting Social Security.

From **Sleeper**
Screenplay by
Woody Allen and
Marshall Brickman

T here is no issue higher on the agenda for seventy-eight million baby boomers than that of retirement lifestyles. Will our savings be enough? Will Social Security and Medicare be adequate? Will our children grow to resent us because of the personal and public financial burdens we will place on them?

Short answers? No, maybe, no, and probably not.

These may be the most diverse, complex, and important issues that the boomer generation has ever faced. If the social safety nets fail to hold up under the strain of retiring boomers in a global economy, it might well be disastrous for the United States.

Working without a Net?

Dr. Dychtwald is something less than optimistic: "Neither Social Security nor Medicare was designed to match the size and extended longevity of the baby boomer generation. When Roosevelt instituted the Social Security program, there were forty workers paying taxes for each retiree. That number has steadily shrunk.

"When the U.S. government cut the first Social Security check to Ida May Fuller back in the Depression era, no one knew what a great deal it would turn out to be for her generation. She had paid a total of just $24.75 in Social Security taxes in her working years.

She lived to be a hundred and collected a total of $22,889 in lifetime benefits. No one complained that Fuller was getting almost a thousand times more than she paid. In her day, there were almost forty-two workers for each Social Security beneficiary. The payments weren't a problem.

"By 2040, it is projected that there will only be two workers, and perhaps as few as 1.6, to support each boomer retiree, who could be living as many as thirty to forty years in retirement."

Ida May Fuller (Social Security Number 1) paid $24.75 in Social Security taxes, lived to be a hundred, and collected $22,889 in lifetime benefits. Congressman Tom Price suggests that today's retiree will be lucky to see a 2 percent return on his Social Security "investment."

Sounds dire. What we need here is a primer on all aspects of the economics of aging from a Harvard-educated PhD in economics with experience at the highest levels of government. Of course, we just happen to have one—Dr. D. Quinn Mills: "The Social Security System narrowly looked at its ability to provide the promised benefits to baby boomers as they retire, and it's not in bad shape. It has a problem to deal with, which is that in another decade or so it's going to be flooded with people, and it's going to have to get the money to pay. It's basically a 'pay as you go' system. We tax people now and turn that money over to retirees. Probably we can continue to do that.

"There are two other problems. One is the collapse of the private pension system. Companies are backing out of providing pension benefits and health care benefits for retirees as rapidly as they can. The government, by law, is trying to force many of them to keep paying these costs, but, in a highly competitive environment both nationally and internationally, many of those companies required to continue the payments are just collapsing. They're going bankrupt, and they're going out of business. As for the matter of the self-managed 401(k) plans, et cetera, basically Wall Street has walked away with a huge amount of that money. The people don't manage them well. . . . So we have a very serious problem. Social Security as it's currently defined is not in bad shape, but it's going to be handed a huge problem unless baby boomers keep working at some kind of jobs and have an income stream.

"Then you add to that where the huge problem is in the federal budget, and that's in Medicare, Medicaid, in the health insurance area, which is a problem that's simply a time bomb that can undo the tax and financial system."

"At one time, the pay-as-you-go system made sense," says Dr. Dychtwald. "The government used the tax receipts of current workers to fund the benefits of current retirees. In fact, at the time they actually worried that the system would be overwhelmed with resources that could never be fully used. In 1937, Senator Arthur Vandenberg said, 'The reserves that finance the system could eventually be so big that they will inundate the federal government.'

"But in the years ahead, there will be too many retirees living far too long for the system to remain solvent."

On March 15, 2005, Alan Greenspan, then chairman of the Federal Reserve, appeared before the U.S. Senate Special Committee on Aging and addressed the issue of the solvency of our safety net. He testified at that time that "in 2008, the leading edge of what must surely be the largest shift from retirement in our nation's history will become evident as some baby boomers become eligible for Social Security. This huge change in the structure of our population will expose all our financial retirement systems to severe stress and will require adjustments for which there are no historical precedents.

"At present, the Social Security trustees estimate that the unfunded liability over the indefinite future to be $10.4 trillion. The shortfall in Medicare is calculated at several multiples of the one in Social Security.

"These numbers suggest that either very large tax increases will be required to meet the shortfalls, or benefits will have to be pared back. [The federal budget] is on an unsustainable path, in which large deficits result in rising interest rates and ever-growing interest payments that augment deficits in future years.

"Unless the trend is reversed, at some point these deficits would cause the economy to stagnate, or worse."

On August 17, 2006, President Bush signed the Pension Protection Act of 2006. Its stated purpose was to increase stability of pensions, close loopholes in existing laws, and to at least make it more difficult for companies to default on pension payments in hard times.

Corporate-sponsored pension plans have been vanishing at an astonishing rate over the past twenty-five years. In that time frame, eighty-two thousand such plans have ceased to exist, and the remaining thirty thousand are underfunded to the tune of almost a half *trillion* dollars. These systems might have survived intact were it not for the fact that boomers have decided to live decades longer than our parents did.

Dr. Dychtwald tells us that it is the failure of the system to anticipate these longer life spans that has sent them into default: "Employers never expected former employees to live into their eighties and nineties. For that and other reasons they failed to set aside enough money to keep their pension plans viable. . . . Failing pension plans are now overwhelming the Pension Guaranty

The Pension Protection Act of 2006 will help shore up our pension insurance system in several key ways. It requires companies who underfund their pension plans to pay additional premiums. It extends the requirement that companies that terminate their pensions must provide extra funding for the system. This legislation insists that companies measure their obligations of their pension plans more accurately. It closes loopholes that allow underfunded plans to skip pension payments. It raises caps on the amount that employers can put into their pension plans so they can add more money during good times and build up a cushion that can keep pensions solvent in lean times.

Finally, this legislation prevents companies with underfunded pension plans from digging the hole deeper by promising extra benefits to their workers without paying for those promises up front.

President George W. Bush
On Signing the Pension Protection Act of 2006

Corporation which insures pensions up to a point and has been technically insolvent for years."*

Of course, Democrats see the legislation as the death knell of the already comatose traditional pension plans, as it pushes companies toward the more Republican concept of "individual ownership and individual responsibility." That is, 401(k)s.

While this is a significant piece of legislation, it was an aside at the end of President Bush's speech that put the future of our entire

---

*Ken Dychtwald and Daniel J. Kadlec, The Power Years (New York: Wiley, 2005), 88.

generation into a very sobering perspective: "To ensure more secure retirement for all Americans, we've got more work to do. We must also prepare for the impact of the baby boomer generation's retirement, and what that impact will have on federal entitlement programs like Social Security and Medicare. As more baby boomers stop contributing payroll taxes and start collecting benefits—people like me—it will create an enormous strain on our programs. Entitlement programs are projected to grow faster than the economy, faster than the population, and faster than the rate of inflation. If we fail to act, spending on Social Security and Medicare and Medicaid will be almost 60 percent of the entire federal budget in the year 2030. And that's going to leave future generations with impossible choices: staggering tax increases, immense deficits, or deep cuts in benefits."

The more pessimistic among us might edit the president's comments to read, "staggering tax increases, immense deficits, *and* deep cuts in benefits." Congressman Tom Price, a member of the president's own party, suggests that Bush's numbers may even be optimistic: "By 2030, if you add Social Security, Medicare, and Medicaid together, it will be *one hundred percent* of the Federal Budget. That means no military, no roads, no transportation, no NASA, no FAA, no education, no labor. . . . All the good things that we count on the federal government to do—all gone."

These are issues that have been hanging over our heads for decades, but the politicians have failed to respond in any significant way. They failed to anticipate us entering elementary school, they failed to anticipate us entering college, and now, even though they have anticipated our passage into retirement for half a century, they continue to bury their heads in the sand and hope the problem will simply go away. Nobody wants to touch that high voltage middle rail of American politics.

This doesn't mean that they are bad people. It simply means that our leaders are trapped in a system that actually discourages leadership. There are 435 congressmen who must face the voters every two years. Therefore, each and every one of them spends approximately half of his or her time in office campaigning for reelection, which means they devote their lives to not ticking anybody off. A vote that would make the rest of us retire later will result in their own retirement coming sooner. This means that short-term thinking was built into the system by our Founding Fathers, and nothing short of a constitutional amendment will change it.

"It'll get done when the crisis comes," says Congressman Price. "Of course it would be much easier to fix now, all of these issues would, but until it reaches crisis proportions all we will get is demagoguery from both sides. Will it even get done then? Sure it'll get done. Our system works in confounding ways, but it works. It will be a huge challenge, but we can think creatively. The ingenuity of Americans can be astounding. There's an answer out there that hasn't even been put on the table yet, but we're capable of outside-of-the-box thinking when push comes to shove."

Regardless of the politicians' reluctance to address them, the solvency of Social Security, Medicare, and Medicaid are very complex and important issues, so it seems that we may require something more than only a primer. You may recall that in previous chapters we have turned the floor over to a member of our panel with particularly impressive credentials in order to allow for an in-depth analysis in his or her particular field.

> President Bush has started to make plans for what he's going to do after he leaves the White House. He'd better hurry up because under his plan he sure won't be able to live on Social Security.
>
> *Jay Leno*

Dr. Fernando Torres-Gil earned a PhD in social policy, planning, and research and is the associate dean of academic affairs at UCLA, where he also serves as professor of social welfare and public policy. He is the director of the Center for Policy Research on Aging. Professor Torres-Gil is an expert in the fields of health and long-term care and in the politics of aging, social policy, ethnicity, and disability. He is the author of four books and more than eighty articles in his field.

The Future of Public Old-Age Entitlement Programs
Dr. Fernando Torres-Gil

"Let me present some potential scenarios over the next twenty to thirty years about where baby boomers as a generation might go vis-à-vis their needs in old age and the role of government and the private sector.

"One scenario we will see within that generation as they get older is what we see now in the population at large—a growing gap between the haves and the have-nots. . . . So in the old age of baby boomers, there will be many of us that will have our condos in Newport Beach with our Bayliners and our convertibles, and multiple sources of income and good health care coverage, and we will be doing very well, thank you. But that scenario will also have many baby boomers, maybe a quarter, maybe even up to a third, that will be dependent—minimal income, no depth, no guaranteed pension, no retirement health care coverage, and dependent on whatever public programs might be in existence. These boomers do not have a college degree. They do not own their home. They do not have a pension or retirement plan of any consequential sum of money that will give them an affordable lifestyle when they get older. And then you have that group in the middle that is just living day to day. . . .

"That's one scenario, and it's not a pretty scenario. But that's the direction we're going.

"Another scenario may see the following: We may see government stepping back in, restoring the solvency of Medicare, Medicaid, Social Security, maybe even expanding that coverage. Maybe we'll see retirement plans come back into vogue; maybe employers will take greater responsibility for providing long-term care and health care. And maybe the baby boomers will work longer, stay in the workforce longer, and have an additional source of income. If that happens, then we may not have as many baby boomers that are vulnerable or at risk.

"We're at a crossroads in American public life and what we call 'the politics of aging,' where we don't yet know whether it'll be a negative scenario, with many at-risk baby boomers, or whether we'll have a more positive scenario where baby boomers and government are recognizing that we had better invest in this population or else they'll be totally dependent on others in their old age. We're at that crossroads. . . .

"Right now, if I were to bet, I would not be too hopeful. [Dominant conservative politics] at the national and the local and the state levels are buying into what we call 'individual responsibility' or the 'opportunity society,' where individuals are expected to depend on themselves as they grow older, and there you have the health care accounts; you have 401(k)s, you have the proposal to privatize Social Security. Now there are proposals to privatize the Medicare program. So at least in terms of political trends, it's all about reducing the role of government and leaving it to individuals to take care of themselves in old age. Not unlike, by the way, the 1920s and the 1930s.

"What is different is that many baby boomers are buying into that. In fact, they don't trust government. They don't believe that government can do good things and can do it efficiently. So many baby boomers are opting to say, 'I'll take care of myself. I'll take care of my family.' . . . So what we're seeing right now is a great gamble by many baby boomers in their fifties moving into their sixties that they can somehow accrue the resources to live a good life as they live longer.

"But the other thing that kind of complicates baby boomers' expectations is they actually expect to continue a quality of life in retirement that they're having right now in the workforce. They're actually expecting that they can continue spending the same amounts, have the same kind of housing and transportation, and the same kind of good life. They actually think they're entitled to continue that lifestyle well into retirement. No generation up to this point of time had been able to maintain a retirement lifestyle similar to a working lifestyle. So baby boomers may be in for some interesting surprises. We shall see!"

Of course Professor Torres-Gil represents one side of the political spectrum. Congressman Tom Price represents the other: "Two workers to support every retiree . . . it's an unsustainable system. President Bush's plan to allow people to invest their own money in their own retirement plans was defeated by sound bites. The Democrats could say, 'They're trying to kill Social Security,' and it makes every newscast. It takes ninety seconds to two minutes to explain why that's not true. You can't explain it in a seven-second sound bite.

"In truth, you pay into Social Security all of your life and realize a 2 percent annualized rate of return. If you were dealing with a stock broker, you wouldn't tolerate a 2 percent return over a long period of time. Why should we tolerate it with the government?"

And so between solvency and bankruptcy lies a political divide that may seem insurmountable, but Tony Snow agrees with Congressman Price that eventually these complex issues will all get fixed: "Democrats tend to mistrust government when Republicans are in charge, and Republicans tend to mistrust government when Democrats are in charge.

"We all know that we're going to have to deal with issues like Medicare, Medicaid, and Social Security. We sort of put it off for a little while, but it's out there, and when people feel sufficient political pressure, they'll figure out a way to solve it as well.

"There's always a tendency for people to say, 'Okay, I'm going to insist on getting mine.' Well, we pretty much *have* gotten ours. And I'll just rely on my own sentiments as a parent. I don't want my kids to be lugging around my bills for the rest of their lives. I want my kids to be able to stand free and enjoy themselves. I think a lot of parents feel the same way. I also think that what's happened with a lot of baby boomers is even though there may be a lot of clamor for this government program or that government program, we've all prepared as if the programs aren't going to be there. Social Security? How many people do you know who have set aside their own investment programs? And this isn't just rich folks; this is everybody. They figured out, 'You know what? I'd better be covered just in case that's not there.' When it comes to health care, you go out and get the Medigap Plans. They've already figured out what happens if government isn't there to provide for them. The answer is, 'I'd better provide for myself.' A lot of people have already taken that move."

David Gergen has served as an adviser to four presidents—three Republicans and one Democrat. This being the only empirical evidence we have, it might be assumed that Mr. Gergen is three-quarters Republican, but he does not share Mr. Snow's optimism that "when people feel sufficient political pressure, they'll figure out a way to solve it": "We're not getting ready, and to me that is an indictment of our political leadership. The big challenge to me is, can the baby boom generation essentially pull itself together in a way that it has not since the sixties and really face up to the big realities of our time and protect the future of the country, protect our kids and grandkids? Because if we don't do that, I can tell you America is heading for trouble—serious trouble—and we're going to be in a world in which we're going to find ourselves no longer preeminent. Indeed, we're going to be in a world, if we're not careful, in which the standards of living are going to be going down, and we're going to create tensions among the investor class and everybody else, because investors are still going to make money in this new world. You can go invest in China and India and make money, but you can't get a job in China and India if you're here as an average American citizen, and a lot of people living here are going to get left behind if we're not careful."

"A lot of people"? *Gulp*. What exactly is "a lot" of people?

"If you have everybody spending everything then you've got a very stimulated economy, and people think things are going great," Dr. Dychtwald believes. "That's fine in the here and now, but payday comes; payback is waiting. And so a third of the boomers right now have less than a thousand dollars in their total net lifetime assets. A third!"

Economist Dr. Lester Thurow doesn't paint a cheerier picture: "If you look at the baby boomer generation, I think it's an 80/20 split. Twenty percent will have the assets to retire nicely; 80 percent will scramble. . . . So there will be a tremendous pressure on government to do something about their benefits. Remember, the average person gets most of their money from Social Security. They don't get it from the money they save."

Okay, so 80/20, huh? Eighty percent of seventy-eight million is . . . *Holy welfare dole, Batman!* Sixty-two point four million of us will have to "scramble"? But what about my investments? What about my 401(k)? What about the value of my house?

It might be helpful at this point to hear from an expert in financial planning, a columnist for *Kiplinger's Personal Finance* magazine and a regular contributor to the *Wall Street Journal, Barron's,* and the *Financial Times,* Wall Street guru Jeremy Siegel: "I think a lot of boomers have underestimated how much money they're actually going to need going forward through their life, especially with Social Security and Medicare under threat. They've been forecasting too optimistic a future for returns, and they're going to find themselves running out of money, because we're living longer all the time. But, if returns aren't going to be any greater in the next twenty years than they were the last twenty years—and they very well might be less—most likely they're going to find themselves either telling the government, 'Hey, I don't have enough money myself; I need your services,' or they're going to have to cut back to a lifestyle that's much below what they had hoped to achieve.

"What we worry about is a big fraction of those who have not planned for the future who say, 'Oh, my parents did well; house prices kept on going up; stock prices have kept on going up; something good is going to happen to me. It's going to happen. I don't have to worry about that.' And the truth of the matter is, the returns from real estate and the stock market in the next twenty years are not going to be as good as they were for the past twenty years.

"I think we have to take a much broader view and say, 'Hey, you know what, we promised ourselves too many benefits. And if we would have understood the population trends and the fact that there's not enough people coming up, we would have seen that we can't pay for all of them.' So it's something that I think all the generations have to come together about. We have some benefits; we can pay. All right. We're not going to stick you guys, you younger people, with the bill to pay for our retirement going forward, because that could lead to a generational war."

So Does This Mean War?

What did he say? *"Generational war"?* Hopefully Mr. Siegel has sprinkled his rhetoric with a touch of hyperbole, but the point is well taken. First of all, rightly or wrongly, it has been widely reported that Generation Xers don't expect to see a dime from Social Security when their time rolls around, or at least that they are taking the cautious route and not counting on it.

But that is not the immediate issue. The most immediate issue is, how do we, as a society, pay for the retirement security and medical needs of this gigantic cohort of boomers? When all is said and done, there is only so much that the government, the insurance companies, and all the doctors and nurses in the world can do. Ultimately, the responsibility for the care of aging parents will fall on the shoulders of our children.

Sociologist Dr. Steven Nock contends that financially, emotionally, and in every other way, it is our sons and daughters who will feel both the pain and the rewards of caring for a loved one in need: "The functions of the family have always been the same, and that is to care for dependent individuals. No government has ever managed to pull that off. We've never yet had a society on this earth that can depend upon the government to care for the ill and the aging and the old. It has always been what families do, regardless of the form of the family. . . . We derive our meaning as individuals from caring for one another."

In researching his book *Social Intelligence,* Dr. Daniel Goleman has come to believe that familial bonds may be more than only cultural or social institutions. The urge to care for those we love may well be hardwired into our brains: "I discovered something that I think will be very significant for the new social forms that are going to emerge among the boomers in later life. That is the fact of what's called the 'social brain.' It's a newly discovered circuitry, which means we're all connected brain to brain, physiology to physiology, and these connections are strongest among the people that we love the most. That means that some other person can actually help my physiology recover from stress, and it's done with neurons that are like a neural Wi-Fi that connects brains unconsciously, automatically, and very powerfully—especially the emotional centers. This means that in later life, as we become more fragile biologically, friendships and caring relationships are going to matter more and more."

Yes, human beings have cared for one another within a family or tribal structure for thousands of years, but even that dynamic is changing drastically because one generation is having children later in life and their parents are living longer. This makes us boomers what is called a "sandwich generation," caring for parents and children at the same time. It will be a dilemma, Dr. Nock says, that will only be worse for the Gen Xers: "More and more people live into their late seventies and eighties now, so that while it was true that our grandparents' generation expected to care for one another, there were a lot fewer people to care for and for a lot shorter time. What's happening now is that the baby boom and their children are both postponing childbearing into their late twenties and thirties, and at the same time, their parents are living into their late seventies and eighties. So the combination of delayed childbearing and prolonged life of the other generation means this period of simultaneously caring for younger and older people has been extended greatly."

But there is only so much families can do as well. What if medical science is able to extend our lives for fifteen or twenty years more? What then will we do with a large population of long-lived elders who struggle with chronic health problems—heart disease, cancer, arthritis, diabetes, osteoporosis, and Alzheimer's—illnesses that our medical system is ill prepared to treat or prevent?

What if we, as a nation, are forced to raise the Social Security taxes and the Gen Xers will have to pay to an exorbitant percentage? What if our kids as taxpayers have to assume the financial responsibility of warehousing the mindless bodies of fifteen million Alzheimer's sufferers, their own mothers and fathers, for fifteen or twenty years each? Hyperbole or no, some experts tell us that it could result in a sociological disaster.

In the coming years, the me generation may raise its ugly head again and do what we've done for decades—demand the very best for ourselves. For thirty years we have notoriously strived to drive the best cars, live in the best houses, and own the best technology, and as we move from "young-old" to "old-old," there is no reason to believe that we will not demand the best services, the most comfortable retirement, and the finest health care that the miracles of modern science can possibly provide.

In the near future, for the first time, the issues that will dominate the political spectrum will be (as they should be) "all about us." These issues will no longer be about vague or nuanced political ideologies. They will be life or death issues that will impact all of us who are not the very rich. Consequently, we may at last unite politically into the single most powerful voting bloc in the history of democracy, and we may use that unprecedented power to get everything we want. At last, we may have found something we can all agree on, but it may cost our children dearly, creating tensions (a new kind of generation gap, if you will), as Gen Xers have to pick up the tab for our "entitlements."

Economist Dr. Lester Thurow believes that this potential intergenerational conflict may be significant: "The tension is very simple. It has to do with pensions, and it has to do with health care. The health care especially, because pensions were at least partially funded. But who's going to pay for the health care? The young people can't pay for the health care because there are fewer of them than the old people. So the whole question of how do we pay for health care becomes an important question. After a while, you can't get blood out of the turnip."

Professor Torres-Gil understands how government policy in one issue can overlap with many others. A solution to the entitlements problem may not come out of the Social Security Adminis-tration or Medicare, but from those in our government who deal with education and immigration: "There is a racial ethnic compo-nent to this generational relationship. When we look at the future workforce, they will be heavily immigrant, minority, and female. So we must also ask ourselves, are we investing in both generation X and Y, and are we investing in today's young immigrants, young minority populations, and women in those cohorts? Because they will be supporting baby boomers in our retirement."

Nonetheless, David Gergen fears that the old me generation attitudes may continue ad infinitum: "The baby boom generation got spoiled early and became self-indulgent early, and it was all about 'me.' And we've now brought that into our politics, and we're never going to grow up."

That seems a bit harsh. Regardless of the me generation thing, there's little doubt that we care for our children, and even the most narcissistic among us isn't going to stand for impoverishing our progeny so that we can play golf three times a week. Or will we?

Dr. Mills shares Gergen's concern: "I think that there is a seri-ous risk that baby boomers in the political environment in the next two decades, three decades, will vote their own interest, not the broader social concerns, and therefore do a good bit of damage to the younger generations. And I think the younger generations are very concerned about that. They don't articulate it quite that way, but they perceive the danger and the difficulty. I think that the society is increasingly separated. People, when they get older, they move to the Sunbelt; they move away from their extended families. We lose touch, and in areas where we're all gathered together, we reinforce our fears and we act more as a voting bloc. The sociological studies of that are very clear that that is a phenomenon of human activity.

"So, I think there is a real danger there. The politicians of course will pander to that as they do to other things, and as a result I think that that could be a very serious problem for the country."

Dr. Dychtwald explains: "Younger generations, growing percent-ages of whom will be nonwhite, will have grown up in a different world than most of today's elders or the boomers. It's not likely that they will quietly agree to pay for millions of boomers' green fees, middle-class lifestyles, and medical expenses.

"The result: younger Americans could rebel, and the newly elder boomers will become the target of their frustrations."*

Whoa! Maybe there wasn't any hyperbole after all!

Dr. Dychtwald recommends a multifaceted approach that could "turn a potential social disaster into a new era of intergenerational cooperation." Among other things, he recommends that boomers not "retreat and retire," as our fathers did. Our kids are not going to like paying for us to migrate into gated, youth-prohibited fortresses to play golf and watch TV, where we will get our vision of "them" from the media, which, of course, will show us only the most violent, imbecilic, and degenerate. He points out that there are more than twenty million "at-risk" young people who could use our guidance and wisdom. He recommends the establishment of an "Elder Corps" to facilitate bringing elders and young people together, so we can get out and mentor those young people and, maybe more important, get to know each other.

We all remember the generation gap of the sixties, and, while Dr. Dychtwald seems to believe that we may be hell-bent for another, Leonard Steinhorn, author of *The Greater Generation: In Defense of the Baby Boom Legacy*, thinks probably not: "The funny thing about the baby boom era is that there really isn't a generation gap any more. And it's largely because those boomer values of openness and transparency and being able to appreciate the diversity of life are so consistent with what young people feel today. In fact, some researchers have found that in the history of polling, they've never seen closer generations between, let's say, parents and kids. They've never seen it closer than they are today. I think, to a great extent, that's because the boomer world view not only is youthful because it's open, but it also accepts the ideals of equality and freedom that mean so much to every young person. So today, for example, you see greater interracial dating and interracial friendships among

*Ken Dychtwald, Age Power (Putnam, NY: Jeremy P. Tarcher, 1999), 215.

young people, or interethnic or interfaith. The interesting thing about it is that if you wanted to do it years ago, across the board, the parent would say, 'No, that's not good, that's not healthy, I don't accept it.' But when they ask kids who are dating interracially, in one survey, 90 percent of them said their parents didn't have a problem with it. That's a fundamental shift in world views that we've seen, and that's why the generation gap really doesn't exist, and that's why today's young people are really boomers without the sixties. They share the same values, the same norms, the same attitudes that arose out of the great baby boom era."

Time for another brief recap. Depending on whom you believe, our children may or may not turn against us. We're going to have to keep working through our seventies and maybe even into our eighties. Social Security, even if solvent, won't be adequate to support anywhere near the lifestyle to which we had hoped to become accustomed. In fact, in order to avoid bankrupting America, we may be asked to give some of our paltry benefits back. Remember, according to our president, we are facing "staggering tax increases, immense deficits, or deep cuts in benefits."

There's a "buzz killer" for you!

chapter 12

At Least You've Got Your Health

D r. Ken Dychtwald offers us a brief history of life: "If you had been alive in the year 1000, the last time we entered a new millennium, you could expect to live to the ripe old age of twenty-five. That was the life expectancy a thousand years ago. And that's up from eighteen a thousand years before that. Life was indeed 'short and brutish.'

"Throughout 99 percent of human history, people have died young. Although a few lived to fifty or sixty or even eighty, infectious diseases, accidents, and violence brought life to an early end for almost everyone else.

"In the last century, life expectancy rose more than any period before. Improvements in public health, sanitation, medicine, and nutrition have added about one hundred days of longevity for each year that passed—approximately two days per week. Boomers who turn sixty this year have an actuarial life expectancy of 82.3 years. And that's without anticipating any major medical advances in the next twenty-five to fifty years. Our generation will live longer than any previous generation in America."

At last, some good news! Cool!

When President Franklin Roosevelt proposed the "pay-as-you-go" Social Security system during the Great Depression, there were more than forty workers paying in for every retiree taking out. Today we can foresee a time when the worker-to-retiree ratio will be 2:1 or worse.

Bill Novelli of AARP has kudos for boomers for their attitudes toward healthy aging: "The way we think about it is people are growing older right now—men and women. And what's happening is, as people live longer, they're going to live in better health. There'll be fewer people going into nursing homes; there'll be more people living longer independently. Part of this will be the result of good health care and new technologies coming along. But part of it will be personal responsibility—people taking responsibility for their own health and their own independent living. So the future can be very rosy, and I think that boomers have a lot to look forward to in the coming periods of their lives."

Sixty-five was established as the marker for retirement more than a century ago by Chancellor Otto von Bismarck. When he was preparing his country's first pension plan, the average life expectancy in Germany was forty-five. Using that same formula today (average life expectancy plus twenty years), Americans would be able to apply for Social Security somewhere between the ages of ninety-five and one hundred.

Social Security can be saved, and we are going to live longer and healthier than any other generation in the history of the world! We *rock!* Don't we?

Economist Dr. Lester Thurow thinks maybe yes, maybe not so much: "Social Security is in good shape. Health care is in horrible shape. In health care, there is no fund to pay for it. How are you going to pay for health care, because in health care it's unpredictable and you have rising expenses? Doctors learn new expensive things they can give you. In 1860, the doctor had nothing to give except a little opium, which was cheap. Today, the doctor can give you expensive operations in the best general hospital room, and it costs a lot of money. And so the question is, how do you ration that health care? The real problem is health care, not pensions.

"If you look at General Motors, it's going broke, and it's going broke because it pays for the health care of 1 percent of the American population. Think about that. You pay for the health care for 1 percent of the American population, and some crazy doctor figures that there's a $100,000 thing to do, and General Motors has to pay for it. So if you look at General Motors versus Toyota, the big difference is health care. Toyota doesn't have a lot of old Americans they have to pay for. General Motors does.

"We are going to do national health insurance because the *business community* has decided to do national health insurance."

Fellow economist Dr. D. Quinn Mills agrees: "The government is going to have to pay for most of the health care, and health care is a very significant problem in this country. . . . There are too many different players in [the industry], doing too many different kinds of things, and then we have two totally different approaches to straightening it out. One is having more competition and letting people buy and purchase health care, with the notion that if they actually spend their own money directly, they'll look more into it and be a better and more cautious buyer. The other one is that we need to centralize everything more into some kind of national health insurance system. What we have now is right in the middle and being pulled both ways, and it is a glorious mess.

"In order to resolve the health care problem, the government has got to take a positive role. It can support market solutions or it can support a centralized solution, but it has to lead us in one way or another.

"The baby boomers' traditional suspicion and distrust of government is a very serious problem here, and I don't see that going away. It is possible the baby boom generation will not be able to successfully address the health care problem and that it will be left to the generation that follows, by which time the problem would be much worse. Unless we straighten this out, it has the potential to bankrupt the United States."

So, if for no other reason than to forestall national bankruptcy, we're well on our way to a system of "national health care insurance." Most leading-edge boomers remember the sixties and seventies when such a thing was called "socialized medicine," and just the mention of it would send doctors and politicians of all stripes into violent and uncontrollable convulsions. Socialized medicine was the first deadly step down a slippery slope that led directly to godless communism. We don't hear much about socialized medicine anymore. We hear a little, but not much.

As the director of the Marriage Matters project at the University of Virginia, Dr. Steven Nock is obviously concerned with how health care costs affect the family, and he agrees—national health care is virtually a fait accompli: "My own prediction is that we are halfway along toward socialized health care. We will not be able to afford a purely free-market system of health care for much longer. As the baby boom enters retirement and frail health, its needs will necessarily have to be socialized in order to be met. And once we socialize health care, the question of who gets more or less takes on a different tone, because now everybody will be contributing at approximately equal levels, with the expectation that all will derive what is needed or what is available as they age, and that is not the case right now. With free-market health care, obviously, those who can afford it receive better care. And that is one of the battles I think that the baby boom will bring to an end. We will see the end of completely free-market health care and will evolve into something closer to a Canadian or a European system."

Tom Price is a conservative Republican congressman and an orthopedic surgeon: "Like Social Security, the stability of the Medicare system is subject to the numbers. . . . More and more people will be coming under the umbrella of Medicare, with fewer and fewer workers to pay for it. But that's not the only problem. Medicare is flawed in nature because it rests on a belief that the federal government has the wisdom and ability to determine what medical treatment is appropriate for all elder citizens. The solution to that problem is to create a system that allows for flexibility in treating patients, and to do that you've got to put physicians 277 and patients in charge. I believe that's imperative. Health care is very personal, and the further we get away from allowing those decisions to be made personally, the worse the health care system will become."

Okay, that sounds like a pretty basic difference of opinion. But another question arises: If we have a national health care system, how will it be rationed? Will absolutely everyone be entitled to an MRI on request? Will absolutely everyone be entitled to a mechanical heart? If not, will that blood pump be denied to people because of age or IQ or the size of their bank account? If it's based on wealth, does that mean that Gordon Gekko gets one and your dear, sainted mother who devoted her life to the care and feeding of orphans doesn't?

To complicate matters, these decisions are not often as cut and dried as they may appear. To spend $20,000 a day to keep someone breathing in a vegetative state seems obviously excessive. But what if a quarter-of-a-million-dollar artificial heart can keep your mother or father or wife or husband alive and coherent for five months? Now it becomes an entirely different question.

In September 2006, the FDA approved just such a device for use in four thousand patients a year. The grapefruit-sized, fully implantable artificial heart is called the AbioCor heart. It had, at the time, been "installed" in the chests of twelve people who were not expected to live for more than a single month. Those twelve people survived an average of 5.2 months. How much money is five months worth?

Note the number above: four thousand. More than fifty-seven thousand people die from chronic heart failure each year in America.* That means that fifty-three thousand people will *not* get AbioCor hearts.

Dr. Fernando Torres-Gil is professor of social welfare and public policy, and director of the Center for Policy Research on Aging at UCLA. It's his job to understand the social ramifications of public policy and his view of the future is not bright: "The way

---

*http://www.medicalnewstoday.com/healthnews.php?newsid=51289.

things are going, twenty years from now the health care system will be a three-tier system. The top-quality medical care will be for those with the best insurance plan. A second tier will be for those who are affluent enough to pay for it with cash, who have their own private doctors and their own private clinic. And the third tier will be Medicaid and charity care and pro bono care, which will be just barely adequate and of the lowest quality and the highest rationing. That will not be good for American democracy."

"We don't have a health care system," says integrative medicine advocate Dr. Andrew Weil. "We have a 'disease management system' that doesn't work. And that system is on the verge of collapse now. Imagine what's going to happen when the baby boomers get into the age ranges where they become the chief consumers of medical care.

"We know that the greatest health care expenses are incurred in the last years of life. And also think about what's going to happen when the generation of fat kids that we're raising now get into the ages where they develop the cardiovascular complications of obesity, which, by the way, is going to occur in their late twenties and thirties. That's the interval usually between the development of the conditions of type-2 diabetes and cardiovascular disease. So these two things are going to hit at once, that is, an epidemic of cardiovascular disease in the young and an epidemic of age-related disease in this enormous population bulge. So, from my point of view, I think the health care system has to collapse if we're going to be able to reconstitute it in some better form. It just doesn't work now. We need to do things completely differently.

"And I don't think the collapse is going to be very pretty. I think it's going to be larger and larger numbers of people uninsured. I think it's going to be bankruptcy at many hospitals and clinics."

Okay! We get it. There is not a single member of our distinguished panel who has spoken up to defend the current system of providing health care to the people of the United States. So what's a boomer to do?

Well, we're going to do what we've always done. No, we're not going to stand on the Capitol steps and burn our Social Security cards. But we *are* going to question authority. We're going to refuse **279**

> The sick they tend with great affection; but, if the disease be incurable and full of anguish, the priests exhort them that they should die.
>
> **From Sir Thomas More's Utopia**
> **(1516)**

to accept the status quo. We're going to innovate. And we're going to think for ourselves. We are going to take control of our own, personal health care. We're going to use herbs and do yoga. We're going to meditate and jog. Whatever it takes, because, according to Faith Popcorn, the government simply isn't going to be there for us: "Our icons are just, like, falling over. The government, oh my, my, we don't believe in them anymore—the FBI, the CIA. Taxes . . . there are potholes in the streets, but we're paying. We felt we should invade Iraq. 'Oh. we invaded the wrong country. Oh, I'm sorry.' We don't believe in anything.

"One of the icons they don't believe in anymore, of course, is doctors. So they started weaning off doctors. Well, you know, the HMOs helped us with that. So it's physician assistants and nurse practitioners. We believe in them a little more. Then we're starting to look into other [options] like acupuncture and meditation. And the other thing is self-prescription. I think we're starting to believe that the nutritionist becomes the doctor of the future."

Naturally our panel includes perhaps the world's foremost expert on such things, Dr. Andrew Weil. Dr. Weil is director of the program in integrative medicine of the University of Arizona College of Medicine, and he advocates a blending of the modern medical philosophies of the West with the ancient approaches of the East. He quotes Buddha, praises yoga, teaches breathing techniques, and insists that supplemental nutrients are just that, supplemental, and excuses no one from maintaining a healthy diet. He is the author of seven books including *Eight Weeks to Optimum Health*.

IN DEPTH

Integrated and Alternative Medicine

Dr. Andrew Weil

"I have looked at health care from a very particular vantage point since I have been a proponent of integrated medicine, which is the thoughtful combination of conventional and alternative medicine. And all over the world today, you see a movement of people toward this system. I think there are many reasons for it, but a very deep one is a desire for empowerment, and I think that's often overlooked. And I think this is a very profound sociocultural change with very deep roots. I think people all over the world want to be more in charge of their own destiny, and they're increasingly dissatisfied with authoritarian care, with paternalistic care, in all spheres. But there have been huge changes in medicine as a result of that shift in attitude.

"It's been very hard for doctors to adjust to patients asking questions, often coming in with more knowledge than the doctor has because they've looked things up on the Internet. So I think the playing field has been really leveled in medicine. Many doctors have had a hard time with that. But they're going to have to get used to it. I mean, it's the way things are. And from my point of view, this is great, because I think the integrated medicine movement is still largely consumer driven, and one of the attitudes behind that force is this incredible desire for empowerment.

"I think this is consistent with the general philosophy of the boomer generation. First of all, not only questioning the authority of the traditional system, but also being interested in alternatives, being interested in things that are more natural, being suspicious of things that are synthetic and artificial. I think it's just consistent with all the values and attitudes of that generation.

"I think that there is the possibility of creating something different. I do very much believe that integrated medicine is one of the solutions [to the health care dilemma], because it offers the promise of bringing lower cost treatments into the mainstream that in many cases produce *better* outcomes.

"For example, I have long been a proponent of breathing techniques to affect physiology. There are very effective, simple breathing methods that can lower high blood pressure, that can correct gastrointestinal conditions, improve circulation, heart function, and so forth. They're free. They use no technology. And doctors never think to try these out because they didn't learn about them in their medical education. This is an example of something integrated medicine can bring into the mainstream that could save a lot of money.

"So I think that one of the solutions is that by looking outside of the conventional medical framework we can find lower cost, lower tech methods of dealing with common health problems. And I think integrated medicine also puts a great deal of real emphasis on prevention, which conventional medicine now doesn't, despite lip service to it. And I think with the age-related diseases—cardiovascular disease, cancer, and neurodegenerative disease—the key there is really prevention. There are things that you can do, in how you choose to eat, rest, exercise, handle stress, and so forth, that have a very significant impact on your risk of developing these diseases at earlier ages.

"Integrated medicine is a real movement now around the world, especially in the United States. It's attempting to restore the focus of medicine on health and healing rather than on disease. It is looking at people as whole persons, meaning bodies, minds, spirits, and community members. Looking at all aspects of lifestyle as relevant to health and illness, emphasizing the practitioner-patient relationship, and then looking at all treatments, whether within conventional medicine or outside, to see what might be most appropriate and most cost effective for managing disease."

Congressman Price (remember that he is also an orthopedic surgeon) thinks that healthy living and longer lives are a very, very good thing. He wants to make certain that everyone knows that he is a huge advocate of such things. But, he says, "it is a fallacy to believe that the healthier we are, the less health care will cost. By living well, we are *postponing* health care costs, but just postponing them. Of course we need preventive care, but it's incorrect to say it will save money."

Former President Carter is unquestionably the world's best role model for how to age well. He does all of those things the good Dr. Weil and others urge regarding exercise and diet and wearing seatbelts and all the rest. But he also does something more: "A diverse life—filled with changes, experiments, different kinds of repose, innovations, and adventures—is one that is much less likely to be afflicted with illness. This means that a few dollars or days spent pursuing a hobby or pastime is a sound investment, paying off in both enjoyment and in avoided medical expenses.

"The bottom line is to take on almost any tasks that are interesting and challenging—the more the better. We all know from experience that talking, touching, and relating to other people are necessary for our development and happiness, from infancy through all other stages of life. As we get older, it is important to avoid mental dormancy and to keep our minds occupied.

"Even when we become feeble in some ways, it is better to be as independent as possible, resisting the temptation to rely on others to do things we are able to do ourselves. It is dangerous to sink into inactivity by accepting help or services that we can provide for ourselves. The best intentions of others can change us into television-watching vegetables."*

It's almost a truism that exercise, diet, and a sense of purpose can keep us maturing rather than simply getting old. But Americans also have access to all the miraculous high-tech gadgets, with all the flashing lights and bells and whistles, and things that would

---

*Jimmy Carter, The Virtues of Aging (New York: Ballantine, 1998), 66.

have killed our fathers not many years ago are now "managed" with "minimally invasive" outpatient procedures. We're not living longer *solely* because we eat broccoli for breakfast!

We also have information available to us that our fathers could never have imagined. In fact, our fathers may never have paid any attention to it, even if they did. They would have listened (perhaps not even very closely), nodded to the authority figure with the white coat and a stethoscope around his neck, and said, "Whatever you say. You're the doctor."

Today we know more than our parents did. Dr. Dychtwald observes that we may or may not use that information wisely, but at least we have it: "We've got people who don't take care of themselves, who abuse their bodies with junk food. And a third of the population is obese; two-thirds are overweight. You can't be that unhealthy as a society and age and not have it buckle the economy.

"We understand now that you can grow old and be healthy. It used to be that everybody thought growing old was all about illness. And now that you see an eighty-year-old athlete or a ninety-year-old weightlifter, people say, 'Oh, I get it. You *can* have a healthy version of aging. How do I do that?'"

Of course there is more to it than spending hours on the treadmill and downing megadoses of vitamins. There is what Dr. Dychtwald calls "good medicine"—preventive medicine like prostate exams and colonoscopies.

President Bush's press secretary, Tony Snow, is a cancer survivor and can personally attest to the miracles of modern medicine: "I'm living testimony that medicine gets better. And the things that could prolong life and save you from otherwise crippling diseases are going to become more widely available. Still, you're going to die, you know. You can't avoid that. But I think extending life spans and the quality of life during that span, I think is something that we not only expect, it's something that we're going to be able to enjoy. Sooner or later, societies figure out ways to deal with the problem of how to afford it."

Dr. Torres-Gil thinks a war should be declared against the "big three" conditions that are likely to affect boomers: "If we can solve the issues of dementia, incontinence, and arthritis, the baby boomers will have little to fear as they grow older. Those are the three great fears of growing old. Losing your mind to Alzheimer's, incontinence because your body gives out, and arthritis because your bones can't keep up with old age. If we can find some kind of solutions, whether through biomedical advances, technological advances, new drugs—we will pretty much eliminate the need for nursing homes and most long-term care."

Excuse me, Dr. Torres-Gil. Did you imply that we might be able to find a "solution" for Alzheimer's? It's possible, right? After all, members of the Greatest Generation cured polio, didn't they?

They Cured Polio, Didn't They?

They did indeed. The cure for polio is another incredibly important accomplishment credited to the Greatest Generation.

Dr. Fernando Torres-Gil, however, was among those who contracted the debilitating disease before the "miracle cure" was found: "I, unfortunately, contracted polio just a few years before the Salk vaccine came out in 1954. But I'm grateful that as a generation, polio has been eradicated, so my children and grandchildren don't have to face it. But as we get older, we're going to find other types of medical crises and diseases. Whether it's the avian flu or AIDS or Alzheimer's or who knows what else is going to come on the scene. The difference between now and 1954 is that we no longer have a public infrastructure or a political system that is willing to invest the monies and the resources to bring us together, to combat these dreaded diseases."

Alzheimer's is the polio of our generation. It is, of course, a crippling disease that robs the elderly of their memories, frequently making it impossible for them to recognize their own children or to recall their names. More than 4.5 million people suffer from Alzheimer's, a number that will approach fifteen million by the end of the boomer century. It is a heartrending tragedy for the sufferers, and it is no less agonizing for their families. It is also a huge financial drain on the health care system.

Alzheimer's has become almost an obsession with leading-edge boomers. Many of us have witnessed it in our mothers and fathers. We have felt the frustration and the hopelessness and the anguish of seeing our once strong and vibrant parents, our childhood heroes, turned weak and mindless in a body that is only biologically alive.

This is not a me generation thing. Perhaps more than even death itself, Alzheimer's has become our greatest fear, for ourselves but perhaps even more so for our children. We do not want our sons and daughters and spouses to mourn over us for an entire decade or longer before we are finally "laid to rest." We also don't want them to suffer the potentially devastating financial burden of keeping that empty body "alive."

It is here then, Dr. Dychtwald says, that because of Alzheimer's, increased longevity moves over to the "bad news" side of the "good news/bad news" equation: "Because we're knocking out other diseases, instead of Alzheimer's lasting ten years, it's projected to go for twenty to twenty-five years. That alone would wipe out our society, would wipe out our economy!

"Currently almost half of people over age eighty-five suffer from some form of dementia. Alzheimer's has often been referred to as 'elderly AIDS' and could become the scourge of the twenty-first century. Unless a cure or treatment is found in our lifetimes, fifteen million boomers will be stricken with dementia by the middle of the century, and tens of millions of adult children will be shackled by bills and countless hours of care.

"If we continue to elevate life expectancy without fostering healthy aging, too many of us will live on for decades, riddled with decay and pain. The average twenty-first-century American will actually spend more years caring for parents than for children."

Nancy Reagan calls this phenomenon "the long good-bye."

While the cause of Alzheimer's is not certain, the bad guy here may be the buildup of a protein called beta-amyloid. Think of it as plaque.

Now, as to Dr. Torres-Gil's implication that a "solution" might be found: Do you remember Dr. Cynthia Kenyon's tiny worms? *C. elegans?* Do you remember the genetic pathway called insulin/IGF-1?

Scientists at California's Salk Institute for Biological Studies have used *C. elegans* and insulin/IGF-1 to delay the onset of amyloid buildup in roundworms. Roundworms may not be people, but, hey, it's a start.

And what about stem cells, you ask?

The media have told us about the amazing possibilities that can result from doing research on stem cells. The possibility exists, they tell us, that cures might be found for Parkinson's disease; that from these cells tissues can be made to regenerate damaged heart and liver cells; and that "tissue engineering" might be used "to grow a new pancreas for diabetics or a new liver for people who have hepatitis.* Other possible uses might include help for people who suffer from spinal cord injuries, diabetes, strokes, burns, leukemia . . .

And Alzheimer's. There is no question that the possibilities are endless. And in some areas they are more than only possibilities.

At Duke University, doctors use stem cells to save babies born with Krabbe disease, a rare genetic and usually fatal disorder that prevents brain development. Infants with Krabbe disease received transplants from another baby's cord blood and the stem cells that blood contains. The afflicted children were cured. That's right. Cured.

The keen eye may have made note of the words *cord blood,* as in "umbilical cord." These stem-cell-rich strains are harvested from umbilical cords and placenta. They are *not* embryonic stem cells. Unlike cord cells, which are already organ specific, embryonic stem cells can grow into an almost unlimited number of different types of cells—and a seemingly endless contentious political and moral debate.

---

*http://www.cord-blood-video.com/quesharris.html.

After five and a half years in office, President George W. Bush used his veto pen for the very first time to reject an attempt by Congress, led by some of his most conservative fellow Republicans, to use federal monies to fund embryonic stem cell research, which he has opposed on moral grounds since his earliest days in office. The "harvesting" of embryonic stem cells requires the destruction of frozen human embryos that have been set aside during the in vitro fertilization process. Regardless of the fact that, in all probability, these cells will be destroyed anyway, President Bush and some deeply religious Americans consider these "clusters of cells" to be human beings, and find the use of them for research to be deplorable.

> I strongly oppose human cloning, as do most Americans. We recoil at the idea of growing human beings for spare body parts, or creating life for our convenience. And while we must devote enormous energy to conquering disease, it is equally important that we pay attention to the moral concerns raised by the new frontier of human embryo stem cell research. Even the most noble ends do not justify any means.
>
> **President George W. Bush**
> **Address to Nation**
> **August 9, 2004**

U.S. researchers are not forbidden to do research on embryonic stem cells; they are only denied federal dollars with which to conduct that research. Many research laboratories are forced to have two different facilities to ensure that private funds are not commingled with federal funds in order to stay in compliance with the law and to protect themselves against the potential loss of federal grants that permit them to do research on "other" forms of stem cells. One such facility has even gone so far as to insist on the use of two different brands of ink pens—one to be used in the free-market laboratory and the other in the federally funded one. The pens from the laboratory that receives federal funding are not permitted to be used in the free-market one so that there cannot be an accusation that they used a buck and a quarter of taxpayer money to write down the results of an embryonic stem cell test.

For better or for worse, this is the status quo. But as we know, boomers historically and notoriously refuse to accept any status quo.

So, again, what is this generation going to do? Are we going to hope for politicians to become enlightened, or sit around and wait decades for the "possible" breakthroughs promised by incredibly complex genetic experimentation on microscopic worms? Or are we going to educate ourselves, innovate new procedures, and do our damndest to keep the beast called Alzheimer's at bay?

Given what we know about boomers, Dr. Weil contends that the latter seems most likely: "While treatments for Alzheimer's are still dismal, I think there're a number of strategies that you can recommend to people for reducing risk. And this is everything from taking low doses of antiinflammatory drugs like ibuprofen; using natural antiinflammatory agents like turmeric, the yellow spice which there's good reason to believe is Alzheimer's protective; taking antioxidant vitamins and minerals; getting adequate rest and sleep; and doing brain workouts. And you know, this can be everything from puzzles of various kinds to learning a new computer operating system periodically. You know my favorite? Learning other languages. There's very interesting evidence that people who speak more than one language have generally better brain function and are protected against age-related cognitive decline. So I think that while we don't understand what Alzheimer's disease is yet or what causes it, and can't treat it, we do know something about how to reduce the risk."

Nonetheless, Dr. Dychtwald says a cure would be better: "If the U.S. could wipe out polio when we were children, why can't we wage a similar campaign now to knock out Alzheimer's? Instead of

Science has presented us with a hope called stem cell research, which may provide our scientists with many answers that for so long have been beyond our grasp. I just don't see how we can turn our backs on this. We have lost so much time already. I just really can't bear to lose any more.

Former First Lady Nancy Reagan

spending $1 trillion over the years ahead to treat it, what if we spent $10 billion now to eliminate it? And I think stem cell research is where the real hope lies. If you could somehow knock out Alzheimer's and knock out Parkinson's and maybe even knock out heart disease or cancer, you might have people living a hundred _healthy_ years."

A hundred healthy years of life, one week of illness, and gone. That is, in fact, the perfect life.

But Dr. Dychtwald contends that a life span of one hundred years may actually be a pessimistic prognostication: "The present biological potential of the human body is somewhere between 120 and 140 years. But given these scientific enhancements, all bets are off regarding how long we might live in the twenty-first century."

A hundred and forty years? Should the very first boomer achieve that mark, she will make her transition in the year 2086, the youngest in 2104. Were there an American soul alive today who had reached that high-water mark, she would have been born in 1866, the year after the Civil War ended, and would probably be a great-great-great-great-great-grandmother. Or so.

Let's go back to a still optimistic but more reasonable possibility of a life span of four score and five. Should we actually "retire" at sixty-five, that gives us twenty years. We have already discussed what we might do with the first ten of those years—continue to work, volunteer, travel, help raise the grandkids. And golf. Don't forget golf. But, what's that old saying?

All Good Things Must *What?*

Lynn Humer was not a boomer. She was one of the Greatest Generation. She was a cancer survivor in her forties, widowed in her fifties, and continued to live in the home she had shared with her husband until the week before she was to turn ninety-one. She went to the hospital and passed away one day prior to her birthday. She never spent a day in a nursing home. She never lived a day in assisted living. She underwent surgery for her throat cancer in the fifties and never went under the knife again. She put the finishing touches on her final painting the day before she checked into the hospital.

She laughed on her death bed.

She owned that home that she occupied for more than forty years. She lived on Social Security and the dividends from her modest stock holdings, and she left no debt. Medicare and Medigap insurance covered her medical expenses to such an extent that even they never put a serious strain on her finances.

By the Numbers

- In summer 2004, there were 36,300,000 Americans over sixty-five years of age, 4,900,000 Americans over eighty-five years of age, and 64,658 Americans one hundred years old or older.

- By 2050, there will be 86,700,000 Americans over sixty-five years of age, an increase of 147 percent. Nine million baby boomers will survive into their late nineties, and three million will reach one hundred.

From the U.S. Bureau of the Census

We will call this nearly perfect life a "Lynn Life." This should be the goal of everyone in the medical profession, everyone in the pharmaceutical industry, everyone in the health care bureaucracy, everyone in the insurance business, and the personal goal of each and every boomer alive today. Should a Lynn Life become the rule rather than the exception, none of the fiscal difficulties enumerated in previous pages would be of the slightest concern.

"I'm going to give you a statistic that'll scare you," warns Dr. Thurow. "Half of all money spent on health care is spent in the last year of life because everybody has a serious illness in the last year of life. And you're going to die anyway. But we give expensive cancer treatment to 'third-generation' [terminal] cancer patients. Nobody else does. So, in the United States, we have 16 percent of our [gross domestic product] in health care; in France and Germany they are around 10 percent. They live longer than we do, but we make you feel good. You have an incurable disease, and we give you a lot of money anyway.

"We give expensive cancer treatments to people we know they won't help. It doesn't keep them alive longer, but makes them feel good. 'I'm so important, they gave me a $100,000 treatment.'

"Not very many people opt out. People who try and opt out find it very hard because the hospital resists. My father was at the University of Chicago Hospital in intensive care. He wanted to die. He was ninety-five. He started pulling the plugs out. They stopped him. They wanted to keep him alive—at ninety-five.

"For every human being, there is a good day to die, and it's not a day to spend a million dollars."

And yet, that is precisely what we do. Congressman Price offers us a couple of reasons why: "One of the reasons the last two months of life are so expensive is that our physicians are fearful of risk of liability. And it's not always the next of kin that sues. It might be a second cousin twice removed who decides that what was done was not the right thing.

"There are decisions that should be made months or even years in advance. We should all have loving conversations about the quality of life at the end of life. Some people don't want to be kept alive on respirators. I don't want to be misconstrued here—of course everyone should have the highest quality of care at that time, but if we discuss these things in advance, a logical decision can be made. Not one based on emotions and certainly not one based on fear of legal action. Most people don't want to be kept alive for that slow and steady decline."

Intensive care can cost $20,000 a day or more. People are hooked up to what is often called "lifesaving technology" that, in the vast majority of cases, "saves" very few lives. Hundreds of millions of dollars are spent simply to postpone death. People say that they don't want to have their lives extended with these technologies, but we do it anyway.

These life-or-death decisions are often made, not by the dying person, but by someone who loves him. In these most stressful of all situations that eventually occur, sometimes multiple times, in each and every life, economics understandably gets trumped by emotion. Anyone who has ever signed a "Do Not Resuscitate" order understands the anguish involved in making a life-or-death decision for a loved one. The next to the last official document recording Lynn's Life was a Do Not Resuscitate order. As badly as Lynn wanted to go, her family, just as badly, wanted her to stay. They did not want to sign that document.

AARP's Bill Novelli suggests that death may be another "institution" that boomers are going to change: "I think boomers are going to be more involved in their own end of life. They're going to have more advance directives. They're going to have more understanding of what to ask doctors. And they're going to make decisions that will be different from what people are making today. I think boomers are going to be asking, 'For what? Why do I want to live longer if I'm not in good health?' And so you're going to have a clash: I think a clash of ethics, a clash of technologies, a clash of decision making."

Lynn Humer and Dr. Thurow's father both wanted to go when the time came, and "we" wouldn't let them. But what about those who can make that decision for themselves? What about those who cling to the desperate hope of divine intervention? What about those who remain determined to breathe every breath, no matter how hopeless, no matter how painful, no matter how expensive?

"Who tells the patient he can't have the treatment?" Dr. Thurow asks. "Is it the politician? Is it the doctor? Who is it? Nobody. We haven't decided that yet.

"That's the hard problem we have in America. George Bush doesn't want to say that. The doctors don't want to say that. Nobody wants to say, 'You can't have that treatment—it costs too much money.'"

A 2006 study done by the Pew Research Center for the People and the Press tells us that "an overwhelming majority of the public supports laws that give patients the right to decide whether they want to be kept alive through medical treatment. And fully 70 percent say there are circumstances when patients should be allowed to die, while just 22 percent believe that doctors and nurses should always do everything possible to save a patient."

Interestingly, the same study found that 34 percent would want doctors to do "everything possible" to save *their own lives*, "even if faced with a terminal illness and great pain."*

Dr. Weil believes that "an awful lot of people are afraid of finding themselves in the situation where they have lost autonomy and they become victims of a system which is intent on preserving life at all costs. So I think many people have executed living wills and given medical power of attorney to trusted people. They have made clear their wishes—they don't want to be maintained alive if they are not conscious and sentient. And I think that it's very important for people to think proactively about these issues and to try to specify and think ahead as to what conditions they might face and how they want them dealt with."

According to the Pew Research Center report cited above, the American people are more aware and becoming (albeit slowly) more proactive: "Public awareness of living wills, already widespread in 1990, is now virtually universal, and the number saying

---

*Pew Research Center, January 5, 2006, http://people-press.org/reports/display.php3?ReportID=266.

they have a living will has more than doubled from just 12 percent in 1990 to 29 percent today."

Since the oldest boomers are just now turning sixty, and the youngest are only in their forties, hopefully these issues of debilitating disease and death remain in the very distant future. Even the oldest of us still have fifteen to twenty years of vibrant life ahead of us.

> The true Buddha is not a human body: it is Enlightenment. A human body must die, but the Wisdom of Enlightenment will exist forever in truth and in practice.
>
> **The Buddha**

Our panel has already discussed the plethora of options open to us over the course of those years, in terms of working or not working, getting by or not getting by, and staying healthy or getting sick. We have reminisced about our youth and the dramatic impact we have had on the world. We have defended ourselves against the slings and arrows hurled at us by our critics. We have stolen a glimpse into the future to see what the final third of our lives might be like. So that should just about cover it, right?

Well, not really.

chapter 13

What's It All About?

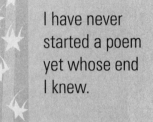

I have never started a poem yet whose end I knew.

Robert Frost

Now it is time for our experts to reminisce about the past, contemplate their hopes and fears for the future, and speculate as to what the legacy of the boomer generation might eventually be.

Up until this moment, I have made a strenuous effort to remain objective, anonymous, and fairly unobtrusive. Now, however, as one of the very first boomers, I have chosen to exercise the birthright of my generation. I shall now rebel against authority, challenge the status quo, and think for myself. I have determined not only that I will, for the first time and at long last, speak in my own voice, but also that I will get to lead off.

Richard Croker, Author

I do not recall when I first was told that I belonged to the least exclusive club in the history of the world. I do remember Red Skelton, my coonskin cap, our first color television set, and roller skates with steel wheels that strapped onto my shoes with flimsy leather bands and were tightened around the soles with an easily losable skate key. I remember double sessions in high school and standing in line for a polio shot.

I also remember the 1960 presidential elections. Even at fourteen years old, it never occurred to me not to participate. I stuffed envelopes and licked stamps at the Fulton County (Georgia) Kennedy for President headquarters and managed to wrangle an invitation to his inauguration at the age of fifteen. As a Georgia boy, it was the first significant snow I ever saw. It was spectacular. I was there on the Capitol lawn when he spoke all those magnificent words—and a baby boomer idealist was born.

A young lawyer named Charles Weltner had taken me under his wing during those campaigning days, and when he decided to run for Congress, I was his first volunteer. Charles was the only congressman from the Deep South (North Carolina, South Carolina, Georgia, Alabama, Mississippi, and Louisiana) to vote *for* the 1964 Civil Rights Act. Four years later, he saw me standing on the sidewalk as he followed the casket of Dr. Martin Luther King Jr. up the Courtland Street hill, and he beckoned me to join him. I stepped off the curb that day and became one of only a very small handful of white southerners to do so. It remains my proudest moment.

Yes, I carried signs and let my opinion be known on Jim Crow and Vietnam. I protested the ejection of Julian Bond from the Georgia legislature. I supported Lyndon Johnson for his incredibly courageous stand on civil rights, and I turned against him on Vietnam.

I was *not* at Woodstock.

I never burned my draft card, and when my number came up, I went. I believed then as I believe now that we are a nation of laws and not of men, my proclivity to question authority notwithstanding. I would reluctantly have gone to Vietnam had they insisted, but, fortunately for me, they never did. I smoked pot and loved the Allman Brothers and still get a flashback buzz whenever I hear "In Memory of Elizabeth Reed."

I confess that I enjoyed Watergate. The magnificence of the United States Constitution is not that it is a set of rules—it's that it is the framework that severely limits the ability of small-minded, power-hungry people to *make* rules. What happened in Watergate was that the Constitution awoke from its slumber, as it was designed to do, and slapped down a tyrant.

For those days, I am proud of us all. I am proud of those who protested against the war, and I am equally proud of those who volunteered to go fight it. Both groups were passionate about their convictions, believed in something greater than themselves, and neither was evil. I am most proud of those who helped bring down Jim Crow. It is so hard to believe today that such a thing as that ever existed in America.

So we did all those magnificent things in the sixties and the seventies. We helped force America "to live up to the meaning of its creed that all men are created equal." We demanded the end of a cruel and senseless war, and (eventually) it ended. We brought down the most powerful man in the world because he used this power immorally. These things are democracy at work, and they changed the world—*we* changed the world—forever and for the better.

But what have we done since? Where are our leaders now?

They are tawdry, partisan politicians playing power games with our lives. They stand opposite each other in Congress and shout across the aisle about such divisive and irrelevant nonissues as gay marriage. They are not trying to make America better but are simply trying to gain the upper hand in the next elections by pandering to the basest fears of the lunatic fringe on both sides.

These so-called leaders are not doing what our generation is supposed to do. They seem not to question authority but to succumb to it blindly. In fact, they cower timidly and submit easily to the control of authoritarians called "whips." They have made no attempt to alter the status quo but have buckled to its tyranny without complaint. They allow the "party leadership" to do all the thinking as they stand meekly in line, like Mr. Bumble's orphans, bowls in hand, hoping for a tiny scrap of pork:

"Please, sir . . . may I have . . . more?"

There are seventy-eight million of us. Can we not put a stop to this? Can we not find just a few good boomers to go to Washington and force the government to do what's right?

We did it when we were children! Why can we not do it now?

Is there not one good boomer out there who can stand up in the well of Congress—as JFK did when he challenged us to go to the moon—and demand that we end our dependence on fossil fuel by the end of the decade? Such a bill would appeal to bleeding-heart, tree-hugging liberals as the most important piece of environmental legislation ever passed, and to truck-driving, immigrant-hating conservatives as vital to our national security.

Can we not do that?

Can we not find one boomer who is willing to touch the "third rail" of American politics and fix the archaic and crumbling Medicare and Medicaid systems that threaten to bankrupt the United States and send it hurtling into beggar nation status?

Can we not *do that*?

No. Sorry. We cannot. We've got to argue about who is going to get the credit.

Right now our legacy is that of a washed-up athlete who mesmerized us with his prowess in his youth, but who has gotten fat and lazy and has to ask people if they want an autograph.

What a shame.

Now, our panel of experts will offer their hopes and fears and perspectives on what our legacy shall be. Some will be long, and some will be short. Some will be optimistic, and some will be downright frightening. Each and every one will be didactic. (Look it up in your *Funk and Wagnalls*.)

Dr. Fernando Torres-Gil, Political Scientist

"My hope is that in our later years, we'll restore our faith in government and politics, and in American public life, and that we can reengage in politics and provide public leadership that can bring us back to where we hope President Kennedy might have lived, had he lived."

David Gergen, Political Scientist

"The reason I'm more committed today to political change than I was thirty years ago is that I think we have not realized the dreams we all talked about in the sixties. I thought by the time I died, this would be a more equal society in which blacks would be integrated into society, in which women would have an equal shot, in which kids growing up poor would have an equal shot, and we're so far beneath that goal that I think a lot of us feel, 'Let's use whatever years we have to see if we can bring that closer to reality.' That's what inspired us when we were young, and we shouldn't shut off the lights just yet."

Eve Ensler, Playwright

"If we're really going to leave the world better, we've got to figure out how to bring the next generation along—how we get them to find their voice; how we get them to stand up; how we get them to believe that because they're so terribly cynical and despaired that they can impact what's going on in the world; how we create a social movement or movements that we leave behind that will stir people to come forward.

"Certainly in the years that I have left, my deepest goals are to connect with this next generation, to serve this next generation, so they will be able to keep doing what we've done.

"And there's a great Bernard Shaw quote, where he says, 'I want to be thoroughly used up when I die,' and I think of that every day. Just use me up. I want to be used up. It's the great life to be used up."

Faith Popcorn, Futurist

"I think the boomers are going to leave the country in a worse place, ecologically. You know, we talked a good game, but we didn't do much about it, really. And I think we're having major problems with nonrenewable resources. And, of course, it's kind of ironic that George Bush is saying that we're 'oil addicts.' I have to say, it's something I agree with him on. And, yeah, I think the state of affairs is not so great."

301

Rob Reiner, Motion Picture Director/Actor

"I think you're going to see idealism in action again. The feeling of wanting to make the world better is going to be out there, and it will hopefully be trickling down through the generations that are following us. You see baby boomers like Al Gore and Laurie David—people who are taking on global warming. That's going to be a big issue. And baby boomers are going to continue to stay engaged and involved, because there is that little ember of wanting to make the world better and wanting to have a perfect and wonderful and great world. That aim is going to be with us all along. . . .

"Sure, I'm proud of what the baby boomer generation was all about, and I'm proud to be part of that. I hope we will have impact beyond the early years when we were in our heyday. It was an important message that we were sending, and that message needs to continue to be heard."

Julian Bond, NAACP Chairman and Civil Rights Activist

"If I look around me today and look at the world and compare it to what my hopes and aspirations were all those years ago, I am disappointed. I thought we would be further along than we are, but I've always been an optimist and always thought that these things would happen. They are not happening on my timetable and they are not *going* to happen on my timetable. But I think they will happen. I think the national sentiment is going to return to some approximation of what I hoped would happen. I am not ready to throw up my hands and say it's all over. On the contrary, it's going to happen. I am not sure I am going to be here to see it happen, but it's going to happen."

Jeremy Siegel, Financial Analyst

"There are parts of the great social revolution of the 1960s, of which the boomers were the chief architects, that they didn't complete. One of those, I think, is the struggle for equal rights for gay and lesbian couples.

"Baby boomers were on the vanguard of the civil rights movement in the 1960s. But when it came to sexual freedom, they never quite completed that project and provided for full equality for gays and lesbians."

Dr. Steven Nock, Sociologist

"My guess is that future anthropologists and sociologists and historians, when looking back on the baby boom, will credit them with some of the most massive failures in history. They ushered in some horrible changes in the society. They pioneered some of the worst social conditions that one can imagine. But I hope that future historians will understand that those failures were largely a result of being pioneers in causes and battles that had never been fought in the same way before. So we should get credit for having caused havoc, disruption, and disorder, disrespect, breakdown in certain social institutions. There's no doubt in my mind that the baby boom gets credit for a lot of that. . . .

"Our children and our children's children are still going to inherit those problems of sexism and racism and all the other things, but they will inherit them in a different way. They will inherit them with some guidance about how it was fought, what worked and what didn't work, what things are feasible, and what things aren't feasible. Is the government the answer to problems? Is it not the answer to problems? Can you have an equitable society and still have personal freedom? These are big questions that no single generation can answer. We failed in many ways, but we succeeded a little bit. And our children will succeed a little bit more, and that is the nature of evolution of societies—the problems are larger than any one generation can confront. We'll be remembered as the first generation to confront many of them."

Dr. Joshua Zeitz, Historian

"It's always hard to say how we're going to look at things in hindsight, but I think that the baby boom generation will be seen as emblematic of what Henry Luce always called 'The

American Century.' The boomers arrived in 1946, and they haven't exited the scene yet. They probably won't for some time. They defined every major trend, every major political movement, and every major economic development of the postwar period. In this sense, they really came to embody and to give shape to the developments that we think of as the American century. And so they'll probably be seen as the key historical actors of their age."

Leonard Steinhorn, Professor of Communications

"I think boomers have to continue to be a voice in favor of environmental protection. They have to continue to be a voice saying that diversity and equality are moral values, and to see it manifested in their families, as they continue to work in the workplace, and continue to rise up as managers and owners of companies or institutions, and to continue to implement those values.

"I think historians will say, 'My gosh! Look at where we started from!' We were starting from a society that had entrenched bigotry and discrimination; that devalued the contributions and the work and the psychology of women; that expected everybody to conform to a certain way of life; that saw progress at any cost and didn't really care about things like pollution and toxic wastes, because it was all in the name of progress. And they'll say, 'My gosh! In those forty years of boomer ascendancy, things really began to change.' We began to implement those values that made America a better and more inclusive and more equal society. . . .

"Being a baby boomer is really being an American today. And I am exhilarated by the incredible freedom and diversity of our culture. . . . I'm proud to be part of a more diverse, a more energetic, a more egalitarian culture. I may not always agree with people, but I love the debate and the dialogue and the possibility that we can influence each other. That is what baby boom culture is all about. It's letting a thousand flowers bloom all over. It's an exhilarating time to be alive, in that sense."

Ken Dychtwald, PhD, Psychologist and Gerontologist

"In our youth we struggled with some of the most vexing problems a society can confront: racism, sexism, war. In our middle years, we rethought work and domestic relationships and tried to achieve a better balance between the two. Now we are becoming sixty-year-olds and facing perhaps our greatest challenges. The world has changed a great deal since our birth and will change even more by the time the first boomer reaches one hundred.

"America's youth generation is going to redo aging—it's going to change it all. The way we look, the way we feel, how long you work, what it means to be sixty, what it means to be ninety, when it's too late to fall in love. The whole landscape and mindscape of adulthood is about to be totally and dramatically changed.

"When we were seventeen, we acted like rebellious seventeen-year-olds. When we were in our thirties, we were often self-centered and self-indulgent. But we have matured as a generation. We have learned from our experiences. We have more time, money, and wisdom to contribute than any generation before us. How will we use these assets in the coming decades? Will we be able to pull together as a generation and find a common purpose? Or will we shatter into separate interest groups with competing agendas? It's clear from our history and our demographics that the boomers are about to transform this country once again, but for better or for worse remains an open question. Will future generations suffer from the world we have left them? Or will they look back at the boomer century and consider it a golden era, a time of innovation, compassion, and new beginnings?

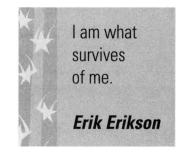

I am what survives of me.

Erik Erikson

The choice is ours."

About the Contributors

KEN DYCHTWALD, PhD, is a psychologist and gerontologist and the author of several successful books on aging, including *Age Power, Bodymind, Age Wave,* and *The Power Years.* He is widely viewed as North America's leading visionary on the personal, social, and cultural implications of what he calls the "Age Wave."

Dr. Dychtwald is a consultant to numerous major corporations and not-for-profit organizations and is a highly sought-after speaker. He has presented to more than two million people worldwide.

Ken is the moving force behind *The Boomer Century* and acted as the host of the PBS documentary for which this book is the companion.

The rest of our panel is listed alphabetically.

CATHLEEN BLACK is president of Hearst Magazines. She graduated from Trinity College in Washington, DC, in 1966. She sold advertising for magazines such as *Holiday* and *Travel and Leisure* before joining *New York* magazine in 1970. She helped launch *Ms.* two years later, becoming associate publisher. Black returned to *New York* and was named publisher in 1979. She was the first woman to publish a weekly consumer magazine. In 1983, she took over a new newspaper, *USA Today,* and by 1991 its circulation had risen to 1.8 million, second only to the *Wall Street Journal.* Black left *USA Today* to head the Newspaper Association of America. In 1995, she was hired to run Hearst Magazines, which publishes *Cosmopolitan, Esquire, Good Housekeeping,* and *Harper's Bazaar,* among others. Black is also on the board of directors of IBM and Coca-Cola.

LEWIS BLACK may be the nation's foremost satiric comedian. He performs before sold-out houses coast to coast, has been featured in

several specials on both HBO and Comedy Central, and is a regular "commentator" on the popular *The Daily Show with Jon Stewart,* also aired by Comedy Central.

JULIAN BOND is chairman of the NAACP, a civil rights activist, and politician. Bond was born on January 14, 1940, in Nashville, Tennessee. He and his family moved to Pennsylvania, where his father, Horace Mann Bond, was appointed president of Lincoln University.

In 1960, Bond was one of several hundred students who helped form the Student Nonviolent Coordinating Committee (SNCC). In 1965, Bond was elected to the Georgia House of Representatives but was barred from taking his seat due to his outspoken statements against the Vietnam War. In December 1966, the U.S. Supreme Court ruled in his favor, and he served four terms as a state representative and six terms in the Georgia State Senate. During the 1968 presidential election, he was the first African American to be nominated for vice president of the United States. He withdrew his name from the ballot, however, because he was too young to serve. Later, Bond hosted *America's Black Forum.*

In addition to serving as chairman of the NAACP, Bond is also president emeritus of the Southern Poverty Law Center. He is a distinguished scholar in residence at American University in Washington, DC, and a faculty member in the history department at the University of Virginia.

BISHOP JOHN CHANE is the Eighth Bishop of the Episcopal Diocese of Washington, where he serves ninety-three congregations and forty-five thousand members in the District of Columbia and Maryland. He is the president and CEO of the Protestant Episcopal Cathedral Foundation and has served as interim dean of the Washington National Cathedral.

RICHARD CHAPMAN is a veteran screenwriter and producer in film and television, with particular interest in the ways journalists re-

port on war. He recently cowrote the Golden Globe–nominated HBO original movie *Live from Baghdad,* which told the behind-the-scenes story of CNN's coverage of the early days of the first Persian Gulf War. He is currently producing *Shooting the Messengers,* a feature-length documentary about how war correspondents in Vietnam covered that conflict.

He also has credits in the entertainment side of the television industry, which includes being producer of the hit series *Simon and Simon.*

Chapman serves as guest lecturer in screenwriting at Washington University in St. Louis.

EVE ENSLER is a playwright. Her Obie Award–winning play, *The Vagina Monologues,* which has been translated into over thirty-five

languages and is running in theaters all over the world, initiated V-Day, a global movement to stop violence against women and girls. Ms. Ensler has devoted her life to stopping violence, envisioning a planet on which women and girls will be free to thrive, rather than merely survive. Her work grows out of her own personal experiences with violence. *The Vagina Monologues* is based on Ensler's interviews with more than two hundred women. The piece celebrates women's sexuality and strength and exposes the violations that women endure throughout the world.

MAYOR SHIRLEY FRANKLIN is the recipient of the 2005 John F. Kennedy Profiles in Courage Award. She became mayor of Atlanta in 2001, having never before run for public office.

She inherited an $82 million budget deficit—about a fifth of the city's total budget—and a crisis of confidence in the public management of the city. Atlanta's sewer system needed immediate and massive repairs, and its homeless population was growing at an alarming rate. While many cities were struggling with budget deficits and other problems, Atlanta's woes were known to be among the most daunting.

Instead of blaming her predecessor or glossing over the depth of the crisis, Franklin responded by leveling with Atlantans about the extent of the city's problems and asked everyone to bear the burden of solving them. She raised property taxes nearly 50 percent, slashed city services, and eliminated one thousand jobs from the city payroll, cut her own staff and salary, and imposed the strictest code of ethics for public employees anywhere in the state.

MARC FREEDMAN is founder and president of Civic Ventures and founder of the Experience Corps, the largest national service program in the United States for Americans fifty-five and older. Formerly vice president of Public/Private Ventures, Freedman is author of the book *Prime Time: How Baby Boomers Will Revolutionize Retirement and Transform America*.

A frequent commentator in the national media, Freedman is a high honors graduate of Swarthmore College, with an MBA from Yale University.

311

DAVID GERGEN is a commentator, editor, teacher, public servant, bestselling author, and adviser to presidents. For thirty years, Ger-

gen has been an active participant in American national life. He served as director of communications for President Reagan and held positions in the administrations of Presidents Nixon and Ford. In 1993, he put his country before politics when he agreed to serve as adviser to President Clinton on both foreign policy and domestic affairs.

Gergen is a professor of public service and the director of the Center for Public Leadership at the John F. Kennedy School of Government at Harvard University. He is also editor-at-large at *U.S. News and World Report,* where he served for two and a half years. During that period, he also teamed up with Mark Shields for political commentary every Friday night for five years on the *MacNeil/Lehrer NewsHour.*

DR. DANIEL GOLEMAN is an internationally known psychologist who lectures frequently to professional groups and business audiences and on college campuses. Working as a science journalist,

Goleman reported on the brain and behavioral sciences for the *New York Times* for many years. His 1995 book, *Emotional Intelligence,* was on the *New York Times* bestseller list for a year and a half, with more than five million copies in print worldwide in thirty languages.

His most recent book is *Social Intelligence: The New Science of Human Relationships.*

ERICA JONG is the author of eight novels, including *Fear of Flying; Fanny, Being the True History of the Adventures of Fanny Hackabout-Jones; Shylock's Daughter; Inventing Memory: A Novel of Mothers and Daughters;* and *Sappho's Leap.* Several of her novels have been worldwide bestsellers. Her other books include the nonfiction works *Fear of Fifty: A Memoir; The Devil at Large: Erica Jong on Henry Miller; Witches;* and *What Do Women Want?,* as well as six volumes of poetry. Her latest book is *Seducing the Demon: Writing for My Life.*

Fear of Flying, which was first published in 1973, is frequently referred to as the genesis of "the sexual revolution" of the seventies.

DR. CYNTHIA KENYON has been internationally recognized for her groundbreaking work in the analysis of the molecular causes of aging and signaling of life span control. Dr. Kenyon, having studied under 2002 Nobel laureate Dr. Sidney Brenner, was one of the first scientists to adopt the small soil nematode, *C. elegans,* as a study system, and now uses it to study aging and longevity.

SHELLY LAZARUS has been CEO of Ogilvy and Mather Worldwide, one of the world's largest advertising agencies, since 1997. She graduated from Smith College in 1968 and earned an MBA from Columbia University in 1970, where she was one of four women in her class.

STANLEY LITOW is president of the IBM Foundation and IBM's vice president for global community relations. He is also a past deputy chancellor of schools for New York City, the nation's largest school system, which serves 1.3 million children.

DR. D. QUINN MILLS consults with major corporations and appears in the Harvard Business School's classrooms to teach about leadership, strategy, and human resources. Mills arrived at the Harvard Business School in 1976. He taught at the MIT Sloan School of Management between 1968 and 1975, and he supplemented his MIT teaching by spending several years in Washington, DC, helping to control inflation during the Vietnam War. Mills has consulted for various government agencies and is a member of the Panel of Thought Leaders of the Peter F. Drucker Foundation. Mills earned his MA and PhD from Harvard, both in economics.

He studied the baby boomers in his book *Not Like Our Parents: How the Baby Boom Generation Is Changing America.*

DR. STEVEN NOCK is professor of sociology and director of the Marriage Matters project at the University of Virginia. He earned his PhD at the University of Massachusetts, Amherst, in 1976. Before coming to the University of Virginia, he was on the faculty of Tulane University and then at the National Academy of Sciences. Dr. Nock is the author of books and articles about the causes and consequences of change in the American family. He has investigated issues of privacy, unmarried fatherhood, cohabitation, commitment, divorce, and marriage. His

most recent book, *Marriage in Men's Lives,* won the William J. Good Book Award from the American Sociological Association for the most outstanding contribution to family scholarship in 1999.

BILL NOVELLI is CEO of AARP, a membership organization of more than thirty-five million people aged fifty and older, half of whom are actively employed.

Prior to joining AARP, Mr. Novelli was president of the Campaign for Tobacco-Free Kids and executive vice president of CARE, the world's largest private relief and development organization.

REV. CAROLE O'CONNELL is minister emerita of the largest New Thought church in the Southeast, Unity North Atlanta. Unity is a nondenominational church that "honors diversity" and subscribes to the principle that "there is one God, but many paths." She is a spiritual life coach and highly sought-after motivational speaker.

O'Connell is the author of *The Power of Choice: Ten Steps to a Joyous Life.*

FAITH POPCORN is the bestselling author of *The Popcorn Report* and chairman of BrainReserve, Inc., the New York–based marketing consulting firm she founded in 1974. She is recognized as one of America's foremost trend experts. Identifying such sweeping societal concepts as "Cocooning," "Cashing Out," "EVEolution," "FemaleThink," and "Pleasure Revenge," she has developed a unique method of understanding consumer needs to prepare her clients for the future marketplace. She has been referred to as the "trend oracle" by the *New York Times*, the

"Nostradamus of marketing" by *Fortune*, and the "Tom Ford of marketing" by her Fortune 500 clients.

DR. TOM PRICE is a conservative Republican congressman from a suburban Atlanta district (Georgia's sixth). He is also an orthopedic surgeon—and a boomer.

ROB REINER is a motion picture producer and director. Fame came knocking for the younger Reiner when Norman Lear cast him as Mike "Meathead" Stivic, Archie Bunker's liberal son-in-law (and straight man), on the classic 1970s series *All in the Family*. The groundbreaking show gave humor to the divisive issues of the seventies and put faces and names to the generation gap.

He wrote and directed a boomer cult favorite, *This Is Spinal Tap,* a mock "rockumentary" that parodied the popular genre of the early boomer generation.

He also directed and/or produced *Stand by Me, The Princess Bride, When Harry Met Sally,* and *Misery. A Few Good Men,* a film he coproduced, was nominated for the Best Picture Oscar in 1992.

JEREMY SIEGEL is a professor of finance at the University of Pennsylvania and a regular columnist for *Kiplinger's Personal Finance* magazine and *Yahoo! Finance* as well as a regular contributor to the *Wall Street Journal, Barron's,* and the *Financial Times.* Siegel is frequently called on by CNN, CNBC, and NPR to share his stock market expertise.

TONY SNOW is President George W. Bush's press secretary. Prior to his current assignment, he was an outspoken conservative presenter for Fox News radio and television and is the first Washington commentator to be appointed to the White House role. Having done a stint as chief speechwriter for President George H. W. Bush, he can claim to straddle both press and politics.

NEIL STEINBERG, in association with Dr. Ken Dychtwald, has produced more than twenty hours of documentary television programming directly related to aging issues. He also has had a diverse career in motion picture and entertainment television production. He is the director/producer of *The Boomer Century 1946–2046*, the PBS documentary for which this book is the companion.

LEONARD STEINHORN is associate professor of communications at American University, where he teaches politics, media, and culture. He is the author of *The Greater Generation: In Defense of the Baby Boom Legacy.* He has written for major media, including the *Washington Post, Baltimore Sun, International Herald Tribune,* Salon.com, and the History News Network and appears frequently on broadcast news shows. He is a former political speechwriter and is coauthor of *By the Color of Our Skin,* a critically acclaimed book on race relations.

OLIVER STONE is a motion picture director and a Vietnam veteran. In 1967, Stone enlisted in the military and went to Vietnam, where he received both a Bronze Star and a Purple Heart.

In 1978, he won his first Oscar for Best Adapted Screenplay for the film *Midnight Express.* In 1986, Stone had his directorial breakthrough with his internationally acclaimed *Platoon,* which won that year's Best Picture award. His other film-directing credits read like a list of the "shared formative experiences" of the boomer generation: *Born on the Fourth of July, The Doors, JFK, Natural Born Killers, Nixon,* and *Wall Street,* to name a few. His most recent film is *World Trade Center.*

JEFF TAYLOR has reinvented the way job hunters seek employment. His "monster idea," conceived at the dawn of the World Wide Web, quickly became one of the first dot-com companies (454th registered domain on the Web), and Monster.com has since become the world's leading online career site.

Taylor left Monster.com in August 2005 to pursue a new unprecedented venture targeting people fifty years old and older, becoming founder and CEO of Eons (Eons.com).

DR. LESTER THUROW has been a professor of management and economics at MIT for more than thirty years, beginning in 1968. He was dean of the MIT Sloan School of Management from 1987 until 1993. His formal academic work focuses on globalization, economic instability, and the distribution of income and wealth.

A prolific writer, Thurow is the author of several books. Among them are *Head to Head: The Coming Economic Battle among Japan, Europe and America; The Future of Capitalism;* and *Building Wealth,* all of which became *New York Times* bestsellers. In the past, Dr. Thurow has served on the editorial board of the *New York Times,* as a contributing editor for *Newsweek,* and as a member of *Time* magazine's board of economists.

DR. FERNANDO TORRES-GIL is associate dean of academic affairs at UCLA, where he also serves as professor of social welfare and pu-

blic policy and director of the Center for Policy Research on Aging. Previously, he was a professor of gerontology and public administration at the University of Southern California and continues as an adjunct professor of gerontology at USC.

His academic accomplishments parallel his extensive government and public policy experience. He served as the first-ever assistant secretary for aging in the U.S. Department of Health and Human Services (HHS). As the Clinton administration's chief advocate on aging, Torres-Gil played a key role in promoting the importance of aging, long-term care, and disability issues, in consolidating federal programs for older persons, and in helping baby boomers redefine retirement in a postpension era.

DR. ANDREW WEIL is director of the program in integrative medicine at the University of Arizona College of Medicine. He also holds

appointments as clinical professor of internal medicine and clinical assistant professor of family and community medicine. He has a general practice in Tucson, focusing on natural and preventive medicine and diagnosis. Dr. Weil is also the founder of the Foundation for Integrative Medicine in Tucson and editor-in-chief of the journal *Integrative Medicine*.

Dr. Weil is the author of many scientific and popular articles and books: *The Natural Mind; The Marriage of the Sun and Moon; From Chocolate to Morphine* (with Winifred Rosen); *Health and Healing; Natural Health, Natural Medicine; Spontaneous Healing; Eight Weeks to Optimum Health;* and *Healthy Aging.*

JOEL WESTBROOK is an Emmy-winning documentary producer (*Lost Civilizations,* Time-Life/NBC). As director of original programming at Turner Broadcasting, he oversaw the production of several seasons of *National Geographic Explorer* and Jacques Cousteau's specials. Other documentary series produced by Westbrook have appeared on TLC, NBC, Discovery, TBS, and other broadcasters.

Westbrook is the producer of the documentary for which this book is the companion.

DR. JOSHUA ZEITZ is a former editor at *American Heritage* magazine and teaches history at the University of Cambridge in England. He is the author of *White Ethnic New York: Religion, Ethnicity and Political Culture in Post-War Gotham, 1945–1970.* He also wrote *Flapper: A Madcap Story of Sex, Style, Celebrity, and the Women Who Made America Modern.*

Photo and Lyric Credits

Photo Credits

Alexandria Productions: 307, 308, 309, 310 (bottom), 311 (top), 312, 313, 314 (bottom), 315 (top, middle), 316 (bottom), 317 (top, middle), 318, 319 (top), 320, 321 (bottom); **AP/Wide World Photos:** iii (Gloria Steinem), 48; **Bachrach:** 319 (bottom); **Aimee Brillhart:** 8; **Hope Burleigh:** 317 (bottom); **Corbis:** iii (couple with surfboard); **Ken Dychtwald:** 113; **Lois Eiler:** 315 (bottom); **Alfred Eisenstaedt/Getty Images:** 6; *GeezerJock Magazine:* 215, 218; **Getty Images:** iii (couple in kayak); **Bob Gomel/Getty Images:** 2, 16; **IBM:** 314 (top); **iStockphoto:** iii (car, yo-yo); **Cyd M. Johnson/The Image Works:** iii (laptop); **Nancy Kane:** 310 (top); **Cynthia Kenyon, PhD:** 207; **Library of Congress:** 4, 33, 42, 51, 55, 61, 63, 87, 105, 121, 127, 179, 180, 213; **Liz Lynch:** 311 (bottom); **NASA:** ix, 109, 90, 189; **NASA Glenn Research Center:** 110; **National Archives:** vii, 1, 32, 49, 80; **National Park Service:** 219; **Ogilvy & Mather Worldwide:** 89; **Photofest:** viii, 19, 22, 43, 114, 129, 149, 160; **Pictorial Press Ltd./ Alamy:** iii (The Rolling Stones); **Bill Pierce/Getty Images:** 118; **Faith Popcorn:** 316 (top); **Franklin D. Roosevelt Library:** 274; **Shutterstock:** iii (smiley face, cell phone, Slinky); **Social Security Administration:** 256; **SSA History Archives:** 275; **U.S. House of Representatives:** 91, 316 (middle); **U.S. State Department:** 173; **Joel Westbrook:** 321 (top).

Lyric Credits

"Alice's Restaurant" by Arlo Guthrie
Copyright © 1966 (renewed) by Appleseed Music, Inc.
All Rights reserved. Used by permission.

"(I Can't Get No) Satisfaction" written by Mick Jagger and Keith
    Richards
Published by ABKCO Music, Inc.
Copyright © 1965 (renewed) by ABKCO Music, Inc.
www.abkco.com

"Imagine" words and music by John Lennon
Copyright © 1971 (renewed 1999) by Lenono Music
All rights controlled and administered by EMI Blackwood Music, Inc.
All rights reserved. International copyright secured. Used by
    permission.

"Oompa Loompa" by Leslie Bricusse and Anthony Newley
Copyright © 1970, 1971 by Taradam Music, Inc.

"The Times They Are A-Changin'"
Copyright © 1963 by Warner Bros., Inc. Copyright renewed 1991
    by Special Rider Music.
All rights reserved. International copyright secured. Reprinted
    by permission.

"Where Have All the Flowers Gone?" by Pete Seeger
Copyright © 1961 (renewed) by Sanga Music, Inc.
    All rights reserved. Used by permission.

Acknowledgments

Thanks, obviously, to Dr. Ken Dychtwald, who is the moving force behind the television documentary, *The Boomer Century,* and hence this book as well.

Thanks go out to all of the scholars, entrepreneurs, authors, playwrights, celebrities, pundits, preachers, and politicos who agreed to be interviewed for both the program and the book. Special thanks go out to several individuals who gave unique or additional interviews for the book alone. They are Richard Chapman; Bishop John Chane; Rev. Carole O'Connell; president of the IBM Foundation, Mr. Stanley Litow; and U.S. Congressman Tom Price (R-Georgia).

Thanks to Joel Westbrook to whom I am indebted for things far too numerous to list, and to Aimée Brillhart, who, on many, many occasions, had to deal with both Mr. Westbrook and myself multiple times in a single day.

Thanks also to producer/director Neil Steinberg, also of the companion documentary, and to Mark Jonathan Harris, who wrote the screenplay. I have borrowed liberally from his script. Allen Feuer hired on as supervising producer for the show and ended up clearing rights for the book. Many, many thanks to him as well.

I am grateful also to Peter Kaufman of Intelligent TV for marrying television and publishing, to our most excellent editor, Karen Murgolo of Springboard Press, and to her able associate, Tom Hardej, as well as copyeditor, Marie Salter.

Thanks also to Al Gore for inventing the Internet, without which this book would never have been completed on time, and to IMBd.com, which claims to be the world's largest Internet movie database. I have no reason to doubt it.

Thanks to boomer Bill Gates or to whomever invented word processors. Without spell-check, cut and paste, and undo, none of my books would ever have been written.

And thanks to my fellow boomers—especially the leading-edge Boomers—for making America, and, for that matter, the whole world, a better, freer, more diverse, and interesting place to live.

About the Author

RICHARD CROKER worked for eighteen years at Turner Broadcasting, writing, producing, and directing, before leaving to become a writer and independent documentary filmmaker. His television credits have appeared on TBS, The Learning Channel, and Discovery Digital Networks. He is the author of *To Make Men Free* (William Morrow, 2004) and *No Greater Courage* (William Morrow, 2006).